THE
GENERAL RADIO STORY

Frederick Van Veen

ISBN   978-0-6151-7665-9

Foreword

Most company histories are works in progress. They are written, often to mark some anniversary or other milestone, as a celebration of what has happened so far and as a promise of an even better future. This history is different. General Radio, which was renamed GenRad in 1975, ceased to exist in 2001. Its stock-trading symbol GEN disappeared from the New York Stock Exchange, its 1300 employees were swallowed by a larger company, and its many retirees were suddenly the alumni of an institution that no longer existed.

General Radio was not the first company to disappear amid the frequent upheavals of the world of high tech. The Massachusetts business landscape is filled with ghosts: Digital Equipment, Data General, Prime, Computervision, GCA, Wang Labs, and many other once-renowned companies came and went, in many cases after only 15 or 20 years of life. In Silicon Valley, few start-ups lasted even that long. High tech was a pot of gold for many, but it could also be unforgiving to a company that missed a turn in the technology roadmap or that failed to translate a successful product (and every company had one, for a while) into a successful business model.

General Radio was no one-trick pony. It lasted for 86 years, an eternity in high tech (and in baseball, as every Red Sox fan knows). But what makes "GR" worth our time is not its longevity, but what it did during those 86 years. It produced measuring instruments without which the pioneers could not have given us electronics as we know it. The first commercial signal generators, oscillators, wavemeters, oscilloscopes, and impedance bridges wore the General Radio monogram, as did sound-level meters, stroboscopes, and variable autotransformers ("Variacs"). As the test and measurement industry morphed into "ATE" (automatic test equipment), GR was first off the mark with automatic circuit board testers and the software to make them hum.

General Radio never became a really big company – its annual sales never hit $350 million – but in terms of its contributions to the growth of electronics in the twentieth century, it was a juggernaut.

My association with General Radio began in 1955, when I joined the Company's Publicity Department, headed by Charlie Worthen. Charlie, who joined GR on graduating from MIT in 1928, headed a small group responsible for the Company's catalogs, instruction manuals, and the General Radio *Experimenter*, a monthly journal bringing news of new products and measurement techniques to an audience of more than 100,000 readers. Charlie wrote and edited virtually the entire output of the Department, and Martin Gilman, his assistant (and another MIT alumnus) supervised production and printing. Early that year, Charlie decided that he needed another writer to take instruction manuals off his hands. Calls were made, interviews were held, and I was hired.

I knew next to nothing about the Company at the outset, except that it had a good reputation for quality products and that the people I met in the interviewing process were impressive. My first assignment was to overhaul the Company's instruction manuals, and, since the first draft of each manual was written by the instrument designer, I found myself working closely with the Company's engineers, and I soon began to appreciate that I was in the company of giants. It was not just that they were the world's leading authorities on electronic measurement; they all seemed to be renaissance men, as comfortable discussing music and literature as they were discussing signal generators and sound level meters. As a liberal arts graduate, I found it unsettling to learn that my boss Charlie

Worthen, MIT '28, knew more about the essays of Orwell and the novels of Tolken than I did.

Lunch times were a special treat at General Radio. Worthen, Gilman, and I would usually join a group of engineers, usually including Arnold Peterson, Jim Faran, Charlie Burke, and Horatio Lamson, for a spirited discussion that rarely had anything to do with General Radio business or General Radio products. Years later, I would look back and wonder whether this was a telltale sign of a company flaw, but at the time those wide-ranging lunch-table conversations were the days' highlights. No faculty club offered a richer menu of intellectual stimulation.

My tenure at GR lasted 13 years. I enjoyed those years immensely, and I treasure the friendships I made while working there. I left GR to join another company in 1968, and the two companies became competitors. Thus I stayed reasonably familiar with events at my former employer. In the late 1990s, as the world started to unravel for GR, I had distinctly mixed feelings – a vindication of my decision to move on in 1968 and regret that a Company that had been such an important part of the history of electronics (and of my own career) seemed headed for oblivion.

This history is an attempt to thwart oblivion. General Radio, the General Radio I knew, should not be allowed to vanish without a trace. When future historians try to identify the people and the companies that gave us the electronics miracles of the twentieth century, I want them to know about General Radio.

Acknowledgments

This is not the first history of General Radio. In 1965, when GR was celebrating its fiftieth anniversary, Arthur Thiessen, the Company's Chairman, produced a history of the Company to that point. At about the same time, Donald Sinclair, GR's President, wrote a shorter version of GR's history, which he presented at a meeting of the Newcomen Society. The Sinclair version was basically a condensation of the Thiessen book, plus a few of Sinclair's own observations.

I worked closely with Thiessen on his history, editing copy and helping with the layout, but the writing was all his. Arthur was a highly intelligent, literate, and dynamic executive, and his history is valuable not only for its factual contents but also as a window on management's thinking in 1965. I am deeply indebted to Arthur Thiessen for leaving such an authoritative record of the Company's first half century. Without it, I wouldn't have dared to embark on this project.

Because relatively few readers of this history will have read Thiessen's, and because I felt this book should stand on its own as a one-volume history, I decided to include much of the Thiessen material, adding other material from that era that I was able to find and omitting whatever seemed to be of marginal importance.

In preparing this history I had access to a formidable volume of printed material. For much of this I am indebted to Gus Lahanas, Bob Fulks, and especially Henry Hall, who worked conscientiously over the years to catalog the archives at the GR museum now taking shape. Henry has also scanned every copy of the General Radio Experimenter as well as many other valuable documents and has burned this material onto CD-ROMs, which are available from him (http://www.teradyne.com/corp/grhs/).

The General Radio Story

The full Thiessen history and other historical material are accessible on the same site.

Others were also generous with their time and assistance. Harold McAleer responded to countless questions regarding the events that occurred during his many years as an employee and officer. CEOs Bill Thurston, Bob Anderson, Bob Dutkowski and long-time directors Jim Wright and Bill Scheerer submitted to long interviews and responded fully to follow-up questions via phone and e-mail. A great many other former employees helped me piece together the story, and I am grateful to them all, as well as to several Teradyne colleagues for sharing their reminiscences of GR as seen from across the competitive divide.

Finally, I want to thank my wife Jill for her considerable help in proofreading and debugging the copy.

Kennebunkport, Maine
November 2006

Contents

1	A Meeting in Waltham	1
2	The Birth of a Company	4
3.	Setting a Course	13
4.	Creating a Technology Powerhouse	16
5.	The Great Depression	22
6.	Filling the GR Catalog	25
7.	An Engineer's Company	30
8.	World War 2	35
9.	The Golden Age	44
10.	Rumbles of Thunder	50
11.	Concord	55
12.	The Young Turks	64
13.	The Sinclair Years	68
14.	Tensions at the Top	80
15.	GR Enters the Systems Business	84
16.	The Acquisition Bug Bites	88
17.	The Fulks Manifestos	97
18.	The Thurston Era Begins	110
19.	The Turnaround	124
20.	GenRad	128
21.	All Systems Go	135
22.	GR Goes Public	141
23.	The Money Keeps Rolling In	144
24.	GenRad Goes for Broke	151
25.	Doug Hajjar Arrives	163
26.	Thurston's Last Hurrah	174
27.	The Wheels Come Off	178
28.	The Anderson Years	193
29.	Hard Times	205
30.	Jim Lyons Takes Over	215
31.	The Last Climb	225
32.	Boom	234
33.	Bust	237
	Afterthoughts	243
	Appendix: Sales, Net, 1915-2001	245

Chapter 1

A Meeting in Waltham

June 5, 2001: Bob Dutkowsky maneuvered his Audi up the ramp from Route 128 to Totten Pond Road, swung right, and pulled into the Westin Hotel parking lot. A GenRad meeting was underway at the hotel, but Dutkowsky's mind was elsewhere. George Chamillard, CEO at Teradyne, had called him a few days earlier to suggest a meeting, and it was not hard to guess what was on his mind. It would be just the two of them, off in the Westin's Garfield Room, out of sight of any stray GenRad employees wandering around.

Dutkowsky knew that as GenRad's CEO he was not dealing from strength. The banks were closing in. Debt stood at more than $80 million, and GenRad was in violation of its loan covenants. The first quarter had been blown, and the second quarter looked horrendous. The banks, led by Fleet, had agreed to waive default only through June 15 – 10 days away. By that date the banks wanted to hear precisely how GenRad intended to pay off the debt.

The crisis had come with almost incredible swiftness, like a tornado on the prairie. Only the year before – Dutkowsky's first year as CEO – the Company reported a net profit of more than $21 million on sales of $342 million, a record. The year before that, sales were $302 million, net profit $47 million. But the boom times of 1999 led to the crash of 2000, when the orders stopped coming, not just for GenRad, but for virtually every other company in the electronics industry. The violent business downturn savaged even the largest companies, with many losing 70 or 80 percent of their stock-market value in a year. If you were trying to pilot your company through this

1

storm, you needed, above all, a strong balance sheet. GenRad's balance sheet, as Bob Dutkowsky knew too well, was shaky, owing to a string of ill-timed acquisitions.

George Chamillard lined up his thoughts as he drove his Mercedes into the hotel lot. He had two major agenda items: first, to find out what was left of GenRad after the beating it was taking; second, to size up Dutkowsky, whom he had never met. On both counts, he had done some research, and the results were encouraging. GenRad still had some good people and some good products, and the feedback on Dutkowsky was positive. The GenRad CEO had been in place for only a little more than a year, but his earlier experience at IBM and EMC was impressive.

GenRad and Teradyne competed in one business: circuit board testing. At GenRad, board test was the heart of the Company; at Teradyne, it was less than 10 percent of a company focused mainly on semiconductor testing. Both companies had been brutalized by the downturn, but Teradyne's total sales were still well over a billion dollars (down from a $3 billion peak in 1999), and its balance sheet was reasonably healthy. Its stock price was in the 30s, GenRad's in single digits. GenRad's share of the board test market was much larger than Teradyne's, though both trailed the market leader, Agilent.

Agilent was in fact a silent player in the discussion in the Garfield Room that day. Chamillard and Dutkowsky agreed that there was little chance that either of their companies could overtake Agilent on its own. Agilent, the spun-off testing operation of Hewlett-Packard, was a multibillion-dollar giant with formidable engineering resources and a worldwide distribution network. Only if GenRad and Teradyne joined forces was there a realistic chance of overtaking the market leader.

"We can spend $20 million to develop a new tester, and you can spend $20 million to develop a new tester – or we can get together and spend $20 million – once - on a

2

new tester," said Chamillard. "If we can pull it off, it makes sense." Dutkowsky nodded.

Chamillard then turned the subject to Dutkowsky's career. Would he be interested in running the combined board test business?

Teradyne's board test business unit was called the Assembly Test Division (ATD), and if GenRad's board test business was folded into ATD, Chamillard wanted Dutkowsky at the top. An added consideration, for Chamillard, was that Teradyne would acquire a senior executive who might one day be a candidate for the CEO slot. Chamillard was 63 at the time, Dutkowsky 45.

Both men left the Westin in good spirits, reported quickly to their management teams and directors (and in GenRad's case, to its banks and its investment banker, William Blair & Co.), and almost immediately the acquisition machinery started grinding away. The two companies signed a confidentiality agreement on June 25, and soon thereafter Teradyne hired Goldman Sachs to look out for its interests. Intense discussions went on throughout July, and on August 2, before the market opened, GenRad issued a press release announcing that the two companies were talking.

Throughout their negotiations, Dutkowsky and Chamillard remained focused on the future, hardly pausing to reflect on the fact that they were drafting the obituary of a once-proud company founded long before either man was born. Dutkowsky was working to avoid bankruptcy and to salvage a future for GenRad's employees and a few dollars for its stockholders. Chamillard was seeking to shore up his faltering board test business. As an engineering student at Northeastern he had used General Radio instruments, and as a young test engineer at Teradyne he had encountered GR decade boxes, but to him GenRad's glorious past was irrelevant; all that mattered was GenRad as it was in 2001.

To the dwindling band of long-time GenRad employees and to the Company's retirees, the acquisition was bittersweet news. On the positive side, Teradyne would provide employment and continue retiree benefits, including health insurance. But to those old enough to remember the General Radio of the 40s, 50s, and 60s, the sight of their grand old Company, hounded by its bankers, fleeing to the arms of a competitor, was hardly a cause for celebration. What would Melville Eastham have thought?

Chapter 2

The Birth of a Company

The public's fascination with wireless had been building for years. Instant point-to-point communication had been available ever since Samuel Morse wondered "what hath God wrought" back in 1844, and three decades later Alexander Graham Bell's invention carried voices long distances, but still over wires. Then, on December 12, 1901, two men in St. John's, Newfoundland sat before a strange-looking device connected by a wire to a kite flying 400 feet above them. At precisely noon, the two heard in their earphones three quick buzzes – Morse code for the letter "S" – and the wireless age was born. Under the direction of Guglielmo Marconi, a signal had been sent from Cornwall, England to North America without wires or cables. In the years that followed, as transmitting and receiving devices continuously improved, trans-Atlantic communication became routine. All that was left was to replace wireless Morse code with wireless voice communication, and for that the pieces were rapidly falling into place. A triode vacuum tube (the "Audion") invented by Lee DeForest and a new regenerative circuit invented by Howard Armstrong were the chief catalysts.

Somehow, "wireless" seemed an inadequate term to describe the miracle unfolding, and the word "radio" – suggesting radiated electromagnetic waves – soon gained currency. (The term "wireless" would thus drop out of sight, only to make a roaring comeback a century later.) In 1912, the Institute of Radio Engineers was organized to serve the growing legions of professional and amateur experimenters who were busily assembling receivers and transmitters in their laboratories and homes. The amateur radio operators, with tall makeshift antennas towering over their houses, were regarded as curiosities by their neighbors, who must have wondered why anyone would want to listen to so much static and so little intelligence.

But public indifference to radio communication disappeared in April of 1912, when the Titanic, the most ballyhooed ocean liner ever built, struck an iceberg and sank in the Atlantic. The drama, endlessly replayed in the press, told of radio distress calls ignored and other calls received and acted upon. The failure of radio communications between the Titanic and the nearby California was widely blamed for the loss of 1500 passengers at sea. On the other hand, successful communications between the Titanic and the Carpathia directly led to the rescue of 706 people still alive in lifeboats - 706 souls who owed their lives to the radio operators on the two ships.

Radio had seized center stage. The demand for radio operators quickly outstripped the supply, and a Marconi radio school opened in New York. The price of Marconi shares soared on the stock exchange. Suddenly, thousands of people wanted to build their own receivers. To many, the Titanic disaster was a call to arms. ("The next time a ship at sea sends a distress call, by God, I'll be listening, and I'll know what to do!") Within a short time, department stores in New York City were selling radio components.

In Boston, at 100 Boylston Street, the Clapp-Eastham Company, a maker of x-ray equipment, had seen the first wave of radio enthusiasm a few years earlier, when its high-voltage spark coils were snapped up by radio amateurs for use in transmitters. The Company went with the flow, drifting out of x-ray and adding variable capacitors and crystal detectors to their line. By 1910, when the Company moved to Cambridge, it had become a favorite supplier to radio experimenters, including some of the giants of the infant technology – Fessenden, Armstrong, Pierce, etc.

By 1915, it was clear that the future of radio was virtually unlimited, but it was far from clear how one should invest one's time and money. It was likely that thousands or even millions of people would want access to the radio waves and would somehow build or buy radio receivers, but to what end? As an alternative to telephony, radio was considered a point-to-point (e.g.,Titanic-to-Carpathia) medium, and the thought of "broadcasting" was widely seen as a liability. What good was a communications channel that allowed everyone to listen to your private conversations? Still, the fact that the world was clamoring for radio equipment could not be ignored. Moreover, the U.S. military, preparing for war and aware that undersea cables were highly vulnerable, was investing heavily in powerful wireless transmitters and sensitive receivers.

Melville Eastham, a young, self-taught engineer at Clapp-Eastham, surveyed the scene and decided that, wherever history might take radio, one thing was certain: there would be a growing need for instruments that could measure the properties of radio signals and for specialized radio components. With that conviction, and with capital of $9,000 from investors Ralph Emery, Ralph Watrous, and Cyrus Brown, Melville Eastham founded General Radio Company. The investors received a half interest in the

Company, and one-quarter each went to Eastham and O. Kerro Luscomb, a principal of Clapp-Eastham, in which Eastham retained an interest. Luscomb would also help Eastham get the new company off the ground.

Melville Eastham was born on June 26, 1885, in Oregon City, Oregon, the second of five children born to Edward and Clara Eastham. He was educated at the local public schools, and on graduation from high school moved to San Francisco to take a job with an electric utility company (his father's field, back in Oregon). Then, in 1905, at the invitation of a friend, he moved to New York to take a job at the Ovington X-Ray Company. The following year he and two Ovington associates, engineer W.O. Eddy and salesman J. Emory Clapp, launched their own x-ray company, Clapp, Eddy, and Eastham. Since Clapp financed the venture, the trio located their new Company in his hometown, Boston. With Eddy's departure in 1907, the Company became Clapp-Eastham, where we first met Eastham a few paragraphs earlier.

General Radio's first home was rented space on the third floor of a flat-iron building at the corner of Massachusetts Avenue and Windsor Street in Cambridge – just a few blocks from the Massachusetts Institute of Technology, which would play a central role in the Company's history.

We should not pass lightly over the fact that the 30-year-old Eastham was staking his claim to a company name potentially of enormous value. Just as General Motors would become the colossus of the automobile industry and General Electric the titan of power generation, the infant General Radio was in effect aspiring to become the leader of the wireless telegraphy universe. Although Eastham would have denied any such grandiose ambition, his "Statement of Purpose," filed with the Commonwealth of Massachusetts on June 14,1915, was broad enough to cover practically any territory the new Company might want to conquer.

Statement of Purpose

> Manufacturing, buying, selling, leasing, and generally dealing in electrical machines, apparatus, appliances, and devices of all kinds and for all purposes and doing all things incidental and appertaining thereto.

Like any start-up, General Radio needed a quick revenue stream, and this was provided by several companies eager to exploit the new radio technology. George Cabot, a founder of the Holtzer-Cabot Electric Company, was among the first customers and remained a buyer of GR instruments for many years thereafter. An inventor of a talking-movie scheme approached Eastham in the fall of 1915, asking for a device that could amplify the output of a microphone and thus transfer sound patterns to fine iron filings cemented to the film. Eastham responded by producing a two-stage amplifier to deliver the sound to the filings and to reproduce the audio output at a loudspeaker. The transformers designed for this application may have been the first audio transformers available for sale, and these were subsequently sold in great quantities to experimenters.

Then came a breakthrough order, from American Telephone and Telegraph. In 1915 AT&T successfully transmitted speech signals across the Atlantic, from a Navy transmitter at Arlington, Virginia, to a receiver mounted on the Eiffel Tower. Now the Company wanted to upgrade its transmitter, and to supply the high plate voltage required to drive several hundred vacuum tubes, it asked General Radio to supply a nine-phase, synchronous, commutator-type rectifier. And serious money started coming in.

Eastham, who never attended college, had taught himself the basic principles underlying the radio art, and he had a seemingly limitless supply of ideas. In 1916, with the Company only a year out of the gate, the first General Radio catalog listed a Precision Variable Air Condenser ($25), a Decade Resistance Box ($19), a Precision Variable Inductor ($24), and an Absorption Wave Meter ($60). To help turn his ideas into products, Eastham recruited several employees from Clapp-Eastham, including Knut Johnson, a machinist, and Ashley Zwicker, who joined in 1916 as the first foreman, overseeing most of the 30 people then on the workforce. Both men were fixtures at GR for many years.

Below: An early variable air condenser from General Radio

The entry of the United States into the war in 1917 triggered a torrent of orders for portable wavemeters, crystal sets, and other devices needed by the military, and the work force quickly expanded to about 100. The action in Europe also gave GR a place in radio history. Captain E.H. Armstrong, who had patented his regenerative circuit in 1914, was working for the U.S. Army Signal Corps at a laboratory in Paris. His efforts led to a landmark invention: the superheterodyne receiver, a fundamental advance incorporated in virtually all radio and television receivers ever since. For his first receiver, Armstrong required a variable air condenser and, finding none readily available, appropriated the laboratory's standard condenser, made by General Radio. Thus the Company secured a place in the first superheterodyne radio receiver – and in history.

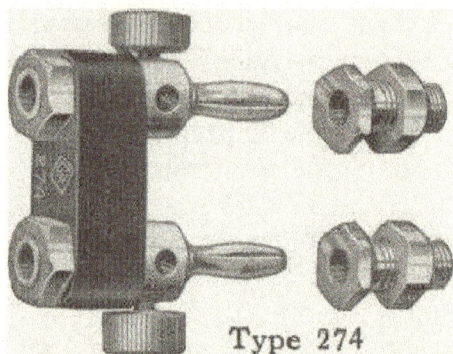

Type 274

Eastham's fertile imagination produced another seminal product: the Type 274 banana plug, offered as an assembled pair, separated by 3/4 inch. The 3/4-inch spacing, like a standard railroad gauge, would persist through the ages, as would GR's double plug. It was initially made of nickel silver, brass, and hard rubber, with exposed setscrews. Over the years, the silver would give way to bronze and then copper, and the rubber would give way to phenolic and then polystyrene, but the critical design and dimensions remained the same, and there is probably not an electronics engineer alive who is not familiar with the double banana plug, which was offered, together with mating jacks, in the 1926 GR Catalog, for exactly one dollar.

General Radio's Flat-Iron Building in Cambridge

The war-induced demand for its products saw GR migrate to other floors of the flat-iron building in Cambridge, and, in 1917, the Company bought the entire building for $70,000. The same year, Eastham parted ways with Luscomb, swapping his interest in Clapp-Eastham for Luscomb's interest in GR.

Building a business around the growth of radio instrumentation was one goal of Melville Eastham. Another, which he pursued with equal passion, was to build a company whose employees were treated as members of a family, entitled to as many benefits as the company could afford, along with the assurance of job security.

The war brought Eastham in contact with a man who was to become a key partner in piloting the Company for the next three-plus decades. Henry Shaw, son of a textile industry executive and a Harvard graduate, class of '06, was also an avid radio amateur and GR customer. Now in his early 30s, Shaw approached Eastham to ask if he might help the Company and thus his country in its war

11

effort. Eastham hired him as a designer but soon realized that his executive talents were even more valuable (he had been an officer at the Saco-Lowell Shops, where his father was Treasurer), and placed him in charge of the office. Shaw was by nature an extremely magnanimous gentleman, and Eastham's passion to build a company based on humanitarian principles found in Shaw the perfect partner.

In 1917, for instance, - the year Shaw came aboard – GR instituted a profit-sharing bonus plan, paying every employee of more than one year's service an extra week's pay twice a year, with the option of taking an extra week's vacation (two weeks was standard) in lieu of either bonus. In 1918, every employee was given a $1000 life insurance policy, with all premiums paid by the Company. In 1919, the workweek was set at 40 hours (it had been 44, which itself was below the industry average). The number of paid holidays was increased to nine, and the bonus plan was made even more generous and was more closely linked to profitability. Word quickly spread in and around Cambridge that General Radio was *the* place to work.

Henry Shaw and Melville Eastham

Chapter 3

Setting a Course

The end of the war brought order cancellations and a temporary sales slump, partly offset by the public's growing interest in radio communication. Investors began dreaming of huge bonanzas awaiting those who bet on the right horses, in a pattern that would be repeated throughout the twentieth century. The most obvious business strategy was to build radio receivers, which would give the general public access to the wonders of radio that were then available only to amateur radio operators and experimenters. Eastham's investors were in this camp, but Eastham was wary of the radio receiver business, feeling that the patent situation was too uncertain. (In this he was prescient, as the long, bitter patent battles among DeForest, Armstrong, Sarnoff, and others would prove.) General Radio, then, found itself at a fork in the road. Half the ownership wanted to chase the radio business; the other half – the founder and leader - wanted to stay focused on measuring instruments.

Eastham prevailed when, in 1918 and 1919, Henry Shaw bought out the three restless investors for a total of $17,976. He also made an additional equity investment of $22,525 in the Company and purchased an outstanding $30,000 mortgage on the flat-iron building. Thus Henry Shaw was backing the young Company to the tune of about $70,000. His was the last outside capital invested in the Company for many years. It gave the two men, Eastham and Shaw, complete ownership of the firm.

Shaw's investment earned him a place on the Board of Directors, along with Shaw's uncle, Lawrence Mayo. In the same year, Errol Locke, a young Harvard graduate, joined the Company as a salesman but soon moved to the production side of the business, where his talents led to a

13

quick promotion to Vice President. In 1919, Harold Richmond, an MIT engineering graduate and a war veteran, was recruited by Eastham on his way to a teaching career at MIT, and he, too, was soon tabbed as a rising star, becoming Treasurer and, years later, Chairman of the Board.

Thus the "first team" of Eastham, Shaw, Locke, and Richmond was in place as the decade of the 20s dawned, and this team, with only a few additions, would manage the Company for the next 20 years.

In 1920, Eastham and Shaw began to transfer some of their shares in the Company to Locke and Richmond, in keeping with their strong belief that the Company's future success would be best ensured through employee ownership. Neither man was particularly interested in amassing a personal fortune. Shaw was already well off, and Eastham's ambition was to build his fortune by making General Radio the world's leading supplier of radio instruments. His game plan was simple: Just down Massachusetts Avenue at MIT, and just up the same street at Harvard, was a steady supply of young science and engineering graduates already aware of the possibilities of radio-frequency measurement. It was necessary only to hire them and direct their talents and energies.

Although military contracts dried up with the war's end, by then GR had established a reputation as a trustworthy supplier to the government. Shortly after the armistice, therefore, the Navy gave the young Cambridge firm a sizeable contract to assemble hydrophones. These were rubber-covered, carbon-granule microphones designed to be placed below a ship's waterline to detect the sound of submarines. The microphones themselves were designed by Professor G.W. Pierce of Harvard, and GR contributed the talents of two new newly hired engineers, Horatio Lamson and Paul ("P.K.") McElroy. Lamson was an MIT graduate with a Master's from Harvard; McElroy's undergraduate and graduate degrees were both from Harvard. Both men would have illustrious careers with General Radio until they retired in 1958 and 1964.

The hydrophone project had little to do with the measurement technology Eastham wanted his Company to pursue, but the money was good, and it helped fund the development of a growing catalog of instruments and precision components. Eastham was confident that once the hydrophone contract was completed, General Radio would recommit itself exclusively to the field of measurement.

In 1920, however, a historic event transformed the world of radio, and its shock waves soon hit General Radio. The event was the birth of broadcasting, when Westinghouse's station KDKA in Pittsburgh broadcast the results of the Harding – Cox presidential race in November. Suddenly it was clear to all, as it had never been before, that radio was destined to become much more than simply a means of private communications, but a technological marvel capable of bringing news and entertainment to millions of listeners - instantly. In fact, it was the first true, real-time "mass medium" in human history.

The trickle of people who had built radio receivers and thus heard the Harding-Cox news now became a flood of people lined up to buy the parts needed to build their own receivers. Within a year, about 30 broadcast stations were on the air, and the entire country was swept by radio fever. General Radio, well known as a source of quality radio products (its name didn't hurt), was soon swamped with orders for components, not by the accustomed dozens or hundreds, but by the tens of thousands. Audio transformers, needed to drive the radios' loudspeakers, were an especially hot item.

The do-it-yourself craze lasted a few years, until an industry was formed to supply complete, assembled receivers to the masses. Then, as quickly as it had arrived, the parts demand stopped. The new receivers would need components, of course, but these would be mass-produced, inexpensive, and of no interest to Melville Eastham, who now put his ship back on the course he had charted in 1915 – the creation of quality measuring instruments.

Chapter 4

Creating a Technology Powerhouse

The appetite for General Radio instruments soon validated Eastham's fateful decision to devote his company to the business of measurement, as hundreds of radio manufacturers raced to equip their engineers with the instruments they desperately needed in order to compete in the exploding market for radio receivers. Nor were the manufacturers the only customers; hundreds of newly licensed radio stations required monitoring and measuring instruments to ensure that their signals were within prescribed frequency and power limitations. The radio mania was not limited to the United States, and by 1922 the volume of orders landing at General Radio's Cambridge plant was enough to justify the appointment of the Company's first overseas distributor, A.A. Posthumus, which represented GR in Holland and Belgium. Sales representatives in the U.K., Italy, and France also signed on in the next few years.

These were heady days for General Radio. Not only was the market for its products soaring, but competition was almost nonexistent, as Eastham and his small band of brilliant engineers produced one ingenious instrument after another – not copies, but original inventions, many of which served as industry standards for many years. Typical of the new breed of GR instruments was the Type 216 Capacitance Bridge, introduced in 1921. The 216 was virtually unchallenged for 15 years, until it was replaced by the Type 716-A. Audio oscillators, beat-frequency oscillators, broadcast frequency monitors, wavemeters, thermionic voltmeters (the first vacuum-tube voltmeters) – these and dozens of other General Radio instruments, along with standards of resistance and capacitance, filled the pages of the General Radio catalog, which became a standard reference source in the laboratories of the world. Amazingly, this impressive product flow represented the intellectual output of just five engineers, all graduates of the region's most prestigious universities - and all led by the formidable Melville Eastham, whose formal education had ended with a high school diploma.

In 1925 the acquisition of a building adjacent to the Company's Cambridge headquarters site doubled capacity, to 42,000 square feet. At this point, the head count was 139 employees. Annual sales were about $1 million, and the Company was comfortably in the black.

The excursion into radio parts in the early 20s had forced GR to take on a network of sales representatives, and in 1926, with the Company back in the instrument business for good, the "rep" network was disbanded, and GR began to build its own direct sales force. This in turn allowed the Company to return to a practice it had embraced in its infancy, but dropped when agent discounts were necessary: the publication of prices. Eastham had always felt that an instrument's price was every bit as important as its accuracy or precision, and it deserved to be included in all sales literature. Thus, starting in 1926, prices were stated in every catalog and advertisement – and in a new, monthly journal introduced in 1926: The General Radio *Experimenter*. The *Experimenter* soon became a "must-read" for thousands of engineers around the world, eventually amassing a circulation of over 130,000 readers. Its purpose, obviously, was to promote new General Radio instruments, but it described these products in a way that made each issue a tutorial on the principles of measurement. It was also a highly literate publication, thanks to the writing skills of three MIT graduates: Charlie Burke, its first editor, John Crawford, its second, and, most of all, Charlie Worthen, who took over as editor in 1932 and held that post until his retirement in 1966. Other companies used the *Experimenter* as a model for their own publications, and David Packard, in his book "The HP Way," freely acknowledged that the *Hewlett-Packard Journal* was inspired by the *Experimenter*.

Among the most avid of *Experimenter* readers were thousands of amateur radio operators. By this time, the line between these hobbyists and professional engineers was blurred, with many amateurs also working in industry. GR was a hotbed of amateur activity, with most of the Company's engineers holding amateur licenses. Thus it was not surprising that the second issue of the *Experimenter* described a new wavemeter designed for amateurs, and the third boasted that "the General Radio Company is now able to supply quartz plates for amateurs." In 1924 Henry Shaw had authored an article on "Oscillating Crystals" in the amateur radio journal QST, and his own transmitter, built the same year, is thought to have been the first to use crystal frequency control.

In 1928, Eastham doubled the engineering staff (to 10) and was able to attract a noted engineer from the Bell Telephone Laboratories. So impressed was he by his new recruit that he soon surrendered the title "Chief Engineer" to him. J. Warren Horton was also given stock in the Company. Horton proved to be a good catch, and the flow of new instruments from GR's engineers turned into a flood.

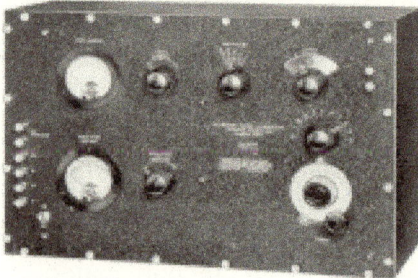

The 403 Standard-Signal Generator

Prominent among the new products was the Type 403 Standard Signal Generator, designed by Dr. Lewis Hull, on loan from Aircraft Radio. In the early days of radio, receiver makers often advertised their products in terms of range ("Hear stations 500 miles away!"). As any engineer knows, such claims are ludicrous, since the ability of a radio to detect signals depends on transmitter power, propagation conditions, and the radio's inherent sensitivity – which means its ability to detect a very weak voltage at a given frequency. Measuring this ability is a job for a standard-signal generator, which places a known electrical stimulus (100 microvolts, say) at a specific frequency at the radio's input. With the help of this instrument, the true sensitivity of a radio receiver can be measured and specified. The 403, described in GR's Catalog E of 1928, delivered a signal of from 1 to 200,000 microvolts over a frequency range of from 500 to 1500 kilocycles per second (the broadcast band), with internally supplied 400-cycle amplitude modulation (AM). This instrument and its many successors established GR as the preeminent source of what was to become an essential tool in every radio laboratory.

The signal generator, along with hundreds of other products, was included in the 136-page Catalog E, published in 1928. This was GR's fifth catalog (letters being assigned serially), and, like the *Experimenter*, it became standard fare in engineering laboratories, serving as a reference book as well as a product list. In Catalog E, for instance, there appeared a detailed description of a new unit of electrical measurement called the Transmission Unit (TU), which was the forerunner of the decibel.

Electrical technology was also impacting the motion-picture industry, and General Radio took notice quickly. The advent of "talkies" set in motion a contest between two competing methods of adding sound to picture. One of these methods, pursued by Vitaphone (backed by Warner Brothers and Bell Telephone Laboratories) impressed the sound onto large phonograph records, whose playback was synchronized to the movie film. Since more than one record was needed for most pictures, the studio faced the challenge of switching records noiselessly. Enter GR engineer Horatio Lamson, with his Vitaphone Fader, described in the January 1927 *Experimenter*. Vitaphone was to lose its competitive battle, but Lamson, seeing countless opportunities for electrical measurement in the motion-picture revolution unfolding, was quick to author the tutorial "How and Why the Talkies," which ran in back-to-back issues starting in December 1928, and "How and Why the Fader," in which he adapted his earlier ideas to the new motion picture sound technology.

There was no limit to Horatio Lamson's field of interest. Power supplies, radio-frequency chokes, vacuum tubes, a new time-measuring device called the Synchronometer, magneto-striction oscillators - the ideas flowed from his brain to commercial reality and the pages of the *Experimenter* month after month. At this point the circulation of the monthly *Experimenter* was 20,000, so articles like Lamson's were seen by an extremely large portion of the scientific community.

Not even television escaped GR's attention, although the Company emphatically declared that the technology was not yet ready for prime time. The following note appeared in the January, 1929 issue of the *Experimenter*:

> TELEVISION: We have received many inquiries as to whether we were contemplating putting out any television apparatus. The answer has been uniformly "No."

At the end of 1929 GR's new Chief Engineer, J. Warren Horton, offered a more temperate view of television ("Television: a Comparison with Other Kinds of Electrical Communication," Dec. 1929 *Experimenter*). It was not so much a matter of technology, Horton explained; the technology, assuming adequate bandwidth, was reasonably well understood. The issue was purely and simply one of economics.

In 1929 the Company introduced the world's first commercial primary frequency standard. Designed by engineer Jim Clapp, the son of Eastham's old partner Emory Clapp, another of GR's MIT graduates, and an enthusiastic radio amateur, the standard's frequency source was a precision 50-kilocycle quartz bar, housed in a temperature-controlled oven. The output of the quartz oscillator drove a synchronous clock, which could be precisely compared with a signal from the U.S. Naval Observatory. The over-all accuracy of the standard was one part per million. Lest his ham radio friends think he was selling out to the giants who could afford primary frequency standards, in the very same year his "A Better Frequency Meter for the Amateur" appeared in the *Experimenter*. The new meter was priced at $18.

In late 1929 Eastham snared another heavyweight for his engineering staff. Robert F. Field (to be forever known, of course, as R.F. Field), a graduate of Brown with a Master's from Harvard, had been an Assistant Professor of Applied Physics at Harvard's Cruft Laboratories. In his 22 years with GR, Field developed many of the Company's most famous products, including the iconic 650-A Impedance Bridge, and became the Company's (and the industry's) resident expert on the effects of temperature, humidity, and frequency on dielectrics.

Although the Company's reputation soared during the 20s, sales did not, holding at just under a million dollars a year. This fact did not seriously bother Eastham or his colleagues. The notion that a company could not be successful unless it grew, or that its worth was measured by its growth rate, would not take root until decades later. General Radio was nicely profitable, and it provided steady employment and generous benefits to its workers. As for the management team, annual stock bonuses steadily increased their stakes. In 1929, the ownership circle was again enlarged with the addition of seven engineers. There was no public market for their stock, of course, but, with book value increasing every year, one could confidently expect that, upon retirement, one would be able to sell his stock back to the Company at a handsome profit. Thus there was no pressure whatever on the management team to accelerate growth. In fact, some years later the Company would run an advertisement under the headline "We Don't Want to Grow Too Large," the point being that bigness begets sloppiness and that only a small company could pay proper heed to the things that really matter.

Chapter 5

The Great Depression

The stock-market crash of 1929 was shrugged off at first. Sales, which were $975,000 in 1929, sagged to $850,000 in 1930, a decrease of about 13 percent, but the Company was still profitable. Having outgrown its quarters, the Company bought another building in its Cambridge neighborhood, increasing plant space to a total of 66,500 square feet. The expansion was ill-timed, as the Great Depression began to bite. Sales fell sharply the next year, to $600,000, and the Company lost money for the first time since the post-war cutbacks of 1918. Sales declined further in 1932 and were not much better in 1933. Yet Eastham and Shaw were determined to ride through the depression without laying off a single employee, and they did just that, trimming the work week (reduced by 40 percent at its low) rather than the payroll. Of the 142 people working for General Radio in 1930, not one was to be a casualty of the Great Depression.

As if that weren't enough, the Company came to the rescue of employees whose funds were threatened by the failure of a Cambridge bank, the Central Trust Company.

The General Radio Story

In a decision that speaks volumes about the generosity of Eastham and Shaw, the Board voted to give each employee cash equal to the amount on deposit. Part of this payout was recovered when the bank was reorganized, but that doesn't lessen the significance of the Company's action.

The effects of the Depression highlighted a problem that would beset most high-technology companies throughout history: How does one maintain a high-fixed-cost business in the face of cyclical downturns? Specifically, how can a company afford to pay its engineering staff when sales plunge and profits turn into losses? To slash the engineering budget is to sacrifice the new products desperately needed to turn sales around. To keep engineers on staff, even in the face of deepening losses, is to threaten the very viability of the enterprise.

The Depression brought this dilemma into focus at General Radio, and it caused Melville Eastham to craft a solution that he had been considering for several years. Thus, in 1932, General Radio instituted the "K Plan," which is so ingenious and which played such an important role in the mid-life history of the Company that it deserves a detailed discussion here.

Two basic principles formed the foundation for the K Plan. First, Eastham was a firm believer in providing job security for his employees. Thus, the Company would deal with slack times, not by cutting the workforce, but by cutting the workweek. If production had to be trimmed by 20 percent, the 40-hour week would become 32 hours, with a commensurate reduction in pay.

That much was fairly straightforward. The thornier issue involved the engineers and other salaried workers. On the one hand, equity demanded that they share in the sacrifice. On the other hand, it would be fatal to cut engineering hours at the very time when they were needed to turn business around. Furthermore, a valuable engineer whose salary is reduced in bad times is likely to find a job elsewhere. But Eastham had thought of that, and his K Plan

23

was designed to offer salaried workers an upside as well as a downside.

The plan's operation began with an estimate by the Company's management of the coming year's orders and shipments (usually about the same). This sum was then divided by 24, to create a monthly target. Then each month's orders and shipments were averaged, and that average was compared with the K quota. If the average was only 80 percent of quota, K was then posted at 0.80, and each person on the K Plan saw his or her salary for that month reduced by 20 percent. If the average was 20 percent above quota, K became 1.20 for that month, and the K-based salaries were inflated by 20 percent.

Two refinements to this simple formula made it work: First, people were invited, not forced, to be on the K Plan, and only those people in positions to influence the Company's fortunes (engineers and managers, mostly) were offered the opportunity. Second, the K factor was allowed to move only between limits of 0.50 and 1.50. If the arithmetic yielded a K of, say 1.60, the excess would be rolled over into a future payment.

When the K Plan was launched in early 1933, the K factor worked out to 0.5 for its first month, but the next month it rose to 0.6, by September it was pegged at 0.80, and it hit 0.95 in January, 1934. It eventually became a valuable supplement to the salaries of key employees, holding well above 1.0 throughout most of the next 40 years. To add to the plan's attractiveness, management, in setting each year's quotas, in effect stacked the deck by ensuring that if sales and orders were right on target, K would be 1.10

Chapter 6

Filling the GR Catalog

Throughout the worst years of the Depression, the flow of new instruments continued, many of them directed at the still-growing radio broadcast industry. In 1931, GR produced the first commercial instruments capable of measuring the modulation percentage and the audio distortion of radio transmitters. These were designed by W. Norris Tuttle, who joined GR in 1930. Tuttle, a Harvard PhD, was a gentle man of broad interests (for years a member of a chamber music group in his home town of Concord) who, like most of his colleagues, spent his entire career with General Radio. The same year, the Company introduced the first commercial frequency monitor, designed by L.B. Arguimbau. And in 1931 Robert Field authored an *Experimenter* article called "Field Intensity Measurements" (in other words, R.F. Field on RF fields).

Radio broadcasting had by now taken a firm hold on the general public, whose appetite for news, sporting events, music, and various other entertainments was insatiable. In response, broadcast stations crowded the spectrum, and government regulations were tightened to minimize interference. These created an expanding market for frequency standards and monitors, distortion monitors, and modulation meters. For the next 30 years, GR remained a leading supplier of such equipment to radio (and eventually, television) stations throughout the world.

Depression or no depression, Melville Eastham knew that innovative instruments were the tickets to recovery, and, instead of retrenching, GR accelerated its efforts to introduce new products. Eastham had a first-class engineering team at his disposal, men such as Horton, Field, Scott, McElroy, Lamson, Tuttle, Arguimbau, and a brilliant Austrian import named Eduard Karplus. McElroy, one of the Company's first engineers, was hired fresh out of Harvard and spent over 40 years at GR. Tall, wry, and never known by any label other than "P.K.," he could be gracious or brusque, depending on circumstances. Karplus, a tall, gaunt, man whose precisely phrased utterances were delivered with a crisp German accent, looked like a baron in a Viennese operetta. Lamson, whose career at GR also spanned four decades, had a professorial air straight out of central casting and in later years was in fact a part-time professor of electrical engineering at Northeastern University.

H. Lamson   **E. Karplus**   **W.N. Tuttle**

In 1932 and 1933, with the United States still in the depths of depression, Eastham turned loose his engineering juggernaut, with astonishing results.

In 1932, Robert Field designed the first radio-frequency bridge, the 516-A, Tuttle turned out the 561-A Bridge for vacuum-tube measurements, and the Company introduced the Type 548-A "Edgerton Stroboscope," a ground-breaking development that was to launch one of GR's most successful product lines. Professor Harold Edgerton of MIT had developed a lamp capable of producing a light flash of very short duration, and this lamp, when triggered by the appropriate electronic circuits, could be used for high-speed photography or for measuring the cyclic rate of machine parts. (The stroboscopic phenomenon is nicely illustrated by the apparent backward motion of wagon wheels in old western movies.) GR's first stroboscope and its many successors, marketed under the Strobotac trade name, were produced under a license owned by Edgerton and, later, by the firm Edgerton, Germeshausen, and Grier. Edgerton, deservedly known as the father of stroboscopy, worked closely with GR engineers for decades, contributing not only his flash-tube expertise but also his extraordinary flair for promoting his brainchild. (Those interested in learning more about the history of the stroboscope can do no better than "Inventing Instruments and Users – Harold Edgerton and the General Radio Company, 1932-1970," Richard L. Kremer, Dartmouth College, 2006.)

In 1933 a GR engineer, Hermon Hosmer Scott, developed the first sound-level meter, the 559-A. (Many years later Scott's own company, H.H. Scott, would become a respected supplier of high-fidelity audio equipment.) But the most noteworthy introduction of 1933 was the Type 650-A Impedance Bridge, the work of GR engineers Horton and Field. Priced at $175, the 650 was one of the most successful instruments in the Company's history, remaining in the GR catalog for the next quarter century.

There seemed to be no limit to what this group of no more than a dozen brilliant engineers could invent. The June-July 1933 issue of the *Experimenter* headlined, not one, but three revolutionary products.

The first was an adjustable autotransformer, designed by Karplus, which could convert ac power-line voltage into any voltage from zero to something above line voltage, at the turn of a knob. The trade name Variac was coined by Norris Tuttle (who collaborated in the development), and the initial 5-ampere model was quickly followed by 2-ampere and 20-ampere versions and, later, autotransformers in every conceivable size, plus ganged assemblies and a wide variety of motor speed controls.

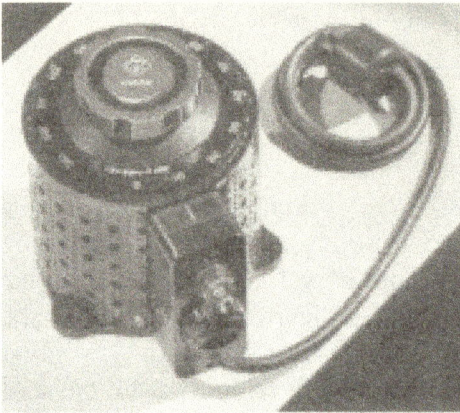

The first Variac autotransformer, introduced in 1933

Karplus's refinement of an old idea was simple in concept but difficult in execution. The copper windings of the toroidal autotransformer were contacted by a brush made of graphite, chosen both for its lubricity and for its resistivity. If the brush resistance was too low, it would short-circuit the adjacent windings as it straddled them. If the resistance was too high, then, because it was carrying the full output current, it would overheat and self-destruct. Karplus's invention dodged both extremes, finding just the right value of brush resistance.

Initially, the Variac was regarded as a useful laboratory tool, but in time it became universally recognized as an elegant way to control the speed of an electric motor or the temperature in a chemical process. It is not too much to say that this invention revolutionized the field of industrial control. For the next 40 years, in fact, the word "Variac" was widely used as a generic term for any adjustable autotransformer – even those made by competitors, and GR was forced to warn the trade press and others that it meant to defend its registered trade name.

Also described in the same issue of the *Experimenter* was the Type 535-A Electron Oscilloscope, the first instrument to combine a cathode-ray tube with a mounting and a power supply. The 535-A was followed in 1934 by the 687-A, which added a sweep circuit to the package, and in 1936 by the 770-A, which included most of the features found in modern oscilloscopes. Thus GR had once again stolen a march on its few competitors by introducing the first commercial oscilloscope, a device that would eventually become a staple of every electronics laboratory. But GR let the opportunity pass, deciding that cathode ray tubes, while accurate enough for radio service technicians, were too erratic for laboratory use, the Company's primary market. Some years later, wartime developments refined the CRT, but by then it was too late for GR.

A Word on "Firsts"

General Radio rightly took pride in its innovations on a number of fronts, and the word "first" has been applied to many electronic inventions that flowed from the laboratories of the Company. But pure inventions are rare in technology, and the historian who claims a "first" on behalf of his subject is often told that, 20 or 30 years earlier, so-and-so in some college laboratory had plowed the same ground. So it is with the Variac (a 1910 paper apparently described a variable, toroidal autotransformer) and the oscilloscope (Professor Bedell of Cornell had developed an earlier version in 1927). Such pioneering efforts deserve full credit, but credit is also due to the company that first translates an engineer's ideas into a commercial product. That process requires both technological prowess and a superior understanding of the needs of the real-world marketplace. Melville Eastham built his Company as much on that understanding as on his engineers' genius.

The third of the 1933 introductions was the wave analyzer, a new breed of instrument capable of making accurate, direct, voltage measurements of the harmonic components of a radio-frequency signal. The wave analyzer was designed by Lawrence Arguimbau, a Harvard graduate known to his associates as "Argie". Arguimbeau was a protégé of Horton, with whom he had worked at Bell Laboratories.

The amazing output of 1932-1933 didn't stop there. Eastham's engineers also designed, in this single two-year period, a frequency deviation meter for broadcast transmitters (the Type 581), a universal bridge (293), a wide-impedance-range power meter (583), a beat-frequency oscillator (613), another standard-signal generator (603), a bridge for testing electrolytic condensers (632), and a larger stroboscope (521), all the while writing tutorials on electrical measurement that were must reading for the growing radio community.

Chapter 7

An Engineer's Company

Buoyed by the sales of such breakthrough products, GR began its own recovery from the recession. Sales crossed the million-dollar threshold in 1934, and the Company returned to profitability, destined not to shed another drop of red ink over the next 37 years. Now, with survival not an issue, and with the Company back on its flight path, Eastham and Shaw, still very much in control, turned their attention to creating their vision of the ideal business enterprise.

Eastham had long been impressed by the paternalistic ways of the Carl Zeiss Works in Jena, Germany. Ernst Abbe, who bought out the Zeiss heirs upon the founder's death in 1888, then deeded the entire Company to a foundation, named for Zeiss, with the following statement of purpose:

To cultivate the branches of precise technical industry of Jena (optics and optical glass); to fulfill higher social duties than personal proprietors would permanently guarantee; to take part in organizations and measures designed for the public good; and to provide permanent solicitude for the economic security of the Zeiss Works and particularly for the further development of their industrial labor organization as a source of substance for a large number of people, and to better the personal and economic rights of those people.

As has been mentioned, General Radio under Eastham and Shaw saw their responsibility to employees much as had Ernst Abbe, and the list of employee benefits was much longer than at most other companies. To provide added "solicitude" for GR employees, the Company had, in 1929, established the "General Radio Special Fund," whose principal and income could be used to help employees who, for one reason or another, were in financial trouble. In 1934, this fund was greatly expanded with Shaw's gift of 2255 shares of his stock (almost a quarter of the Company). The fund was then renamed the Genradco Trust (a harbinger of the Company's rechristening many years later), and the list of employee benefits grew significantly. A prominent physician, Dr. Roy Mabrey, and an ophthalmologist, Dr. Mahlon Easton, were engaged as consultants, and both regularly visited the plant, where they were available gratis to all employees. Company-paid Blue Cross – Blue Shield medical insurance was initiated. Free eyeglasses were supplied. The employee cafeteria was heavily subsidized. An employee house organ, the *General Radio News*, was launched.

All this was happening in the 1930s, when much of the industrial world was being rocked by labor unrest. There was no unrest at General Radio. It lived in its own cocoon, fulfilling "higher social duties than personal proprietors could permanently guarantee." Eastham and his fellow managers were of course personal proprietors, but

31

they were of a unique stripe, proprietors with social consciences.

> *"If there was an ethic shared throughout the early electronics industry it came from General Radio. In what can only be described as a spectacularly successful mixture of idealism and quasi-socialistic management practices, General Radio set the standard not only in the manufacture of electronics gear, but in how a successful electronics company should run. Thus, early competitors fashioned themselves in General Radio's image."*
>
> From *A Passion for Quality – The First Fifty Five Years of Electro Scientific Industries*, by Marshall M. Lee

The Company's largesse all began with engineering excellence, which, when translated into quality products, supplied the profits without which the Company would have quickly succumbed to the downward pressure of a failing economy. Eastham's corps of engineering all-stars kept the whole system viable, and everyone else at the Company knew this to be true. A tag line widely used in GR's recruiting advertisements was "An Engineer's Company." Its meaning was clear: The Company was in the hands of its engineers – and not just those working as engineers. The Sales Manager, the Publicity Manager, and the Treasurer were all electrical engineers. An engineering culture permeated General Radio, and this was a powerful inducement for each year's graduating class at the university a few blocks down Massachusetts Avenue.

The laboratory instruments that accounted for most of the Company's sales were carefully crafted assemblies in which resistors, capacitors, coils, relays, switches, vacuum tubes, meters, and other components were hand-wired from point to point. The volumes were relatively small (typically a few hundred copies a year), so Henry Ford's assembly line techniques were not practical. Instead, each assembler was responsible for the manufacture of a small lot of instruments. Moving from instrument to instrument, with a soldering iron traveling with him on a trolley, he (it was an all-male crew) would execute one assembly step on each product, then the same step on the next product, and so on down the line. Then it was on to the next step, repeated on each product, and the next, until assembly of the lot was complete. Each member of the staff was of necessity a highly skilled artisan, intimately familiar with the whole anatomy of every product. For his work the assembler was paid an hourly rate, plus a piecework incentive that typically added 20 to 30 percent to his base salary.

The quality inside the cabinet was reflected in the instrument's exterior. The front panel was painted with a black-crackle finish, with panel legends engraved in white. The control knobs were made of black molded Bakelite, the cabinet of oak. The whole product looked and smelled of quality, as if it were an instant collector's item - which, in many cases, it turned out to be.

In 1932, overseas sales represented 18 percent of GR's total, and by 1937 the export share had risen to 39 percent of the Company's sales of $1.4 million. Leading the list of overseas destinations was Russia, spending heavily in an effort to modernize its radio industry (now becoming known generally as "electronics"), followed by the United Kingdom, France, Holland, and Belgium. (Curiously, Germany was not among the leaders.)

By the mid-30s, the Company recognized that certain of its product lines had extraordinary potential as revenue producers, and these were the subjects of intense development. The so-called Edgerton stroboscope was one, the Variac autotransformer another, and Hermon Scott's sound-level meter was a third. Bridges, signal sources, and wave analyzers were also by now firmly entrenched in the GR catalog. By this time the Company also was a recognized leader in the field of frequency monitors and standards used in broadcasting and in national laboratories. In 1936, in fact, 18 countries used 60 GR systems as their primary standards of frequency. (Russia alone had eight.)

The Cambridge plant was stretched to support the growing level of shipments, and a fourth floor was added in 1937, bringing the total floor space in Cambridge to 75,000 square feet. In the same year, a Los Angeles sales office was opened, with Myron Smith as Manager. At the New York Office, Smith was succeeded by Fred Ireland.

In the years leading up to the war, a new member of the engineering staff started appearing often in *Experimenter* bylines. This was Donald B. Sinclair, a Canadian who earned his BS, MS, and D.Sc. degrees from MIT. Sinclair joined the Company in late 1936 and soon was contributing to the development of new frequency monitors, radio-frequency bridges, vacuum-tube voltmeters, and oscillators.

In 1937 the Company applied for a patent, later issued, on an R-C oscillator designed by Hermon Scott. The circuit was unique in requiring no inductor, relying instead on a resistor and capacitor in a clever feedback circuit. The invention was of use to GR, but it was even more useful to a fledgling instrument company named Hewlett-Packard. In 1940 GR granted the start-up a license to manufacture under its patent, HP brought out its Type 200 R-C Oscillator, and a star was born.

In *The HP Way*, David Packard tells of a 1939 visit to HP by Melville Eastham, "who gave us some very good advice on how to organize and run a company.......After that meeting, Eastham and his General Radio colleagues continued to be helpful to us, and although we were competitors, we also became good friends." This spirit of professional collegiality was typical of the era, and for the next 20 years or so, senior management of either company would be welcome at the headquarters of the other – *noblesse oblige* – until too large a gulf separated the two.

In 1940, with war in the wings, shipments were $1.25 million, and 215 employees worked at the Cambridge plant and a scattering of sales offices. The balance sheet was solid, the recession losses having been more than offset by the profitable years since. The employees were well paid, with an enviable list of benefits, the growing band of engineers was prolific in the extreme, and some of them showed promise as a potential next generation of management. Melville Eastham had guided his creation through its first quarter century, and the result was a Company that had become the foremost manufacturer of laboratory test instruments in the world.

Chapter 8

World War 2

With the entry of the United States into a world war, once again the armed forces turned to General Radio for help – but with a difference. In 1917, radio was still largely experimental; in 1941, it was recognized as an essential element of warfare, an often decisive factor in air, sea, and land battles. Thus General Radio found itself under mounting pressure from the War Department to undertake the volume manufacture of transmitters and receivers. Eastham, however, argued that, while many companies were able to produce communications equipment, they could do so only if they were equipped with proper instrumentation – something GR was uniquely qualified to provide. His position prevailed, and the Company's assemblers soon found themselves struggling to meet an unprecedented demand for instruments.

In the early part of the war, military planners grew uneasy over the heavy concentration of electronic manufacturing along the east coast, and GR was asked to find a second source of assembly of the more vital instruments – preferably far removed from Cambridge. Melville Eastham, a native of Oregon, found a likely prospect in a small radio shop in an Oregon town he knew well, Klamath Falls. The shop was run by two brothers, Frank and Jesse Brown, and it was given a contract to assemble 400 General Radio Type 650 impedance bridges – in Portland, Oregon, for its larger labor pool. The Brown brothers, thus attuned to the technology of impedance measurement, developed their own bridges after the war (notably, a 650 derivative known as "the Brown bridge" both for its developer and for its color), and on the success of these products they and their colleagues built Electro Scientific Industries (ESI), a moderately successful instrument company.

Over the course of the four wartime years, the Company would see its sales more than quadruple. Thousands of GR frequency meters (called LR interpolators) were installed on the ships of the U.S. Navy, and instruments of all kinds flew off the Cambridge shipping dock, some bound for laboratories engaged in what was called, without further explanation, "the Manhattan Project."

With the draft, able-bodied men were in short supply, and the Company's all-male assembly operation was hard pressed to keep up with the surging demand, even though the workweek had been bumped up to 48 hours. Some of the less complex subassemblies were farmed out to subcontractors, but the labor situation remained a stubborn problem until the woes of a Cambridge neighbor supplied the solution. The neighbor was the New England Confectionery Company, maker of the popular "Necco" candy wafers. Suddenly Necco, finding its sugar supply a wartime casualty, was forced to suspend operations. Eastham thus found a workforce of about 100 young women available for the asking – right across

Massachusetts Avenue from General Radio. The Necco space was leased, the ladies were hired, and a plant that had produced Necco wafers was soon turning out stroboscopes.

The "Necco Girls" were not the only females to take the place of men at war at GR. A group of women known as the GREIFs, for General Radio Emergency Inspection Force, was recruited and then put through a six-week training course in basic electronics to prepare them for jobs in the testing and calibration laboratories. The course was administered by one of GR's most professorial engineers, Horatio Lamson, and the ladies embraced the new world of ohms, farads, and kilocycles with great enthusiasm. The first group of 12 was followed by three more platoons, and the result of the program was highly gratifying to the Company and to the ladies themselves, some of whom were motivated to enroll in evening classes in mathematics and electronics.

In WW2, General Radio went co-ed, with the arrival of the GREIFs.

Employees were regularly reminded of the importance of their work to the war effort. The General Radio News, a monthly employee house organ launched in 1938, was filled with letters from employees now on the battlefields of Europe and the Pacific, and there were

37

constant exhortations to buy War Bonds and to donate blood ("If You Give, They May Live"). Frank Capra's acclaimed propaganda film, "Why We Fight" was screened for the benefit of the GR workforce in November of 1944.

As sales and profits rose, Eastham and Shaw kept expanding the list of employee benefits. The regular two-week vacation period was increased to three weeks for the office staff. (The production workers received an extra week's pay instead.) A generous pension plan was initiated in 1941, and a profit-sharing trust was established in 1943. And of course, with sales and orders increasing sharply, the "K" factor was pegged at its 1.5 limit. The wartime economy inevitably enriched many, but Eastham and Shaw were determined that the wealth being created at General Radio would be shared by the entire work force.

They were also determined to resist the temptation to parlay the demand for GR products into the creation of a giant company. Life was quite good enough, thank you, and as long as GR employees were well paid, well endowed with benefits, and surrounded by congenial people, who needed more? Not General Radio, which ran its famous (or infamous) ad titled "We Don't Want to Grow Too Large!" in the February 1942 issue of MIT's Technology Review. The writer (probably Eastham, with an assist from Burke or Worthen) laid it on the line:

We Don't Want To Grow Too LARGE!

Visitors to the laboratories and factory of General Radio are very often surprised at our size. Some think we occupy a hole-in-the-wall, others that we are spread out over acres. Happily, we occupy a position between both of these undesirables. Our total floor space is 75,000 square feet, divided between three four-story buildings and occupying about a half a city

block. Our total personnel is 287, of which number 30 are engineers.

G-R does not want to grow large; only by following the basic idea on which the company was founded in 1915 can we continue to serve our customers in the instrumentation field. That idea was to have an organization large enough to get instruments turned out, in peace time, in sufficient quantity to satisfy our customers and give us a reasonable profit, and at the same time small enough to enjoy the flexibility essential to adapting research, engineering and manufacture to the ever rapidly changing developments in the electronic art.

The type of equipment manufactured by G-R does not lend itself to production-belt methods; G-R design will never be cheapened to make mass production possible.

As soon as we grow to be a large company, we lose most of the essential direct contact between engineers and customers, and between engineers and the shop; ideas when diluted by eighteen in-betweens in an organization lose some of their sparkle and much of their originality.

Fundamentally we have only one thing to sell: engineering ideas wrapped up in cabinets with control panels. Many concerns can manufacture more economically than we; few have such a large percentage of idea-developing engineers.

If G-R grows too large.....if it grows so large that to change a machine screw from a 6-32 to an 8-32 requires a design conference, a thousand dollars in drafting time and a month's delay for tooling.....we will cease to perform the function for which the company was established: to design and manufacture precision electrical measuring apparatus at a price consistent

with both the quality of the product produced and the type of persons employed.

It should be remembered that a world war had just begun, and Eastham would have viewed the sudden pressure to expand with a jaundiced eye. Nevertheless, General Radio played a major role in the war effort, in terms of the large volume of measuring apparatus produced for the military and military contractors and in terms of engineering talent directly applied to technical wartime challenges. GR's close association with MIT brought it into contact with the Institute's Radiation Laboratory (known as the "RadLab"), which employed a large number of engineers, some on loan from GR, advancing the technologies of radar and communications. Looking for someone to help manage this vital enterprise, the Institute sought out Melville Eastham, by this time well known to the MIT family for his leadership ability. Eastham, then approaching his sixtieth birthday, agreed to give some of his time to the project, and he quickly became one of the leaders of the Office of Scientific Research and Development, where he played a key role in the development of Loran. Don Sinclair, meanwhile, was in charge of search receiver work for radar countermeasures at Harvard's Radio Research Laboratory. He was also a member of the National Defense Research Committee on Guided Missiles, and for his work he received the President's Certificate of Merit in 1948.

Another GR engineer, Frank Lewis, also received the President's Certificate of Merit in 1948. Lewis, like Sinclair, was a member of the National Defense Research Committee and also served as an "expert consultant" to the Secretary of War. Norris Tuttle, one of GR's most prolific engineers, won the Medal of Freedom for work in Europe with the Eighth Air Force, in radar and operational analysis, from October 1942 through October 1944. Dr.

Tuttle's citation noted his extraordinary achievement in "adapting blind bombing equipment" to the needs of the Air Force.

Errol Locke

Eastham's decision to give more time to the war effort left less time for GR, and this brought about a broad reshuffling of General Radio's management. Errol Locke was named President in 1944, succeeding Eastham. (Locke, who was not an engineer, would devote most of his time to personnel and production matters, leaving the technological leadership to Eastham, who would remain active in the Company until he formally retired in 1950.) Harold Richmond was named Chairman of the Board, Charles Carey VP for Manufacturing, Frank Tucker Secretary and Treasurer, and Arthur Thiessen VP for Sales. The Board of Directors now numbered five: Eastham, Shaw, Richmond, Tucker, and Locke.

Shaw, Locke, and Richmond were all hired by Eastham before 1920, and they were thus "the old guard." Carey, a no-nonsense manufacturing type, and Thiessen, a tall, imposing presence out of Johns Hopkins had both joined GR in the '20s, and both had become unchallenged masters of their respective domains. Thiessen's mother and Melville Eastham's father were brother and sister, but there was no hint of nepotism; Thiessen was every inch the corporate executive. Tucker was of a breed new to General Radio – the possessor of an MBA (Harvard), handsome, polished, and arguably the first General Radio executive to specialize in the business of business, rather than the

41

business of technology. Tucker's southwestern roots also set him apart from his mostly Bostonian colleagues, and it is likely that his MIT- and Harvard- educated colleagues were less than impressed with his University of Texas undergraduate degree.

Another building in the same Cambridge block was added to the GR complex in 1943. Formerly a garage leased by Tech Chevrolet Service, it came on the market when a local bank foreclosed on the mortgage and finally, after much haggling, lowered the price to a level GR thought reasonable. A new heating system was installed, architects were hired to integrate the adjoining buildings, and eventually the garage was turned into office space and became the Company's new headquarters address, 275 Massachusetts Avenue.

At about the same time, a new sales office was opened in Chicago, "CHO" thus joining "NYO" and "LAO." The three sales offices allowed management to raise the game of musical chairs to a new level. Luke Packard opened Chicago, turning New York over to Martin Gilman, down from Cambridge. Then, two years later, Gilman returned to Cambridge and was replaced as NYO manager by Ivan Easton. Easton, who had joined GR a few years earlier with an engineering degree from Northeastern and a master's from Harvard, was more engineer than salesman, and before long he was back in Cambridge developing instruments and writing scholarly technical papers on dielectric measurement for the *Experimenter*.

General Radio's Cambridge complex was, for its day, efficient and attractive, although its urban constraints made it clearly inadequate for the longer term. The location was hard to beat. A subway stop a few blocks away made commuting relatively easy for most employees.

For a workforce dispersed as it was throughout Greater Boston, there was a surprisingly long list of employee after-hours activities, including a bowling league

42

and a glee club. The year's highlight was the Winter Party, which featured a catered dinner and a production of the GR Dramatic Society, usually at Boston's New England Mutual Hall or the John Hancock's Dorothy Quincy Suite and auditorium. The dramatic fare consisted of such standards as "You Can't Take it With You," "The Gramercy Ghost," and "Arsenic and Old Lace," the last-named featuring P. K. McElroy as the manic Teddy.

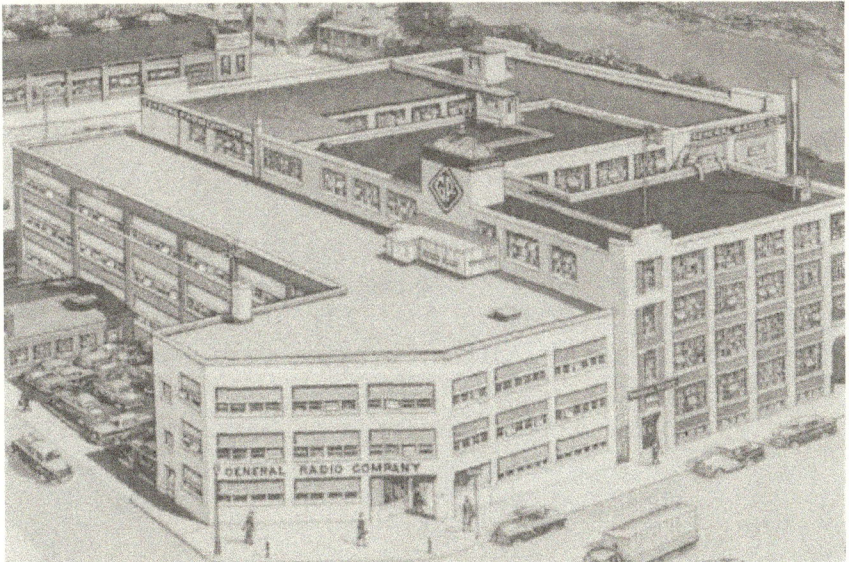

The final GR Cambridge complex, with the converted garage in the foreground.

Sales in 1944 were $5.3 million, and the Company employed 440 workers. This was a short-term peak, as the war's end the following year brought the expected order cancellations. But the damage was slight and fleeting, for the electronics industry, having broken so much new ground during the war, quickly learned how to translate these advances into consumer products. Radar to target enemy aircraft became radar to cook with, and cathode-ray tubes to display sine waves would soon become cathode-ray tubes to show Milton Berle. Best of all, the new consumer markets opening up would create an even larger appetite for General Radio instruments. So, cancellations or not, the Company would remain profitable in every year throughout the 1940s (and the 1950s and the 1960s), and not a single employee would be laid off, even as sales slumped in 1945 and 1946. Most important, the entire development engineering crew, now numbering 27, was still churning out one dazzling new instrument after another.

In 1946, there was a rare defection, when Hermon Scott, who was largely responsible for GR's success in the field of noise measurement, left the Company to start his own "H.H. Scott Company" in Waltham. It was a blow, but its impact was softened by the presence of Arnold P.G. Peterson, who had joined GR in 1941 after earning his doctorate at MIT. In 1947 GR further reinforced its acoustics staff by employing Leo Beranek as consultant. Dr. Beranek, Technical Director of MIT's Acoustics Laboratory, would later co-found Bolt, Beranek, and Newman, a well known firm in the field of acoustics research.

Chapter 9

The Golden Age

By 1947, the Company was again growing, thanks to a series of innovative ideas from its crack engineering team. Among these was the "butterfly circuit," developed by Eduard Karplus and refined by Arnold Peterson. The butterfly circuit was a variable air capacitor through which inductance and capacitance could be simultaneously adjusted, thereby permitting wide frequency control at the turn of a knob. The butterfly circuit (so-shaped) would serve as the key element in a long series of instruments, including the Type 720 Heterodyne Frequency Meter.

Peterson turned out to be one of General Radio's most distinguished design engineers. Scholarly, soft-spoken, and courteous, he would become the Company's (and arguably the world's) leading expert on sound and vibration measurement, the developer of a long and highly successful line of sound-level meters and accessories, and the author, with fellow engineer Ervin Gross, of GR's *Handbook of Noise Measurement*.

Their reputations burnished by bylined articles in the *Experimenter*, GR's engineers enjoyed a certain celebrity in the electronics industry. They also recognized their responsibility to the larger engineering community, and all were members of the Institute of Radio Engineers. The IRE, it will be remembered, was founded just a few years before General Radio, and among its charter members were Melville Eastham (member No. 120, in 1913) and Ashley Zwicker (member No. 105, in 1912). (Between the two, at No. 112, was RCA's David Sarnoff.) Eastham served as Treasurer of the IRE from 1928 through 1940, and Don Sinclair would be elected IRE President in 1952. For the IRE's first 50 years – a period during which membership grew from a few hundred to more than 90,000 – GR's support was a given. GR engineers served on standards committees. GR advertisements regularly graced the rear cover of the Institute's premier journal, *The Proceedings* of *the IRE*, and GR was always a conspicuous presence at the annual convention in New York, part technical conference, part trade show, known to the troops as "The IRE Show." On the eve of opening day of "the Show," a large contingent of GR engineers would typically board the Merchants' Limited at Boston's South Station for the five-hour ride to Manhattan.

The onset of television broadcasting brought with it a need for TV frequency monitors, and the first of these rolled out in 1947. Television's growth also spawned a growing demand for coaxial connectors, and GR responded with a highly ingenious   design known as the "874 line." The connector (and a long list of adapters, extensions, and accessories) was hermaphrodite, meaning that any two could mate, without the usual concern over male and female pairing. The concept came from the prolific Karplus, the engineering details were worked out by Bill Thurston, a recent MIT graduate, and Harold Wilson, a manufacturing engineer who had joined GR two years earlier.

Cutaway of the 874 Connector

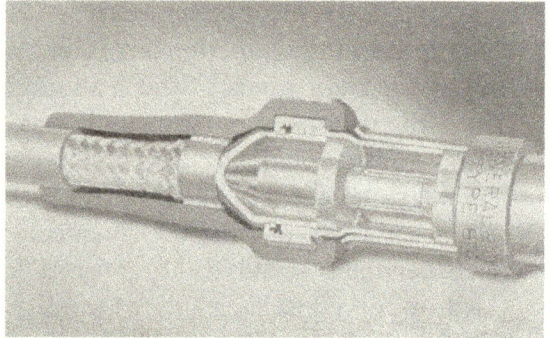

In 1947, with sales again climbing, the Company bought another building in the same Cambridge neighborhood, bringing the total plant space to 145,000 square feet. The buildings abutted one another, and passageways were created to permit indoor transit from building to building, with ramps to compensate for slight differences in floor elevations. To accommodate the growing number of people driving to work, the Company also purchased a nearby garage. This was woefully inadequate for the size of the workforce, and, characteristically, management assigned spaces strictly on a seniority basis. Thus, in the competition for a highly prized indoor parking space, a maintenance worker with 10 years of service outranked a vice president with 9 years of service. Outdoor lots, some of them several blocks away, were leased to handle the overflow. Newly hired employees would be assigned to the Lansdown Street lot (Siberia), and as they acquired seniority they would move to the Columbia Street lot (Mongolia) and, if they lived long enough, eventually to the garage.

All the scrambling notwithstanding, it was clear that General Radio was running out of expansion space in Cambridge, and that its future lay elsewhere. In 1948, therefore, the search began for a suitable suburban site. The chief instigator, ironically, was Melville Eastham, who had sunk deep roots in Cambridge, where he lived with his wife Jesse in the Garden Street house he had designed years before. (A word about Jesse: Jesse Chase was, like Melville, an Oregonian. After graduating from the University of Oregon, she moved to Boston to attend Simmons College, and while there she met Eastham. The couple had one son, Richard. Jesse was a Director of the Cambridge Nursing School and during World War 2 headed the Cambridge Chapter of the Red Cross. She outlived her husband and died in 1979.)

Eastham had no intention of moving to the suburbs, but he was approaching the mandatory retirement age of 65, and personal preferences mattered less than what was best for his Company. So he began consulting maps showing the distribution of the workforce, commuting patterns, etc. The conclusion: A move to the northwest suburbs made the most sense. Not so coincidentally, the officers for the most part lived in the northwest quadrant, in towns like Lexington, Concord, and Lincoln. Moreover, such towns were regarded as attractive communities for the professional workforce GR would need to recruit.

A search led to the purchase of a 66-acre tract in Concord in 1948, and an adjoining 18-acre parcel was bought two years later, giving General Radio a beautiful expanse of open land, bordered by the Assabet River and Route 2 and including its own small pond. It was an idyllic spot, and employees working amid the noise, traffic, and foul air of Cambridge started dreaming of spending their days in a more bucolic setting.

In 1948 the Company introduced its "Unit Line," a series of instruments and matching power supplies whose relatively low prices made them attractive to college laboratories. The idea was Eastham's, and the initial implementation was left to Karplus. For many years, unit oscillators, unit amplifiers, unit modulators, unit power supplies, etc. were listed in GR catalogs. Many thousands of "unit instruments" were sold, again proving Eastham's remarkable ability to sense market opportunities. Many of these instruments were relatively simple circuits, inexpensively produced, and thus highly profitable.

Karplus, whose hand seemed to be in everything, supervised the development of two new standard-signal generators, the 1001-A and the 1021-A Standard-Signal Generators. The 1001-A, designed by Arthur Bousquet, offered solid value for $595, and it quickly became a popular laboratory item. Although other electronics companies made signal generators for hobbyists and service technicians, when it came to quality, laboratory-grade standard-signal generators, General Radio at the time owned the franchise.

In June 1950, Melville Eastham turned 65 and retired, also declining to stand for reelection to the Board of Directors. Henry Shaw did the same. Thus an era ended. The man who conceived and named General Radio, together with his partner in creating the Company's social conscience, yielded the stage to the next generation. Eastham, an inveterate entrepreneur, was far from ready for shuffleboard. In 1936 he had cofounded a company, Mico Instrument Company, to make microtomes (instruments used to cut tissues into thin slices for microscopic examination). Mico, located in Cambridge, was the

48

reincarnation of an earlier company called Mann Instrument Corporation, whose Board included Eastham, Shaw, Locke, and Richmond, GR's "big four" of the thirties. Mann produced, among other things, a weather-resistant anemometer, which in 1934 was installed atop Mount Washington, where it was monitored by Shaw via nightly scheduled radio transmissions from his home in Cambridge. In 1936, Mann was reorganized to pursue "somewhat different interests and purposes," and later that year it was renamed Mico Instruments. With his retirement from GR, Eastham was able to devote more time to his other venture, which became a destination for other GR retirees wishing to remain busy after age 65. Mico was to survive long after Eastham's death on May 7, 1964.

Although Locke had nominally been GR's President for several years, Eastham in fact remained its dominant presence until his retirement in 1950. Locke, though a man of intelligence and talent, was no Eastham, and to fill the void an "office of the president" was recognized in fact if not in name, with the vice presidents in charge of engineering, sales, and manufacturing constituting a ruling troika. This scheme persisted through Locke's tenure and that of his successor.

Carey and Thiessen were elected to take the places of Eastham and Shaw on the Board, joining Locke, Tucker, and Richmond. Don Sinclair, Assistant Chief Engineer since 1944, succeeded Eastham as Chief Engineer, and he and Planning Director Charlie Burke were appointed to the Management Committee. Burke, another in GR's army of MIT graduates, had joined GR in 1924. He was known for a cantankerous personality and a first-class mind. He was also a good writer and was the *Experimenter*'s first editor.

Chapter 10

Rumbles of Thunder

In 1952 GR opened its first Concord plant, a 72,000-square-foot, three-story brick building, described in the *Experimenter* (somewhat disingenuously) as needed "to provide the additional manufacturing facilities necessitated by the nation's defense and rearmament program." Initially this suburban outpost would house only Variac manufacturing, coil winding, and transformer assembly – involving a total of 135 employees, but the 440 employees left in Cambridge could see the writing on the wall, and those who didn't already live in the northwest suburbs began checking out the real-estate listings in the area.

The Variac autotransformer that accounted for the bulk of the Concord activity had become an enormously successful product, but as these units proliferated and ran up thousands of hours of use, a technical shortcoming had been exposed. Cupric oxide would form on the copper windings, increasing resistance at the point of contact with the brush and causing eventual burnout of the unit. As usual at GR, a difficult problem led to a clever engineering solution, this time by engineer Gil Smiley: the rhodium-plating of the brush track to prevent harmless cuprous oxide from turning into harmful cupric oxide. The development was trade-named Duratrak®, and the Variac was given a new long-term lease on life.

In the early '50s, the United States was again at war, and increased spending for military hardware helped provide a tailwind for GR's sales, which grew 18 percent in 1952 and another 17 percent in 1953 (to just under $10 million), with profits growing apace. At the time, annual growth of more than 15 percent was considered more than respectable. General Radio's ambition was to increase the book value of the Company by five to ten percent a year, and this had been achieved with clockwork regularity. Thus, the engineers and other professionals who received annual stock bonuses over a career of four decades or more were virtually assured of a bonanza when they retired and sold their stock back to the Company. Most GR workers were not stockholders, but with good pay supplemented by profit-sharing, a retirement plan, health insurance, and so many other benefits, few had cause to complain. If it was not an employee's paradise, it was the nearest thing to it.

Since the early days of radio, the world of technology that General Radio served had progressed at a measured rate, and, although the Company's engineers had steadily advanced the science of electrical measurement, there had been no dramatic development (or, as it would be termed years later, "disruptive technology") to create competitive opportunities. Thus it was enough for General Radio to design better impedance bridges, better standard-signal generators, better frequency meters, etc. New product lines, like stroboscopes, sound-level meters, and coaxial connectors, would be added from time to time, but the core of the Company, the laboratory instruments, seemed reasonably safe from attack.

Now, however, there were rumbles of thunder in the distance. One came from the West Coast, where Hewlett-Packard was assembling its own catalog full of instruments to challenge GR. HP's sales doubled from 1950 to 1951 (to $5.5 million) and doubled again in 1952, passing General Radio. ("They'll pass us again on the way down," huffed one GR Vice President at the time.)

The other rumble was the transistor, invented a few years before at Bell Laboratories. The era of solid-state electronics was dawning, and GR, like most established electronics companies, was unprepared. MIT offered after-hours courses in semiconductor technology, and GR's engineers dutifully marched down Massachusetts Avenue to learn how to translate plates, cathodes, and grids into collectors, emitters, and gates. Meanwhile, William Shockley, one of the inventors of the transistor, left Bell Laboratories in 1954 and set up shop in Palo Alto, near his alma mater, Stanford. In the coming battle between east and west coasts for semiconductor supremacy, the title contenders would be the chip makers, but in a sense the real competitors were Stanford and General Radio's long-time farm club, MIT. MIT was also the only outside owner of General Radio, having been given a block of stock by Eastham shortly before his retirement in 1950.

By the early fifties the Company's sound and vibration measuring business, led by Arnold Peterson, had completely recovered from the loss of Hermon Scott, and then some. In 1951 Peterson and his small group of engineers produced an octave-band analyzer (the 1550-A) for noise measurements, and the following year saw Peterson's team delivered a bumper crop of new products: a random-noise generator (1390-A), a new sound-level meter (1551-A), and a low-cost version, the 1555-A Sound-Survey Meter. To cement GR's place at the top of acoustics measurement world, new editions of Peterson's *A Handbook of Noise Measurement* kept rolling off the presses.

Instruments for the measurement of resistance, capacitance, and inductance also constituted a market owned by General Radio. These were offered in every conceivable configuration: ac, dc, rf, high-frequency, audio-frequency, precision, etc. If that weren't enough, there were special-purpose instruments like the fuel-gauge calibrator introduced in 1955 by P.K. McElroy's "specials" group. Aircraft fuel gauges were essentially capacitance meters, and, since their accuracy was obviously of vital importance, regular calibration was in order. The air force instinctively looked to GR, the grandmaster of capacitance measurement, and the GR fuel-gauge calibrator was born.

The retirement of Company President Errol Locke in 1955 handed the Board a knotty succession problem. There were five candidates: long-time officer and Chairman Harold Richmond, now 63 years old; Don Sinclair, Chief Engineer, with a wall full of MIT degrees and professional honors; Arthur Thiessen, the Sales VP, with decidedly presidential bearing; Frank Tucker, the Company's Texan CFO; and Charlie Carey, the burly manufacturing VP. As Locke departed to raise prize cattle in Vermont, the office was left vacant for a short time, as the Board agonized over its duty to name his successor. Richmond is said to have favored Tucker, but found no support. In 1956, the Board named Charlie Carey President.

To some, the choice was a shocker. General Radio, which always prided itself on being "An Engineer's Company," had elected as President the candidate with the most modest academic credentials. Of course, it could be pointed out that in this particular he followed in the footsteps of his two predecessors, neither of whom held an engineering degree. But Eastham was *sui generis*, and Locke was Harvard. Frank Tucker in particular seemed to have the perfect resumé: an engineering degree plus a Harvard MBA – a winning hand for hundreds of CEOs in the next few decades. On the other hand, Carey was much more than a shop foreman. He was a voracious reader, said to consume a book a night, and he was a strong-willed manager. The officer corps rallied around their new leader, with one exception: Tucker promptly left the Company, joining the Harvard Business School faculty. His place as Treasurer was taken by Controller Larry Pexton, also a rare MBA at the Company.

Years later, Tucker is said to have quipped, "The reason I left GR is simple: It was going to take too long to get a parking space in the garage."

53

**Charles Carey, President
1956-1963**

Sales in 1956 were $11.5 million, and the head count stood at 650. The Eisenhower economy was strong, the electronics industry was growing rapidly, and the General Radio catalog was bulging with more than 200 pages of products – instruments, Variac transformers, coaxial connectors, stroboscopes, frequency standards, sound and vibration meters – plus reference materials (e.g., Smith charts) for engineers. Profits were good, the K factor held steadily above 1.0, and the Company once again found its Cambridge quarters straining to keep up. The acreage at Concord beckoned, and plans for a second, 80,000-square-foot unit were drawn. This would be a T-shaped building, matching and adjoining the T-shaped building already in place, to produce a letter "H" with an extra crossbar.

To finance construction, the Company took a $2.5-million, five-year revolving loan from the National Shawmut Bank. The addition was completed in 1957, and the entire engineering department headed west, along with Purchasing, the Calibration Laboratory, and Final Assembly. For those left behind in Cambridge, it was clear that it was only a matter of time before they too would move west, the timing depending on the Company's ability to find a buyer for its sprawling urban complex.

The mortgage was modest for a Company with gilt-edged credit, but it did underscore the fact that earnings and bank loans were GR's only sources of capital. In the same year, Hewlett-Packard made its first stock offering to the public – not to fund growth, but to give its employees a new way to build wealth. The initial public offering by its arch-competitor stimulated some conversation at Cambridge, but it was generally agreed that the negatives of public ownership far outweighed the positives.

The fact that HP was now a public company and General Radio still private did not affect the competitive balance, at least at the time. More significant was the fact that in 1954 HP and Stanford University joined forces to establish the Honors Cooperative Program, which allowed HP engineers to pursue advanced degrees. The program enabled HP to recruit engineers with the promise of company-funded graduate education. General Radio, with no similar program at MIT, was seriously disadvantaged, as were other Boston-area high-technology companies.

Chapter 11

Concord

In 1958 opportunity fell into General Radio's lap, when a fast-growing young company called Epsco made an unsolicited offer to buy GR's Cambridge plant, for $800,000. The offer was quickly accepted, and GR ended its 43-year tenure in the City. Among the last to leave Cambridge was the Publicity Department, and for several weeks that group coexisted with the advance wave of Epsconians, on the first floor of the building at 275 Massachusetts Avenue. Then the Publicity crew packed its catalogs and instruction manuals and formally closed the Cambridge chapter of General Radio's history.

The Company's new address was 300 Baker Avenue, Concord, Massachusetts 01742. To most of the Town's residents, the plant site, since it was south of Route 2, was located in West Concord. But politically Concord was one town, notwithstanding the presence of a West Concord Post Office near GR's plant. Baker Avenue was a short street, and the adoption of the number 300 was a conceit suggesting that the new address was in some sense superior to the old 275 Massachusetts Avenue (and to Hewlett-Packard's 275 Page Mill Road, in Palo Alto).

Initials

To those working at General Radio, Don Sinclair was (and is, in memory) DBS. Arthur Thiessen was and is AET, Charlie Burke CTB, Charlie Worthen CEW, etc., etc. Interoffice mail flowed through the corridors carrying such initials, and each new hire would within a matter of months be forever branded by his initials. When district sales offices were opened, they, too, were known by their initials: CHO, LAO, NYO, SFO, etc.

Thus mail directed to WRT/NYO was known by all to be intended for Bill Thurston in New York. Superscripts denoted that action was to be taken or not taken. Superscript "1" meant that the initials next to it were expected to do something, preferably right away. A superscript "2" beside your initials meant that you were sent the memo for information purposes only. A "3" directed you to route the document to the next set of initials on the list. (Any memo worth its salt had at least three or four sets of initials.) It was a childishly simple scene, but it was also elegantly effective.

The initials stuck to their owners like glue, and, amazingly, 50 years later, anyone who worked at GR in the mid-20th century instantly thinks of Arnold Peterson as APGP, Henry Hall as HPH, Bob Soderman as RAS, and so on through the long list.

The significance of the move from Cambridge to Concord cannot be overstated. To the workforce, it was a huge plus. Since World War 2 there had been a massive population shift to the suburbs, and GR employees, as their financial status improved, moved to Arlington, Belmont, Lexington, Concord, and other attractive suburbs. The officers bought handsome, almost palatial homes in the same area: Carey's in Lexington, Thiessen's in Lincoln, Sinclair's in Concord. A few employees were forced to move from homes south of Boston to the northwest corridor, but, although a few secretaries were unwilling to give up public transportation, the move to Concord was made without the loss of a single male employee.

GR's Concord Plant

With the move, GR also surrendered to the irresistible force of the automobile as the nation's preferred transportation system. In Cambridge, many workers commuted to and from their workplace by mass transit. In Concord, though a commuter rail line ran nearby, with a station within walking distance, hardly anyone at GR used it. In Cambridge, parking space was at a premium, with Company lots scattered over a wide area. The Concord acreage, on the other hand, was flat, open, and large enough to accommodate hundreds of cars (or, for that matter, a small airport if one was needed). Moreover, the Concord plant was situated next to Route 2, a major highway from Boston to the western part of the State.

The move also changed the human dynamic. No longer tethered to train or bus schedules, engineers were free to work after hours on important projects. The Company had never pressured its employees in this regard, and no pressure was exerted now, but an engineer facing an easy ten-minute drive to his home was more likely to work late than one facing an hour's commute by train.

Concord quickly became a Company town. A co-ed bowling league was formed. Christmas parties were held at the Concord Armory. Softball games were played on the Company's grounds. Engineers and their wives, many of them Concord residents, socialized regularly. General Radio employees served on various Town boards and committees. General Radio clearly loved Concord, and the feeling was mutual.

There was another view, voiced some years later by then-President Don Sinclair in a conversation with me. Sinclair, one of Concord's most prominent citizens and one who was deeply involved in the Town's government, wondered aloud whether the move to Concord had cost the Company more than it had gained. The Company had become insular, according to this view, and its engineers no longer benefited from the educational and cultural interactions that Cambridge could offer. MIT might have been slower than Stanford to partner with industry, but in Concord there was no MIT.

It was an arguable point, but to the vast majority of the General Radio family Concord was a most pleasant place to spend the workday. The 84-acre (later 88-acre) spread included ample parking space, room enough for the softball games, and a pond beside which one could picnic on the grass at lunchtime. Some Concord residents bicycled to work, and a few walked. GR employees now had a beautiful campus to go with their traditional rich crop of employee benefits. Who could ask for anything more?

The plant itself had been expanded one last time before the grand move, to a total space of 300,000 square feet. It was arranged as a trio of connected three-story "T"-shaped buildings, with a fourth wing added to create a series of three butting "H"s. The configuration maximized the number of offices with windows (an especially important consideration, as the complex was not air-conditioned) and, this being New England and not California, these were real offices with doors, not cubicles. Each engineer had enough room for his own small laboratory (and, in some instances, an assistant), and the third-floor Engineering Department had its own small library. Also on the third floor was the cafeteria, with all but the cost of the food itself funded by the Company. In another wing, the Sales Department was also quartered in third-floor offices. By now, of course, most of the Company's sales force worked at District Offices in New York, Philadelphia, Washington, San Francisco, and other cities in North America. Presiding over the Sales Department was Myron Smith, who reported to Arthur Thiessen. Also reporting to Thiessen were long-time Publicity Manager and *Experimenter* Editor Charlie Worthen, Advertising Manager John Clayton, and Service Manager Howard Dawes.

> ### *Canobie Lake*
>
> *An annual tradition for many years was a family outing at Canobie Lake Park, in Salem, New Hampshire. Here a thousand or more GR employees, spouses, friends, and, especially, children would take over the amusement park for a day of fun and games and good fellowship. The regal Don Sinclair and the continental Eduard Karplus would mingle with shop foremen and assemblers in a family pageant that would have delighted Melville Eastham. At mid-day the crowd would gather under a large pavilion to be served chicken pies and banana fritters by caterer Luther Witham, and then it was back to the roller coaster and canoe rides. The whole scene was pure General Radio, straight out of Norman Rockwell.*

Sales in 1959 were a record $13.4 million, on which the Company netted $523,000. Thus the net margin on sales was an uncharacteristically low 3.9 percent. The return on equity was somewhat higher, as the Company earned money on its investments, but flagging earning power signaled problems to come, especially when long-time senior officers began retiring and cashing out. The good news, if it was that, was that there were no outside stockholders, money managers, or securities analysts to complain.

The engineers, productive as ever, kept turning out superior instruments. Bob Soderman and Bill Thurston developed the Type 1607-A Transfer Function Meter, designed to measure the characteristics of transistors at very high and ultra high frequencies. It was, in fact, no more than a token acknowledgment of the semiconductor revolution, as GR left the measurement of semiconductor parameters mostly to other companies. The ability to measure semiconductor performance at high frequencies was of more than passing interest in Japan, where, if anyone cared to notice, the 1607-A sold particularly well.

The venerable and enormously successful Type 650-A Impedance Bridge was replaced in 1959 by the 1650-A, developed by Henry Hall, who received his graduate degree from MIT a few years before. The 1650-A, whose run would eventually exceed its predecessor's, featured an "Orthonull" circuit to offset the troublesome interactions that had plagued operators attempting to manipulate two interactive balance adjustments. It also included built-in, battery-operated modulation and an ingenious "flip-tilt" cabinet designed by mechanical engineer Henry Littlejohn. If one looks for products representing the heart and soul of GR in its first half century, the 650-A,1650-A, and perhaps the 1001-A Standard-Signal Generator would be among the leading candidates. In terms of longevity, the 650/1650 duo runs away with the prize.

The 1650-A

The elegance of the 1650-A stamped Henry Hall as not only a gifted engineer, as comfortable with microprocessors as he had been with vacuum tubes, but also one who understood the need to wrap his engineering in practicality. The 1650-A was filled with clever touches, but it became a blockbuster because it was easy to use. Hall would design many more bridges for GR, and by the time of his retirement he would be internationally recognized as a preeminent authority on impedance measurement.

Another engineer, working closely with Hall, earned a comparable reputation in the field of laboratory standards and precision bridges. This was John Hersh, who joined GR in 1957 with a PhD from Harvard. Hersh, a quiet, teddy bear of a man, kept GR at the top of the standards game for almost three decades before retiring in 1985.

Harold Wilson

In 1960, Arthur Thiessen was named Chairman of the Board, a post that had been vacant since Richmond's retirement in 1957. At the same time, Don Sinclair was named Executive Vice President, a new title signaling his position as Carey's likely successor, and Ivan Easton and Harold Wilson were named Vice Presidents for Engineering and Manufacturing, respectively. Wilson joined GR in 1946, after a wartime stint with a company that made models for the Radiation Laboratory. He was a laid-back, genial manager and a gentleman farmer in his home town of Bolton.

The Board of Directors, which had numbered five a few years before, had shrunk to three with the departures of Tucker and Richmond. Thus Carey, Sinclair, and Thiessen

62

presided over the semiannual stockholder meetings, held in the cafeteria, with Treasurer Pexton also on hand to report on the financials. The stockholder meetings themselves were reliably uneventful, since there were no outside stockholders to ask potentially embarrassing questions. Except for a five-percent stake held by MIT, every share of stock was owned by employees, either directly or through the Genradco and Profit- Sharing Trusts. Board members were reelected, the auditors appointed by unanimous vote, the profit-sharing bonus announced, and the meeting adjourned.

Thus GR remained insulated from many of the pressures (and opportunities) encountered by other electronics manufacturers. It cherished its independence, and this led it to decline various Defense Department projects that came with strings attached. Reporting1960 sales of about $16 million, management noted that the total would have been much higher had the Company been willing to compromise its policy of self-financed, controlled growth. The "We Don't Want to Grow Too Large" mantra was still alive, although a few of the younger employees were becoming restless.

Europe had long been served By General Radio through resident sales representatives, but in 1960 the time had come to establish a direct presence. The chosen location was Zurich, and to manage the new office the Company called on a young German, Peter Macalka, who had joined GR in 1954. Macalka was an energetic, well-liked marketer clearly slated for bigger things at GR.

Although the Company owned 88 acres of flat, open land in Concord, it was management's contention that the number of employees at Concord, now almost 1000, was approaching a practical limit. It was clear to most that the Concord plant had been an unqualified success, and that the obvious next move should be to replicate the model at some equally attractive site. A 100-acre site in Bolton was thus purchased for the next expansion. Bolton was a farming community about 10 miles southwest of Concord, and the site was on a numbered highway, near a planned major circumferential highway, Interstate 495. The value of the Concord tract had appreciated enormously since GR had bought it, and there was every reason to believe that Bolton would be an equally sound investment, as well as a good place for employees to live.

Chapter 12

The Young Turks

As the Company entered the politically volatile 1960s, it was still at the top of its game. The engineering corps remained remarkably fertile. The first generation of engineers hired by Eastham – men like Lamson, McElroy, Karplus, Clapp, and Tuttle - was now gradually yielding to the class of the '50s: Henry Hall, Mac Holtje, Bob Soderman, Bob Fulks, Dick Frank, Gordon McCouch, Harold McAleer, and the younger generation quickly made its mark. Charlie Worthen's catalog continued to expand, the total product count preposterously large for such a relatively small Company. In fact, few industry observers, as they noted the weight of GR catalogs, read their monthly copies of the *Experimenter*, and noted the Company's long-time claim to the back cover of the *Proceedings of the IRE*, would have guessed that this instrument behemoth was a Company whose annual sales were well under $20 million.

There were competitors, including Hewlett-Packard, Boonton Radio, and John Fluke, but there seemed to be more than enough business to go around. The competition between HP and General Radio was particularly cordial, with Sinclair and Thiessen on excellent terms with Hewlett and Packard. But HP, with its risk-taking west-coast culture, was opening up a widening sales gap over General Radio, still very much a conservative New England institution.

By 1960, the transistor had moved from the laboratory to the production line, and a new, yield-based production model was beginning to take shape in the electronics industry.   Boston-area companies like Transitron and Sylvania, Bay Area start-ups, notably Fairchild Semiconductor, and established industrial giants like Texas Instruments, General Electric, and Raytheon formed the nucleus of the new industry, which was soon to transform the market for test and measurement equipment. Like many of its peers, Fairchild initially designed and produced its own semiconductor testers and then, sensing a new market opportunity, began selling these testers to others. In Boston, Teradyne was founded in 1960 to address the same market.   Fairchild and Teradyne began with strong semiconductor pedigrees. One was a semiconductor maker, the other was founded by a semiconductor engineer. General Radio, Hewlett-Packard, and Tektronix, all rooted in earlier technologies, watched passively, almost indifferently, from the sidelines.

But it was impossible to be indifferent to the implications of semiconductor technology on instrument design. If the future building blocks of instruments were to be monolithic circuits, then a vital part of the Company's intellectual property would shift to the chip suppliers. As Chief Engineer Ivan Easton saw it, the Company, in order to protect its flank, would have to develop its own semiconductor fabrication facility.   This position was endorsed by consultant Arthur D. Little.

The first, tentative step down this path was the creation of a thin-film facility, based on a tantalum sputtering process developed by Western Electric. The operation included a state-of-the-art sputtering machine and a mass spectrometer to monitor impurities in the sputtering chamber. The first product to emerge from the new GR production line was a ceramic 50-ohm termination for the Company's 874 coaxial connector line.

Having established some competence in the new technology, the Company then set its sights on a full-bore semiconductor facility. To run the new operation, GR sought a qualified manager from the semiconductor industry, but three prospects declined offers. The job was then given to one of GR's senior engineers, Mac Holtje, who had just returned from a year at MIT's Advanced Studies Program, where he had specialized, fortuitously, in semiconductor physics. A semiconductor engineer hired from Transitron then designed the production line and bought the necessary equipment.

It soon became clear that a silicon foundry made no economic sense for a Company whose product line consumed only a few thousand circuits a year, and this part of the operation was dropped by Holtje. The thin-film line was another story. Aided by production manager Steve Crowell and engineering manager Nelson Powers, Holtje built the thin-film line into a key in-house component supplier. For the next two decades, the Bolton thin-film line, with automated sputtering machines designed by Holtje, would churn out more than 10 million resistors, hundreds of thousands of pin drivers for test systems, and hybrid circuits for virtually the entire GR product line.

The three-man Board of Directors was expanded to five in 1962, with the addition of Ivan Easton and Harold Wilson. The early 1960s also saw a significant enlargement of the sales network, as sales offices opened in Syracuse, Orlando, Cleveland, and Dallas. To staff the new offices, GR stepped up its recruitment of sales engineers. Sales *engineers*, not salesmen, as it had long been dogma at GR that only a graduate engineer could credibly sell the Company's lines of laboratory instruments to a technically sophisticated customer base. So new engineers were hired from the campuses of MIT, Northeastern, Worcester

Polytech, Cornell, and elsewhere, and, after a brief orientation period, dispatched to the regional sales offices. The typical office had a complement of two to four sales engineers, plus a secretary and perhaps a service technician.

The dictum that only engineers were qualified to sell GR products had a downside. The presumed self-sufficiency of the sales force tended to isolate the development engineers from the customers, leaving them to design instruments on the basis of their own interests rather than on feedback from the market. What feedback there was came chiefly during the annual "Sales Week," when the sales force shmoozed with the headquarters staff, learned about new products, and networked with sales and engineering colleagues. It was also a rare opportunity for a perceptive sales engineer to carry messages from the customer base to the folks at Concord.

Among the more outspoken of the breed was a gregarious sales engineer fresh out of Cornell named Leo Chamberlain. Chamberlain was assigned to the Syracuse Office, but he was soon recognized as a comer and brought to Concord, where he was groomed to succeed the soon-to-retire Myron Smith as Sales Manager.

Leo Chamberlain

Chamberlain hit Concord like a whirlwind. He was energetic, enthusiastic, and unawed by Company traditions. He spoke in machine-gun bursts, and delighted in floating outrageous ideas. He was also among the first at the Company to recognize that, in an increasingly competitive world, a sales

engineer would have to be, first, a good salesman, and he nurtured an abiding interest in human motivation. With a future that was apparently limitless, he bought a large home in one of the more established sections of Concord and set about scaling the corporate ladder.

Chamberlain's counterpart in the Engineering Department was Bob Fulks, who was, like many other GR engineers, a product of MIT's VI-A graduate program. Fulks could hardly have timed his education better. During his undergraduate years he experienced first-hand the replacement of the vacuum tube by the transistor in the engineering curriculum, and his master's thesis was a compendium of the possibilities inherent in various combinations of transistors. When he arrived full-time at GR in 1959, he found the entire product line ripe for solid-state renewal. Of course, not everyone shared his zeal; there were products to be protected, to say nothing of egos.

In 1963, GR brought its new Bolton plant on line. The building was an 80,000-square-foot, T-shaped clone of the first Concord plant. Its first occupants were the engineering and production staffs for signal generators, frequency synthesizers, and coaxial connectors. Bob Soderman was appointed Engineering Manager for the new facility, and a young Harvard graduate named Phil Powers was named Manufacturing Manager.

Chapter 13

The Sinclair Years

On October 17,1963, General Radio lost its President. Charlie Carey, aged 58, died in the course of a heart operation, in Boston. Carey had been contemplating retirement and was in fact building a new home in York, Maine. His death shocked the

Company's employees, but the line of succession was never in doubt, and Don Sinclair was quickly elected President. (Only five weeks later, the United States lost its President to an assassin's bullet.)

As Don Sinclair surveyed the Company over which he now presided, he had reason to be pleased. Once again, GR was a true "Engineer's Company," with a widely respected and much honored engineer at its helm. He could (and did) stroll the engineering corridors, asking penetrating questions along the way and challenging viewpoints at odds with his own. He was a proud man, justly so, and somewhat diffident, so that banter with the factory hands did not come easily to him. But he fully understood that his mission was to be, not chief engineer, but the leader of a business enterprise, so he began reading the literature of business.

Don Sinclair

By 1965, the concept of automating the process of electrical measurement had taken root, principally in the semiconductor industry, where the demand for productivity, commonly defined in terms of throughput, or the number of devices that could be tested per hour, was most pressing. GR's management was aware of the trend, and some recognized it as a possible threat. But it took the young Bob Fulks to catapult GR into the age of automated testing. In late 1964 he led a fact-finding expedition to many of the country's major electronics manufacturers and research laboratories, mostly in the military/aerospace sector. Stops included Hughes Aircraft, Litton Industries, North American Aviation (Autonetics), Sandia Laboratories, IBM, and Lenkhurt Electric. The tour convinced him that GR had a role to play in automated testing, and on his return he pressed his case for an automatic capacitance bridge. Thus, after contributing his transistor design skills to an inductance bridge (the 1633), Fulks turned his full attention to the development of the 1680-A Automatic Capacitance Bridge. Assisting him was Mike Fitzmorris, a young engineer who had taken over the "special products" responsibilities that had once belonged to P.K. McElroy. Sensing that such special products would become a growing part of the GR repertoire, the Company in 1965 formed a Custom Products Operation, headed by MIT graduate Harold McAleer, which would soon be using the 1680-A to penetrate new markets. Also assisting in the bridge project was MIT co-op student Bob Anderson. Of this group, Fitzmorris would soon become a key administrator and Vice President, McAleer would in time become a Senior Vice President, and Anderson, after a detour, would become GR's President.

The 1680 Automatic Capacitance Bridge

The 1680 was described in the April 1965 issue of the *Experimenter*. The article began with the following prophetic statement:

"The ideal measuring instrument is one that requires only that the unknown be connected to its terminals and which thereupon indicates the measured value, with not so much as a single control being manipulated."

Thus the writer (Fulks) was in effect tolling the knell for the entire GR instrument line, the very lifeblood of the Company. Fulks goes on to claim that the new product "selects range, balances capacitance and loss simultaneously, generates coded digital output data, and displays the measured values, complete with decimal point and units, on illuminated indicators – all in a half second or so." This, then, was to be the wave of the future: automatic testers for the electronic factories of the world, with manually controlled instruments slipping into commercial irrelevance.

In taking GR into the digital world, Fulks enjoyed the enthusiastic support of Don Sinclair, who was too good an engineer to miss the signs of a sea change in the test and measurement industry, and too good not to recognize true talent. There were skeptics at GR, but Sinclair was not among them, and Fulks was backed to the hilt.

In 1965, sales were about $20 million, net profit $844,000. Of the Company's 1123 employees, 793 worked at Concord, 227 at Bolton, and 103 at sales offices in the U.S. and Europe. "Foreign" sales were about 17 percent of the total, sales to the U.S. Government about 15 percent. In 1965 GR "went direct" in the United Kingdom, severing its relationship with long-time representative Claude Lyons Ltd and placing the UK under its own London office. At the same time, GR announced that it would open an office in southern Germany in the following year.

The best sellers in 1965 were the Variac (orders up 21 percent), the 874 line of coaxial connectors, the Strobotac stroboscope, the line of frequency synthesizers, the 1680 automatic capacitance bridge, and the 1650 impedance bridge. These were outstanding products, all worthy of a place in the GR pantheon, but the sales and orders in the aggregate were surprisingly low. The 1680, for instance, brought in $657,000 in orders, the synthesizer line $644,700. The five best sellers (exclusive of Variacs) generated only $1.3 million worth of the Company's $20 million in total bookings.

In 1965 half the Company was owned by about 150 employee stockholders, 40 percent by the GR Profit-Sharing Trust, and five percent each by the Genradco Trust and MIT. The employee stockholders enlarged their holdings through bonuses granted three times a year. Departing employees (retirees, mostly; up to that point very few stockholders left the Company for greener pastures) were compelled to sell their shares back to the Company. The machinery was, in short, still functioning as smoothly as Melville Eastham had left it, with the Company serving its employees, the community, and its customers magnificently.

Yet the Company was not growing fast enough to create new opportunities for the younger professionals – or, as would soon become clear, to sustain the system of self-ownership. Sales growth in the five-year period from 1960 through 1965 had averaged only about four percent a year – at a time when the electronics industry was getting into high gear. Hewlett-Packard had become a major threat, picking off one GR product line after another. And the imminent retirements of senior officers, each with large stockholdings, would soon begin taxing the Company's treasury.

Such concerns were put aside as the Company celebrated its fiftieth anniversary on a gloriously sunny day in June. Families were treated to a band concert and a picnic lunch on the Concord grounds, VIP customers were escorted through a "living catalog" of GR products, and there were balloons for the children, "golden rulers" and other mementos for the adults. Thiessen's "History of the

General Radio Company" was published in a handsome red, hardcover binding, and a condensed version by Don Sinclair appeared as a monograph published under the auspices of the Newcomen Society.

To some veteran employees, that day in June 1965 marked the high point of General Radio's illustrious history, There would be many other noteworthy achievements. Sales would eventually increase more than tenfold, the Company's stock would trade on the New York Stock Exchange, GR would carve out a leadership position in the ATE industry, and thousands of new employees would be added to the rolls. But, to those who were there, there was on that June day in 1965 a special feeling that to work at General Radio was one of life's greatest pleasures.

GR's Fiftieth Birthday Celebration, June 12, 1965

General Radio had always been noted for the quality of its products, the instruments in their walnut cabinets and black-crackle panels being emblematic of the best in electronics. But quality alone was no longer enough. A company had to be able to point to a Quality Program. Accordingly, GR went with the flow, adopting a Zero Defects program, complete with slogan ("GRQ=ZD"). It is not clear whether any measurable improvement was effected, but the signs reassured visiting customers.

GR's moves to establish its own sales force in Europe had begun paying dividends, and GRO (General Radio Overseas) streamlined the Company's export logistics by opening a warehouse in a customs-free area of the Zurich Airport. Every week, a shipment of instruments would travel by truck to Logan Airport in Boston, then fly to New York, whence it would fly via Swissair to the warehouse. This routing was impractical for the heavy Variacs, which traveled by sea monthly from Boston to Antwerp. The European Variac demand was also satisfied by GR's French sales representative, Radiophon, which manufactured Variacs under license. (In 1968 GR would buy Radiophon's Variac plant.)

In May 1966, the serenity of GR's pastoral setting was shattered when, in broad daylight, three armed men robbed the Company of $70,000 and drove off in a cloud of dust. The cash was obligingly on hand for the weekly shop payroll, the assumption being that no one would ever think of pulling a payroll heist in tranquil Concord. The incident prompted the Company to issue paychecks in lieu of cash.

At the end of 1966, the *Experimenter*'s long-time editor, Charlie Worthen, retired. For more than 30 years, Worthen was personally responsible, not simply for an astonishing volume of technical literature – *Experimenter*, the encyclopedic catalogs, bulletins, manuals – but for a consistently high level of literacy. Among those enriched by Worthen's example was this writer, who succeeded him as *Experimenter* editor and Publicity Manager.

In March 1967, under Sinclair's direction, the Company published the most complete, most detailed statement of policies and objectives ever seen in its 52-year history. Distribution was limited to174 direct shareholders, with copies serially numbered to ensure confidentiality. The document, over 100 pages long, came complete with graphs and formulas setting forth the conditions under which the Company's system of self-ownership could be perpetuated. That it should be perpetuated was announced in paragraph 1.1: "It is desired that this form of ownership continue and that all necessary measures be taken to assure it." (The underlining was Sinclair's.) The following pages laid out the necessary measures. The model would require a growth rate of at least 10 percent, which in turn would require a return on equity of 10 percent (the 1966 figure was 8.8%). Gross margin on equity should be 40 percent (1966: 30%), and the margin on sales should be 20 percent (15.2% in 1966). Inventory was a tricky subject. Because the Company built for stock, inventory was relatively high (20 months of sales), and the near-term objective was to cut this to one year, still a high ratio by most standards.

Arthur Thiessen

The Company's commitment to stable employment was reaffirmed ("Fluctuations in business are taken care of by the adjustment of inventory and hours of work rather than by the size of the work force"), as was a determination to augment employees' salaries by at least 25 percent each year via three bonuses and profit-sharing.

In an appendix, Ivan Easton rigorously set forth the mathematical foundation for the self-ownership model, taking special account of the changing shares of ownership held by the direct stockholders and the Profit-Sharing Trust. The latter's share had grown steadily, from 20 percent in 1955 to almost 40 percent in 1966, and Easton projected that this would stabilize at about 50 percent. The balance among shares sold to the Company by retiring employees, shares recycled to younger employees, and shares acquired by the Profit-Sharing Trust was precarious. The Trust's other investments added to the employees' total return, and there was a remote danger that the Trust would eventually hold nothing but General Radio stock. The solution, Easton emphasized, was growth, which, assuming all other factors fell into line, should average at least 10 percent and which must not be allowed to fall below 7 percent a year.

Ivan Easton

Easton, now one of two Senior Vice Presidents (the other was Harold Wilson) painted a cautionary tale for the readers of the report, but it is likely that few spent time studying his equations. The year before, he had laid out, also in excruciating detail, an analysis of GR's outdated pricing system, based on the costs of labor and materials. Again, the engineering approach to an essentially financial issue yielded bulletproof results, but few converts. Easton would continue to move into the financial realm, becoming Treasurer upon Larry Pexton's retirement in 1971.

In 1967 a comprehensive survey of the fledgling ATE industry was published under the joint authorship of Bob Boole, Bob Fulks, Mac Holtje, Warren Kundert, Hal

76

McAleer, Dave Nixon, Bob Owen, and Jim Skilling. Boole's field was market research; the others were development engineers. The report covered the markets for module and circuit-board testers, integrated-circuit (IC) testers, passive-component testers, and cable testers. It raised the possibility of supplying subsystems to the military/aerospace market, as well as the prospect of selling components to the existing ATE industry. It noted, correctly, that analog testing, a GR strength, was a notable problem in ATE circles. It spelled out the advantages of computer control and noted the importance of software.

At the Company's annual "Sales Week" in 1967, Sales Manager Leo Chamberlain wowed the attendees by driving "on stage" in a new mobile display van, soon to bring General Radio instruments to the far corners of the country. A converted Clark Equipment Cortez, the van featured 12-1/2 feet of well appointed interior space, with an impressive array of GR instruments neatly showcased. An earlier traveling exhibit, called GRAIL (for General Radio Acoustical Instrumentation Lab), had debuted in 1966, but GRAIL had no interior display space; instead, the removal of the van's side panels revealed outward-facing instruments, in a configuration not unlike that of a hot-dog wagon. In Chamberlain's version, the visitors were inside, sheltered from the elements, and they could even sit down and enjoy a drink. The van, christened "Tour-Lab," was soon bound for Los Angeles, San Francisco, and Dallas. The van was a hit, and Chamberlain had laid another marker in his journey to higher office.

The Tour-Lab

Sales growth in 1966 and 1967 exceeded 10 percent in each year, and the Company's long-term history suggested that 10-percent growth was quite doable. At any rate, the "Policy and Objectives" statement of 1967 revealed no doubt about the Company's ability to survive and prosper as a self-owned entity. It was necessary only to tighten up the system, now that the objectives had been so clearly expressed.

This document, so central to an understanding of the Company at that point in its history, also provides a window on the management style of Sinclair, who, as has been mentioned, was determined to apply his undoubted intellectual skills to the broader landscape of business. There was a rich harvest of books on management at the time, many written by business school professors trying to follow Peter Drucker to fame and fortune. High on the hit parade of new management techniques was "Management by Objective," or "MBO," and this was the basis for Sinclair's 1967 tract. The Company also reaffirmed in the 1967 document its long-standing adherence to the committee form of management, with the following standing committees ratified: the Management Committee, the Bolton Administrative Committee, the New Products Committee, the Development Committee, the Marketing Planning Committee, the Pricing Committee, the Patent Committee, the Personnel Committee, and the Data Processing Committee. Committees had always been part of GR's DNA, and management saw no reason to change course. A patient, consensus-driven management style had served the Company well for a long time, and anyway, none of the senior officers was of a type inclined to act impulsively or by fiat.

Yet Sinclair and others sensed that a new management approach was needed to deal with the changes overtaking the industry. The committees, and indeed the entire departmental structure of the Company, were based on functional responsibilities – engineering, sales, production, etc. It would be necessary, concluded Sinclair, to add market-oriented responsibilities to the mix. Thus was born "matrix management," an approach guaranteed to take a complex organization and make it more complex. Under matrix management, there were two axes of responsibility (and authority and accountability). Along the market-oriented axis, four groups were formed: acoustic products, under Bob Boole; industrial products, under Ken Castle; component and network test, under Dick Rogers; and custom products, under Harold McAleer. These were quickly realigned into three formal business areas: acoustic and industrial products, component and network test, and high-frequency equipment. Much more shuffling was in store over the following years, as the process of rationalizing the Company's unwieldy product catalog unfolded.

The memos launching matrix management spoke hopefully of the new level of teamwork that would emerge, and concerns about confusion were dismissed. Within a few years, new memos would appear explaining, with equally powerful logic, why matrix management was not appropriate for General Radio.

Although GR easily met its growth goals in the first years of Sinclair's reign, sales in 1969 and in 1970 failed to grow even 3 percent. The problem, now impossible to ignore, was the impact the semiconductor revolution was having on the electronics industry in general and on the instrument market in particular.

General Radio had historically earned its way by supplying instruments to people who wanted to measure the properties of capacitors, resistors, and inductors – the building blocks of all electronics. Now these components were being incorporated into integrated circuits, which were in turn tested by automatic test systems run by computers. GR had tested the water with Fulks's automatic capacitance bridge, but the tide was running out on the instrument business. Surveying the entire GR product line – instruments, Variacs, stroboscopes, sound and vibration meters, connectors – it was hard to see how the Company could achieve the 10 percent growth that Sinclair and

Easton had set down as a condition of self-ownership when its core business was growing at a rate much less than that. To a point, market-share gains could make up the difference, but against a voracious competitor like Hewlett-Packard, GR had its hands full simply holding share.

In 1967 GR's long-standing Chairman of the Board and Vice President for Sales, Arthur Thiessen, retired. His role atop the sales and marketing organization was taken by Bill Thurston, who became Vice President for Marketing. Cash-strapped GR could ill afford to buy back a block of stock the size of Thiessen's, but the repurchase was made, to the discomfort of some observers. At about the same time, the Company announced that it was amending its policy and would thereafter permit retirees to retain their GR stock. Most, whether out of company loyalty or the hope for a windfall later on, did choose to keep their stock – and were soon to regret it.

Chapter 14

Tensions at the Top

Despite the conservative line taken in the 1967 statement of policies and objectives, Sinclair, Easton, and other senior officers knew that the Company badly needed to accelerate the promotion of the Company's younger generation of managers. Two candidates stood out: Leo Chamberlain, the highly energetic salesman, quick-witted and a self-styled student of human behavior, and Bob Fulks, the first of a new breed of "digital thinkers" on the engineering staff. Chamberlain was appointed Sales Manager in 1966, and Fulks was named Chief Engineer in 1968. Chamberlain, who was much admired by Sinclair among others, was also named to the Management Committee, a signal honor for someone still in his 30s. Slightly older, in his 40s, was Bill Thurston, Vice President for Marketing and a member of the Management Committee. To any interested observer of the GR scene at the time, these three seemed to be the nucleus of the Company's next generation of leaders. There were several other talented managers, including European Manager Peter Macalka and Market Research Manager Dick Rogers, but Chamberlain and Fulks were on the fastest tracks. Thurston was quietly growing in stature by virtue of his attention to detail and his position as the Company's chief marketing manager. There had always been engineers and salesmen at GR, but the marketing professional was a relatively new phenomenon. In fact, when Bill Thurston became the Company's Marketing Research Manager in 1956, his was the first title to include the term "Marketing" in GR's history.

Most significant of all, Bill Thurston was named to the Board of Directors in 1968, one of only five members, all insiders.

Macalka and Rogers would in time climb far in the GR hierarchy. Macalka, who had the distinction of having served in both the German and the U.S. armed forces (the latter tour paving his way to citizenship), was liked and respected. In his position as Manager of "GRO" (General Radio Overseas), he reported to long-time Export Manager Steve DeBlois. It was assumed that it was just a matter of time before he found a senior position in Concord. Rogers, a heavy-set, bespectacled, fellow, looked more like a ward boss from South Boston than a high-tech executive, but he was a young man of great ability and reliable instincts, and in the next decade he would become widely recognized as one of GR's most effective managers.

Only three years after Sinclair had declared the Company's system of self-ownership to be an article of faith, the following appeared over his signature in a report to stockholders dated March 2, 1970:

"It has therefore been unanimously agreed by the present members of the Executive Committee and Management Committee that General Radio will need wider equity participation, leading to "going public" through one mechanism or another at some appropriate time during the next few years."

Peter Macalka   **Dick Rogers**

What had happened in the space of three years to cause General Radio to abandon the system of ownership so carefully crafted by its founder and so steadfastly embraced for 55 years?

The short explanation is that the profitability and growth objectives stated by Sinclair and Easton in 1967 had not been met. Profit on equity fell to 2.6 percent in 1970, versus a goal of 10 percent. Gross margin on sales was 5.4 percent, versus a goal of 20 percent. Inventory was well above target. The Company's growth rate slipped to 2 or 3 percent a year. Thus the Company was performing well below the standards laid down as essential by Sinclair and Easton in their 1967 treatise.

To make matters worse, the system of recycling Company stock from retirees to new employee stockholders was strained by cash-outs on the part of some members of senior management. Over the period from 1963 through 1969, money used to repurchase stock exceeded new inflows by more than $3 million, a significant sum for a Company with a net worth of $12 million. The Profit-Sharing Trust was cushioning the blow, buying in most of the stock being off-loaded by the retirees. By the end of 1970, the PST's share of equity total equity stood at 44 percent, still under the 50 percent that Easton had predicted in his 1967 analysis. But Easton had stated two essentials in that document:

> "Growth is not only possible but is mandatory for long-term stability of the system.
>
> The growth rate must equal or exceed the earnings rate. The minimum acceptable figure is about 7 %."

In short, the system defended by Sinclair and formulated by Easton in 1967 was perfectly sound as long as the Company performed reasonably well. If it did not, all bets were off.

The first reaction to the gathering crisis was of course an attempt to cut costs. Travel budgets were trimmed. Advertising costs were cut by the simple expedient of creating an in-house agency ("GRAD" for General Radio Advertising Department), thus reclaiming the 12-percent commissions that had been paid to outside agencies. The *Experimenter* was considered a wasteful expense, and it became obvious that it could not survive.

The K Plan, the variable compensation scheme under which the monthly pay of key employees was adjusted to track the state of business, was a source of some grumbling on several counts. Those paid under the K formula (stockholder employees) had been used to K factors well above unity, often boosting their monthly salaries by 20 or 25 percent. But in each of the years from 1964 through 1968, K had fallen below 1.00 in at least one month, reaching a low of 0.87 in 1968. In response to growing dissatisfaction, Sinclair, in a memo dated December 4, 1968, announced several revisions to the K formula, setting a new floor at 1.00 and using quarterly, rather than monthly, data in the K calculation. In the wake of these changes, the K factor struggled along for another 11 months, averaging 1.05, and then the whole plan was scrapped, after a 36-year run.

Salvation, everyone realized, lay in sales growth – growth far beyond what could reasonably be expected from the traditional instrument lines. The most promising new product was a circuit-board test system designed by Fulks for in-house use but later turned into a marketable product, the 1790.

Chapter 15

GR Enters the Systems Business

It is not true, as conventional wisdom has it, that GR's initiation into the systems business was via circuit-board testing. In the 1960s there had been several custom products that could only be described as test systems. In 1965, for instance, GR designed a Sound Calibration Console for the Heath laboratory at the Newark (Ohio) Air Force Base. This system became the Air Force's primary calibration laboratory for measuring noise (chiefly from jet engines). An Automatic Cable-Capacitance Measuring System, based on the 1680 Automatic Capacitance Bridge, was designed for Western Electric.

This system required the integration of bridge, scanner, interface unit, and software, and engineers Dick Sette, Peter Jorrens, and Matt Fichtenbaum, working under the direction of Bob Fulks, pulled it off rather well. But these were custom assignments for specific projects, none of which involved production testing. The first GR test system to be offered as a catalog product, designed for use in the factory, was indeed the 1790 board-test system.

The 1790

It began with the Company's struggles to test the complex new circuit boards that products like the 1680 required. Determining whether a board was good or bad was hard enough; if it was bad, it was necessary to find out where the fault lay, so that it could be repaired. Manual fault-diagnosis was theoretically possible, but practically out of the question. The challenge led to the development of an in-house board tester. In bringing the system on line Bob Fulks led a team of engineers, including Matt Fichtenbaum, Bob Cvitkovich, Paul d'Entremont, and Peter Goebel. Fichtenbaum, an intense young engineer in the

Fulks mold, helped design the high-level test language that was so central to the system's ease of use. He arrived at GR as a co-op student at MIT in 1964 and joined the Company as an engineer in 1968. D'Entremont contributed the packaging for the new system, and Goebel was Project Manager.

Customers touring the Concord plant were fascinated by GR's in-house board tester, and in short order management realized the commercial possibilities. The project was moved under the umbrella of Harold McAleer's Custom Products Operation (CPO), now staffed by some of the Company's best engineering talent, including Dick Sette and Dan Abenaim, as well as the aforementioned Goebel and Cvitkovitch. Converting the in-house system to a commercial product meant that sales and marketing skills would be needed, and Bob Anderson, Eric Mudama, Dave Allen, and Dave Osborne were added to the team. The system, christened the 1790, was unveiled at the Wescon conference in San Francisco in August 1969 and then made the trade-show rounds, calling at NEREM (Boston) and NEC (Chicago).

At the Wescon exhibit, Nick DeWolf, the founder of Teradyne and an acknowledged ATE guru, asked the price of the system. When told it was $32,500, DeWolf grinned and remarked, "You guys don't know anything about selling systems."

"He was right," Anderson recalls.

The Company also knew nothing about supporting systems as complex as the 1790. Matt Fichtenbaum recalls describing the 1790 to an assembly of GR service managers from the various sales regions, after which one member of the audience was heard to say, "Boy, I sure hope my district isn't the first to get one of these things."

But the learning process was about to begin. On December 30, the first 1790 left the Concord shipping dock for its new owner, Raytheon's Norwood (MA) plant.

In its initial configuration, the 1790 consisted of GR-developed test hardware (drivers, or stimuli, and detectors to compare outputs against expected values), a Digital Equipment PDP-8 computer, an interface system, a Tektronix display scope, a Teletypewriter (the operator's command post), an optical tape reader, and adaptors to accommodate various board types. The list price - $32,500 for a basic 240-pin system - was determined more by GR's traditional "minimum selling price" formulas than by a realistic assessment of the system's economic value to its owners. (Thus DeWolf's comment.) Terms like economic payback, throughput, yield, and return on investment had yet to be added to the GR sales vocabulary.

With the 1790 the Company was in a position to leapfrog ATE companies focused on semiconductor testing. The situation called for a full-scale marketing campaign, with promotion, trade-show participation, installation of "demo" systems at sales offices, a crash course in ATE for the sales force – in short, for the kind of heavy up-front expenditures GR could ill afford. Nevertheless, as the 1790 quickly began to gain traction in the market, the die was cast: General Radio was forced to transform itself into a systems manufacturer. In fact, what Fulks and company had wrought was the birth of the circuit-board test industry and a new lease on life for General Radio, though the birthing pains would be severe.

The invention of the PDP-8 minicomputer in the mid 60s was central to the creation of the 1790 (and of many other systems throughout the electronics industry), and it was a huge commercial success, helping to make Digital Equipment a stock-market darling. Its headquarters, in old mill buildings in Maynard, was only seven miles from GR's Concord plant. DEC founder and CEO Ken Olsen sat on the Shawmut Bank Board with GR President

Don Sinclair. GR's purchases of PDP-8s, though initially modest, gave promise of an important new business sector for DEC, especially when coupled with the minicomputers being soaked up by other ATE pioneers.

Despite this chummy relationship, Fulks bridled at the PDP-8's limitations, particularly its slow speed, its lack of specialized test instructions, and its 8-bit word length. He also saw that by taking advantage of new "bit slice" integrated circuits one could slash production costs dramatically. At about this time, a band of DEC engineers was laying plans for a competing minicomputer company, to be known as Data General. The DEC renegades invited GR to invest in their enterprise, with a new computer, meeting Fulks's needs, sweetening the pot. Fulks supported the idea, but Sinclair, worried that Olsen would regard it as a betrayal, and even more worried that the Data General group might be accused of stealing technology from their former employer, vetoed the deal. Recognizing that Fulks's technical concerns were valid, however, he gave Fulks the green light to design his own computer. The Fulks computer project was thus launched. It would in time spin its own controversies, about which more later.

Chapter 16

The Acquisition Bug Bites

General Radio had never been an acquisitive company, partly because it viewed itself as technically and financially self-sufficient, partly because, lacking market-priced stock, it could deal only in cash. In 1970, money was getting tight, and the Company's entry into the systems business required heavy investments. Nevertheless, management in 1970 made two acquisitions. Neither acquired company was very large, but then, neither was GR.

One of these, the Grason-Stadler Company, was a Concord neighbor; in fact its plant stood across the Assabet River from GR's campus. Like GR, it had been founded in Cambridge. Its principals were two Harvard graduates, scientist Rufus Grason and businessman Steve Stadler. The Company moved to Concord in 1955. Its products – chiefly audiometers and psychoacoustic equipment – were tangentially related to GR's successful line of sound- and vibration-measuring instruments, developed by Hermon Scott and Arnold Peterson, with the notable assistance of Ervin Gross. Grason-Stadler had been generally profitable, although at the time of its acquisition it was not.

The second acquisition was Time/Data, a young Bay Area manufacturer of digital signal-processing systems, founded in 1966 by scientists from Ampex. Time/Data was a pioneer in the new, promising field of digital time-series analysis, introducing the first commercial digital signal processor based on a breakthrough algorithm known as the Fast Fourier Transform (FFT). The Company enjoyed some initial success, but by the end of 1969 it was running out of cash. Enter General Radio, which saw in Time/Data an opportunity to take its signal analysis and acoustics businesses to a new level. Thus, in March 1970, GR acquired more than 80 percent of the shares of Time/Data. With the acquisition, Time/Data got its cash, and GR entered the world of Fast Fourier Transform. An FFT-based analyzer of the type made by Time/Data could, for instance, be used to extract valuable data in the field of seismic exploration, and it was tempting to imagine a gusher of orders from the oil companies. Time/Data was expected to lose money for a year or so but then, bolstered by GR's technological and sales resources, to become a major contributor to the parent's top and bottom lines.

The two acquisitions were orchestrated with the help of C. J. "Gus" Lahanas, who over the years had risen from Advertising Manager to Sales Promotion Manager to

Assistant to the President. Gus, another of GR's MIT graduates, was a quiet, conscientious, intelligent GR loyalist, with a devotion to detail. The purchase of Grason-Stadler involved cash and stock totaling about $2 million, while Time/Data cost GR $1.25 million, mostly in cash.

Sales Manager Leo Chamberlain was offered the job of Executive Vice President (and de facto CEO) at Time/Data. Although the relocation would effectively remove him from the Company's seat of power, Chamberlain accepted. Having been disappointed when Thurston was named Marketing VP – a title Chamberlain thought he had earned – he had lost some of his affection for GR management, and a 3000-mile separation from Sinclair, Thurston et al was not unwelcome. Also, he liked the Bay Area and was intrigued by the opportunity to run a computer-related business in the heart of Silicon Valley.

Chamberlain's departure from Concord, though a loss for the core Company, spelled opportunity for two up-and-coming managers. Dick Rogers was an easy choice to become board-test product manager, and Peter Macalka was given over-all responsibility for worldwide sales, both men reporting to Marketing VP Thurston.

If there were hopes that Time/Data would quickly recoup its purchase price, they were dashed when Chamberlain predicted, on June 1, that the unit would lose $450,000 on sales of $795,000 for the year. He nevertheless was highly confident that 1971 would bring a major turnaround, with orders of $4 million and a profit of $200,000. The picture at Grason-Stadler was brighter, and it was hoped that profit from one acquisition would partly offset losses from the other in 1970.

With the 1790 successfully launched in Europe, attention turned to Japan, where GR was represented by Midoriya Associates, with Fritz Pfaffman overseeing the relationship from his office in Concord. Midoriya also represented Teradyne, the Boston-based, fast-growing

90

producer of semiconductor test systems. Although the two companies were not yet head-to-head competitors, it seemed likely that they would be in the future. The issue was complicated when Teradyne set up its own organization in Tokyo – staffed by several ex-Midoriya sales engineers – engineers now withdrawn from the pool available to GR. Searching for someone to sell Time/Data's systems in Japan, Leo Chamberlain opened discussions with Tokyo Electron (TEL), which would, in 1972, become GR's systems outlet in the Japanese market.

It can be argued, with the benefit of hindsight, that the two acquisitions were unfortunate distractions at a time when all of GR's energies should have been poured into ATE. The 1790 was clearly destined to be a winner. A bench-top integrated-circuit tester, the 1730, showed some promise. Fulks's line of automatic bridges had been expanded by the addition of the 1-MHz 1682 Capacitor Bridge, designed by Dick Sette, and the 1683 Automatic RLC (resistance-inductance-capacitance) Bridge, designed by Tom Coughlin. The need to focus on ATE had been stressed in a 1969 report of the Concentration Effort Task Force, chaired by engineer Bob Soderman. 'The Committee consensus," Soderman wrote, "strongly favored uncompromising concentration on automatic systems." There was now concentration, certainly, but it was hardly uncompromising.

It could be (and undoubtedly was) argued that Time/Data was foursquare in the automatic systems business, but in 1970 Time/Data was consuming precious cash and diverting even more precious talent. The 1790, for instance, would never have the benefit of Leo Chamberlain's prodigious sales skills.

On the other hand, the products thus added to the GR portfolio complemented the Company's existing lines, and management no doubt concluded that the acquisitions represented a reasonably inexpensive way to augment the Company's R&D program. GR's engineering staff was still, pound for pound, the best in the business, but it would be increasingly consumed by the task of transitioning the Company's instrument technology into the ATE systems business.

Moreover, the broad universe of sound and vibration measurement and analysis was seen at the time as having virtually unlimited potential. Suddenly, agencies of the U.S. government were mandating noise reduction programs in factories and around airports. Ford was promoting its new cars as super-quiet – as proved by a GR sound-level meter in Ford advertisements. Medical science was bringing new attention to hearing loss. And in Time/Data GR was acquiring a true pioneer in the use of the digital computer to extract a whole new world of useful information from acoustic waves.

But the most plausible explanation for GR's new-found appetite for acquisitions is that the Company, in 1970, was desperate for growth, from almost any source. From 1960 to 1970, GR's sales had increased from 16 to 26 million. In the same period, Hewlett-Packard's sales had soared from 60 to 347 million, Tektronix's from 43 to 165 million. In short, the test and measurement business was exploding, and GR was just not in the game. The numbers seemed to scream at Sinclair, Thurston, Easton et al, "Don't just stand there. Do something!"

The same pressures for change were placing many of GR's core values and traditions under siege. The facts were laid on the table at a management conference called by Sinclair and held at a hotel in Hyannis in March 1970. At this meeting, Sinclair stated unequivocally that GR would have to become a public company. This did not cause shock inside the Company. On the contrary, "going public" had become, for the employees of many high-tech companies, something of a holy grail, and the 175 or so direct holders of GR stock began dreaming of an initial public offering and BMWs and homes on the Cape. The dreamers also included a small group of restless retirees holding illiquid GR shares.

If self-ownership was to be abandoned, what other long-standing practices were worth keeping? Not the all-male production workforce, certainly. Soon there were ladies on the production line, and the Management Committee found itself debating the appropriateness of pants suits. The Company's age-old slogan – "Since 1915, Manufacturers of Electronic Instruments for Science and Industry" – was jettisoned as too backward-looking. The familiar, diamond-shaped GR monogram was set in a more modern-looking red rectangular flag. The *Experimenter*, the face of GR to hundreds of thousands of readers for 44 years, was scrapped. Throughout the Company, there was a growing consensus that General Radio would have to change fundamentally in order to survive. The young Turks welcomed the coming changes, while some old-timers groused that GR was "becoming just like any other company."

Tensions were inevitable. Those whose careers had been wrapped up in the instrument business were apprehensive as the systems steamroller began taking over the Company. The systems tide was unavoidable – no thinking person could deny that – but that didn't make things any easier for the old-timers.

In mid-1970 a severe downturn hit the electronics industry, especially the semiconductor sector and companies making capital equipment for that industry. General Radio was not in the direct line of fire, but it did not escape the downdraft. Bookings slowed markedly, and sales forecasts for the year were revised downward. Time/Data showed no improvement, the estimated losses now approaching $600,000.

Entry into the systems business forced a restructuring of the sales force. Over the years, the Company had opened sales offices wherever a critical mass of business was reached. This was a reasonable way to sell instruments, which could be carried around in a salesman's car (or displayed in the traveling sales vans that Chamberlain had introduced a few years earlier). But systems like the1790 were large, heavy, and too expensive to be replicated throughout the sales network. The solution, announced in August 1970, was the creation of four regional sales centers. The Western Center, in Los Angeles, under Frank Thoma; the Central Center, in Chicago, under Tom Fricke; the Southern Center, in Washington, under Bob Delzell; and the Eastern Center, in New York, under John Snook. With this realignment, a number of smaller offices were closed, including those in Cleveland, Atlanta, Syracuse, and Philadelphia. Bob Anderson, who by now had indeed learned how to sell systems, was dispatched to Zurich to stimulate1790 sales in Europe.

Sinclair, in the 1970 annual report, had a somber story to tell. Putting the best face on it, he began by claiming that sales had reached a record. After that opening, the rest of the letter was downhill. The shocker was Time/Data's loss of $789,000 (on shipments of $242,000), leaving the total company barely profitable. It also developed that the record shipments were achieved in part by eating into backlog, leaving the Company at year-end with only seven weeks of work on the order books.

The last paragraph of the letter is worth quoting:

"Several small changes of format have been made in this year's report to take into account the developing importance of subsidiary operations and to show as clearly as possible the interrelationships among the Company elements. You will note, for instance, that the Parent Company is referred to, from time to time, as GR/M (for Massachusetts corporation), and the total company, consolidated for balance-sheet purpose, as GR/W (for world-wide). These abbreviations are preferred as compared with GRM and GRW, because the name General Radio and the initials GR are trademarked, and the suffix letter is not part of the Company name."

This labored explanation of the distinctions between GR/M and GRM and between GR/W and GRW was vintage Sinclair. With so much of moment going on at the Company, the Chief Executive Officer devotes one of the thirteen paragraphs of his annual report letter (and the closing paragraph at that) to what most people would regard as a trivial matter of nomenclature. It was not that Sinclair was incapable of grander thoughts; his was an overpowering intellect. But he sometimes applied that intellect in curious ways.

In January of 1971 GR did the unthinkable: It laid off 70 employees. Not even in the Great Depression had the Company laid off a single employee. But the recession that hit the electronics industry in mid-1970 was sudden and severe, and GR's profits for the year were almost wiped out by the loss at Time/Data. The balance sheet was passable, just, and the backlog was anemic.

GR had now developed a taste for "business relationships," as would-be deals were called in minutes of the Executive Committee. In addition to Grason-Stadler and Time/Data, GR acquired a small, Florida-based supplier of NC-control software, Techware, and in 1971, the Company entered into an agreement with Micronetic Systems, a maker of automatic laser-trimming systems used in the production of hybrid circuits and film resistors. The technology involved the use of a precisely positioned laser beam to evaporate part of a film resistor and thus bring the resistor or a circuit containing the resistor to some desired value. Earlier trim systems had used a jet of abrasive material to blast part of the resistor, but the laser was much faster and could be positioned more accurately, and the laser-trim business seemed promising. (A third trim technique applied an anodizing gel to the resistor, and Mac Holtje's Microelectronics Center at Bolton used such a system to turn out hybrid circuits for a variety of GR products. (GR's Resistance Anodizing Trim System was known by its unfortunate acronym, RATS.)

GR invested $100,000 in Micronetic Systems (the instrument was a debenture convertible into 75,000 shares of Micronetic) and agreed to become Micronetic's exclusive sales agent. Under the terms of the agreement, GR received an option to buy an additional 500,000 shares of Micronetic, potentially giving it a controlling interest. GR saw the relationship providing access to another sector of the ATE industry without taxing its own engineering resources.

Interestingly, though the new "business relationship" with Micronetic Systems was seen by some as an important window of opportunity for GR, the initial agreement was not mentioned by Sinclair in his 1971 Annual Report letter. It was buried in a financial footnote.

In 1971 GR published a five-year plan. Total shipments were projected to grow from $26.5 million in 1971 to $53 million in1975, with profits climbing from less than a million to $3.6 million, and equity increasing from $13.8 million to $21.1 million. The major growth driver would be automatic board-test systems.

The plan seemed reasonable. A doubling of sales in four years meant growing almost 20 percent a year, but other companies were doing that. And the 1790 was starting to roll, with about 40 systems shipped in 1970, despite the second-half downturn. Most people expected an industry recovery in 1971, and sales did come off the bottom, sluggishly at first, then vigorously in the second half, culminating in record monthly sales and profits in December. The 1790 continued to lead the way, but there was also good news from the west coast: Time/Data, GR's problem child, had turned around, converting a loss of $789,000 in 1970 to a pretax profit of $124,000 in 1971.

With the 1790, GR had mastered the art of combining test instrumentation with a PDP-8 minicomputer and some basic software to achieve levels of productivity and performance undreamed of only a few years before. The Custom Products Operation, run by Harold McAleer, took the routine and ran with it, producing a large customized test bench for Western Electric, in which computer-controlled test stations were dedicated to passive components and linear and digital circuits. The system, called the 2200, would spawn several derivatives over the next few years. These and other custom systems would add relatively little to the Company's top line and next to nothing to the bottom line, but they added enormously to the systems capability of the GR engineering staff.

In 1971, GR also appointed its first outside director, James Wright, a Vice President at the Shawmut Bank. Steve Stadler, one of the principals at Grason-Stadler, was also added to the Board, joining Sinclair, Thurston, and Easton. Since Harold Wilson and Larry Pexton retired that year, the Board's complement stayed at five.

Chapter 17

The Fulks Manifestos

Don Sinclair was facing mandatory retirement at the end of 1972. Not that the rules couldn't be bent or scrapped completely, as so many rules had been lately, but the environment had changed, and the new world order – systems and semiconductors – was *terra incognita* to Sinclair. Also, the younger managers were starting to complain about lack of opportunity, and this fact, coupled with the Company's financial situation, meant GR would have to grow fast, soon.

There were really only two candidates to succeed Sinclair: Ivan Easton and Bill Thurston, both Senior Vice

Presidents. At most companies, the Board of Directors would choose one, risking the loss of the other. But GR was not "most companies." It ran by committees and by consensus. (One insider recalled the era thus: "The Board met and talked and talked, and the only real decision that emerged was the date of the next meeting.") So Sinclair summoned Easton and Thurston and asked them to hold a series of meetings throughout the year to decide which of the two would be the next President.

This decision – or nondecision – triggered a year of rising tensions, as managers began to consider the likely effect of an Easton presidency or a Thurston presidency on their own career paths. One might have expected engineers to root for Easton, and the sales force for Thurston, and there was some team cheerleading, but the situation was more complicated than that.

A particularly interested observer was Bob Fulks, who was dead sure the Company was heading in the wrong direction – wrong for General Radio and wrong for him personally. In June, his frustrations finally erupted, first, in a 106-page document presenting a proposed agenda for an upcoming strategy meeting in Hyannis. This was a pull-no-punches critique of the way GR was currently being managed, penned with a bluntness rarely seen at General Radio. On acquisitions: "Attaching other companies will not solve the problem." On the Company's history and traditions: "Delusions of grandeur, a longing for the glory of the past." On management by consensus: "For a great many years the Company has operated without a strong central management. Instead we have created an environment." On the Company's five-year plan: "Some numbers on a piece of paper are not a plan but a manifestation of wishful thinking." On committees: "We generally talk until everyone is worn down and then settle for a compromise on which all can agree and which no one is happy with." Committees should be abolished forthwith, argued Fulks, and responsibilities for achieving results assigned to individuals.

Bob Fulks

There was more, much more, most of it strongly critical, and a reader could not escape the impression that Fulks was questioning whether either of the two candidates for the presidency was capable of leading the Company to the promised land – a position that could be considered suicidal. Thus the document, initially dubbed "the Fulks tome," became known in some quarters as "the Fulks tomb."

In the same month, June, Fulks carried his plea for change directly to Don Sinclair, with a long, impassioned memo framed as "a proposal and request for advice." The memo had two main threads: first, that the Company was being mismanaged; second, that his own career track at GR seemed to be going nowhere financially, compared with those of MIT contemporaries at other companies and, most gallingly, compared with earlier generations of GR management. His proposed solution: Management should name him the manager of General Radio/ Massachusetts - i.e., the entire Company less its subsidiaries. He would then improve GR's performance, take the Company public, and make the kind of real money (on stock options) that such an achievement justified.

A frequent criticism at the time was that the Company offered far too many products for its size ($27 million in 1972, excluding subsidiaries). If one counted all possible variations of Variac autotransformers, coaxial connectors and adaptors, stroboscopes, bridges, signal sources, power supplies, banana plugs, decade boxes, etc., the total ran to several thousand, the vast majority of which brought in less than a few thousand dollars per year. It was painfully clear that such a broad product line could not be maintained, but no one in management was eager to discard products that were woven into the fabric of the Company's history. Thurston expressed his view in May, at a meeting of the Executive Committee, arguing that "this broad base.....should not be permitted to wither. It is an asset built over many years, and it would take considerable effort to recreate it if our position as a broad-based instrument manufacturer were permitted to die."

Some looked for guidance in the experience of other test and measurement companies. Hewlett-Packard was still successfully pursuing a broad-line strategy. Tektronix, on the other hand, had achieved its success on the strength of a single, market-dominating product line, oscilloscopes. Taking those as two successful approaches, some at GR were advocating "a third force," with GR combining a broad line approach with concentration on a single, industry-leading product line, presumably board test systems. Fulks, in his tome, rejected the third-force idea, dryly commenting that a broad product line does not automatically create a major company.

Sinclair, not surprisingly, passed the Fulks memo along to Thurston, who as the year progressed seemed to have the inside track for the presidency. Thurston then shared with Fulks some of his reorganization schemes, which Fulks regarded as more of the same, and his thoughts on the Company's bonus system, which Fulks thought wholly inadequate. In October, Fulks sent an eight-page, handwritten memo to Thurston restating his complaints, in effect concluding that a Thurston presidency was unlikely to change the system significantly.

It was now clear beyond doubt that Bob Fulks presented management with a dilemma. The Company could continue on its present course of management succession and probably lose its most gifted young engineer, the man who brought GR into the world of ATE, or it could give Fulks the power he sought and take its chances. Fulks was known to believe that manufacturing and financial management were in the hands of incompetents (the Fulks tome had argued that GR was too eager to retrain people who should be replaced) and that the sales department was overspending. Once in command, Fulks could be expected to attack these issues with gusto.

Fulks, it is obvious, had much to say, not all of it welcome, but most of it extremely perceptive. Among his more trenchant observations was this comment on GR's management deficiencies, quoted years later in a Harvard case study:

"Eastham was bright and had the entire plan for the Company in his head. He created a number of rules of thumb for managers, which were consistent with his mental plan. When he left the Company, he took the plan and left behind the rules of thumb. The problem was that no one knew how he had arrived at the rules, since no one really knew his plan."

It would be a mistake to characterize Fulks as a lone rebel. His were the most pointed complaints, and he aired them broadly. Leo Chamberlain, running Time/Data, was far from happy at the direction the Company was taking, but he was preoccupied with a developing crisis involving T/D's financial reporting and controls, termed "totally inadequate" by Sinclair in the 1972 Annual Report. Chamberlain, in turn, had complained in August of GR's "increasing lack of support for Time/Data." Peter Macalka joined Fulks in a year-end plea to the Board of Directors to take decisive action. Much as Bill Thurston was respected throughout the Company, some regarded his likely accession to the throne as a continuation of a system that was broken.

GR saw its recently developed taste for acquisitions as a sign of a new, more venturesome General Radio. The cover of the 1972 Annual Report carried a photograph of a signpost displaying the names of the members of the expanding GR family. In addition to the sales subsidiaries (General Radio GmbH, General Radio Canada, General Radio UK, etc.), the family tree now included, in addition to Time/Data, Grason-Stadler, and Techware Computing, Micronetic Systems and a recent Micronetic acquisition, Computerwrap Corporation, billed as "A GR Associate." Even this roster understated the reality: In September, Micronetic Systems formed a subsidiary, Wrapcon, to sell wire-wrapping services using Computerwrap equipment. And the total family size might have been even greater, since, during 1972, GR looked at several other potential acquisitions, including handler maker K. Dixon and Monitor Instruments, a maker of vision-measuring equipment that seemed to complement the Grason-Stadler product line.

Grason-Stadler did well in 1972, but its profits were swamped by Time/Data's losses. GR's hoped-for exit strategy for Time/Data, of which it now owned 85 percent, was to take it public as soon as conditions would allow, and in July, 1972 Leo Chamberlain and Gus Lahanas made the rounds of possible investment bankers, including technology-player Hambrecht & Quist in San Francisco. The bankers suggested a possible public offering in mid-1973, assuming the numbers were good enough. Time/Data sales in 1972 were heading for $3.6 million, about 24 percent higher than in 1971, and the market for FFT analyzers was growing rapidly. There was strong competition from Hewlett-Packard and Spectral Dynamics, both companies outselling T/D in 1972. But Chamberlain was confident that T/D's technology, bolstered by an infusion of talent from Concord (notably engineers Arnold Peterson and Bob Owen), would prevail, and to strengthen his position further he recruited a key HP manager, Tracy Storer, and made him Vice President for Product Development, presiding over a 35-man engineering staff. A new T/D system, the 1923, was rolled out, and HP responded with its 5451, featuring that Company's new 2100 computer. And so the slugfest went on, with Time/Data holding its own.

But financial controls at the Palo Alto subsidiary were just as bad as Sinclair had observed, and late in the year Chamberlain was forced to drop a bombshell on Concord: Time/Data would lose more than a million dollars in 1972. The year was thus blown, both for Time/Data and for GR, and all thoughts of a near-term public stock offering were blown as well. Sinclair's displeasure was on display in his 1972 Annual Report letter. "It is clear," he fumed, "that systems for financial reporting and control have been totally inadequate at T/D, and, to sustain its financial credibility, T/D is now seeking, with GR's help, a strong financial man to institute these systems and to supervise the business aspects of the Company."

Meanwhile, GR's association with Micronetic Systems was growing worrisome. The maker of laser-trim systems had managed to float a public stock offering early in 1972, but the stock, offered at $7 a share, was selling for $4 six months later. GR's direct financial exposure was minimal, but its reputation was on the line. The Micronetic laser-trimming systems were proving unreliable in the field, and General Radio, as its exclusive sales agent, was becoming a target of customer anger. GR thus thought it necessary to apply some engineering talent to the reliability problem, assigning Henry Hall to debug the system's bridge circuits. Hall found the system extremely noisy, and he added power-line filtering and shielding and rerouted cables, but, he recalls, "it was still pretty bad." The

103

problems continued, and aggressive competition was quick to attack the highly vulnerable operation.

In mid-1972, the following very un-General Radio statement appeared in the minutes of the Executive Committee:

"It has been agreed that Micronetic Systems must continue to quote on and deliver systems to get enough revenue to keep going, in spite of the likelihood of continuing service problems."

GR's problems were not confined to its subsidiaries and associates. At GR/M (i.e., the core company) a sales increase of 11.2 percent in 1972 was offset by a 19 percent increase in expenses. Noteworthy was the hiring of 154 people in Manufacturing, as that Department struggled to meet demand. The new, hot systems, like the 1790, couldn't be shipped because of production issues. (Fulks, in one of his memos, claimed that 80 percent of the circuit boards required rework.) And the older, established instruments, which GR could make blindfolded, were under heavy competitive attack. In one incident that must have been galling, GR lost an order for 300 sound-level meters to H.H. Scott, the Company run by the noted GR alumnus.

As 1972 wore on, the balance sheet continued to deteriorate. The cash situation was termed "critical" by Easton in September, and he downgraded this to "serious" in October. Management considered selling the Variac line to avoid having to build a new chemical treatment plant in Concord. A convertible debenture was considered and then deferred when it was learned that lenders would demand a 7 percent coupon. Another $800,000 was borrowed from the bank, and both the bank (Shawmut) and the Company's mortgage holder (New England Mutual) increased their interest rates. To make matters worse, the Company desperately needed but could ill afford to build more manufacturing space in Concord.

Easton, probably more than anyone else in Concord, knew how desperately GR needed financial relief. The Company, he knew, simply did not have the financial wherewithal to exploit the opportunities that the systems business provided. So, when luck seated him next to your scribe (then Assistant to the President at Teradyne) on a shuttle flight from New York, hints were dropped that a merger of General Radio and Teradyne might be worth exploring. Consequently, on April 18, 1972, Easton and Teradyne CEO Alex d'Arbeloff met at my home in Concord to discuss, in the broadest terms, the possible outlines of a union. The conversation was friendly, and both men were amenable to further talks, with one caveat: Easton would have to report the gist of the conversation to Sinclair and Thurston, and only with their consent could discussions proceed. But Easton's colleagues were cold to the idea, and the matter was dropped. The reaction was understandable. General Radio was much larger than Teradyne (in 1972, sales of the two companies were $33 million and $21 million, respectively), but Teradyne had the stronger balance sheet, a publicly traded stock, and, most important, a dynamic founder/CEO who would probably insist on control. A GR-Teradyne combination would be more seriously considered years later, when Teradyne was by far the larger, more prosperous company, but again, GR management was unwilling to yield control.

The unfolding drama at General Radio was being watched with growing interest by a group of businessmen in Phoenix, Arizona. Their company, called Mirco, was using a simulator to create test programs for the 1790. The 1790 was a functional test system, which required the development of a complex test program for each board under test. Such programs could best be created through the use of a fault simulator running on a large computer, and, since the entire process of testing digital circuits depended heavily on the use of simulators, the larger computer makers – companies like IBM, Honeywell, and General Electric – were investing heavily in simulation technology. Mirco, using a GE computer armed with a powerful simulator, was widely recognized as a good source of test programming services. GR, uneasy at the prospect of leaving so much added value on the table, tried to buy Mirco and also made a pass at Telpar, another test services provider. Neither courtship panned out, but the frequent interactions of GR and Mirco had acquainted Mirco's people with Fulks, and the relationship ripened.

Then, in late 1972, a thunderbolt struck. Mirco, backed by a group of wealthy Arizonans and their bankers, offered to buy a controlling interest in General Radio – for cash. It was no secret that GR was being squeezed financially as it struggled to invest in the systems business, and the need to raise outside equity capital had been acknowledged explicitly by Sinclair. It is likely that the "outside investors" Sinclair had in mind were members of the Boston financial establishment, which was beginning to dabble in high technology. But a bunch of cowboys in Arizona?

But the cowboys had done their homework. Their appraisal of GR's spread of prime real estate in Concord revealed that the plant and land were grossly undervalued on its books, so that in buying 51 percent of the Company at book value the investors would in effect be buying General Radio's business for a pittance.

Unwelcome though the Mirco offer may have been to Sinclair and his management team, no offer of cash could be dismissed out of hand. Accordingly, Ivan Easton, GR's financial VP, was dispatched to Phoenix on a reconnaissance mission, accompanied by Fulks. Easton's verdict on returning was that the cowboys were legitimate. Legitimate or not, Sinclair was not interested.

Meanwhile, Fulks and his engineering team were beefing up their prize system, the 1790. The original version, though innovative for its time, was now under siege from several competitors, including Teradyne, with its L100-series featuring a new wrinkle called "guided probing," which walked the user through a series of steps converging on the fault. Other competitors included Cleveland-based Digital General, Computer Automation, and, from the UK, Membrain. In 1970, the GR board tester was the only game in town. In 1972, the customers had choices.

Fulks's response was the 1792, sporting a PDP-8E, 32K of core memory, bidirectional pins, and a real disk operating system. But the most important advance was in the software used to program the system and to aid in fault diagnosis.

General Radio's heritage lay in hardware – from the variable condensers used by Armstrong and other pioneers to the precision instruments in walnut cabinets, with black-crackle panels that seemed to scream "quality." But now the hardware, at least the hardware that represented GR's future, was hostage to the computer and to the test programs and the software needed to create them. This in turn shifted much of the engineering work to a new breed of engineer, less interested in the flow of electrons through a circuit than in the sequences of 1's and 0's by which a computer might orchestrate that flow. Not that the hardware was unimportant – one still had to measure voltages and currents – but, to an increasing degree, the software engineer was playing a key role in the success or failure of a test system.

As a functional test system, the 1790-series attempted to verify a board's ability to do what it was supposed to do. The advantage of this type of tester – versus, say, a tester than looked for manufacturing defects – was that it was more likely to spot a bad board. The disadvantage was that the functional approach required the creation of a complex test program. Thus, competitive battles were fought on the basis of the programming aids available for use with the tester. These aids were usually based on the use of software simulators, sold by test system vendors and independent firms such as Mirco. With a good simulator, the test system programmer could create a software model of the circuit board, then determine which test programs yielded the highest fault coverage.

General Radio's entry in the race was called CAPS, for Computer-Aided Program Simulation. It was developed by a team headed by Lutz Henkels, an MIT doctoral candidate hired by Fulks a few years earlier. With Fulks's encouragement, Henkels assembled a team of software virtuosos, including Rene Haas and Ken Brown. (The trio would in time go their own way, under the name "HHB Associates.") CAPS was enormously successful, first as a programming aid run on the test system, then as the basis for an Automatic Fault Detection scheme offered as a response to Teradyne's Guided Probe. (Later, GR was forced to admit that guided probing had merit, and it introduced its own "look ahead" guided probe, which further exploited its software prowess.)

CAPS was often the decisive factor in competitive shoot-outs, especially against its nearest rival, Teradyne. Teradyne's initial response to CAPS was a sophisticated simulator run on a bank of PDP-11 computers, and in competitive battles it insisted that CAPS, based on the smaller PDP-8, could not possibly yield the kind of performance GR promised. But Henkels and CAPS almost always prevailed, often dazzling prospects with demonstrations. One such CAPS *tour de force* led to GR's largest board-test order to date, a contract for 40 systems at Digital Equipment. (Sixty systems were eventually bought by DEC.) GR soon began flashing its trump card in advertisements proclaiming, "The Difference in Software is the Difference in Testers." It was a catchy and effective advertising slogan, and, to the discomfort of competitors, it was generally true.

108

The cross-currents were intense at General Radio during 1972. Sinclair had announced his intention to retire, and Thurston and Easton were competing (with civility, of course) to succeed him. Bob Fulks was leading the engineering charge into the systems business, triggering convulsions among the old guard. Leo Chamberlain, who had derailed a bright future in taking over at Time/Data, was restless, as was Marketing's Peter Macalka, selling products that Production could not deliver. Gus Lahanas, having orchestrated the Grason-Stadler acquisition, was looking for other quarry. Fretting over the financial health of the Company was Ivan Easton, who, with Thurston closing in on the Presidency and Steve Stadler about to seize the financial reins, was likely to be left without a chair when the music stopped.

In the middle of this supercharged year, the Company held a management strategy session at a hotel in Hyannis. At this meeting, copies of a satirical tale called "The King His Grand Council Did Convene" were distributed to the attendees. It is an ingenious invention, illuminating the personalities and attitudes that prevailed at GR in mid-1972. Its author, somewhat surprisingly, was Steve Stadler, a fairly recent inductee into the world of General Radio, who might have been expected to be wary of rocking the boat. But Stadler, a laconic and insightful gentleman, was sure enough of his own worth to risk skewering some of his new GR associates.

Chapter 18

The Thurston Era Begins

The year 1972 ended with a flurry of activity. On December 29, Sinclair posted his long-awaited announcement – the white smoke rising from the Vatican. Echoing Fulks, Sinclair wrote that "it is clear that one individual should be given the responsibility and the authority to manage all the Company's operations." That person would be Thurston, who would become President and Chief Operating Officer. In addition, he went on, a single individual should be given the full-time responsibility for managing all the Company's finances. That person would be Grason-Stadler cofounder Steve Stadler, who would become Senior Vice President and Chief Financial Officer. Ivan Easton would retire from the Company, remaining on the Board only until the next Annual Meeting. Since Financial Manager and GR veteran Ed Hurlbut joined Easton in departing, Stadler would now have a clear field in managing GR's financial affairs. At the Annual Meeting, wrote Sinclair, two new candidates for the Board would be proposed: Bob Fulks and Peter Macalka, the Company's senior engineering and marketing managers. For the time being, Sinclair would remain Chief Executive Officer, with the title of Chairman of the Board.

Only three days before the Sinclair memo, Fulks weighed in again with his blueprint for the future, in a memo titled "Status of GR and a Plan for the Future." After noting that the success of the new board testers was being undermined by inept manufacturing (lead time for the 1790 had surged to 23 weeks) and poor cost accounting, he posited three options for the Company: The first was to accept Mirco's offer. The second was to raise cash by selling Time/Data and Grason-Stadler and trimming inventory. The third was to retrench drastically to restore profitability. Accepting the Mirco offer would mean bringing in a new manufacturing VP and a new financial VP, scrapping matrix management, and embarking on a program to improve profit margins.

Orders were relatively strong in 1972, but near-term, this was more curse than blessing, as the manufacturing staff in Concord could not keep up with demand. The sharp reversal at Time/Data torpedoed hopes of taking that unit public and helped drive the consolidated results deep into the red for the first time since 1937. The net loss was $2.3 million, chopping a sickening 17.7 percent off GR's book value. By any of the standard financial yardsticks, it was the worst performance in the Company's 57-year history.

Bill Thurston, as he became President in 1973, inherited a Company with a proud tradition, a respected name, a solid entry, in the 1790, into the exciting world of ATE, a world-class engineering staff, and the broadest product line in the test and measurement industry.

He also was taking over a Company that was losing money and whose balance sheet was creaking under the weight of past retiree buyouts, bloated inventory, a self-ownership model that was clearly unsustainable, and no quick prospect of a public offering. The Company's two most promising young stars, Bob Fulks and Leo Chamberlain, were conspicuously unhappy. The broad product line simply meant that the Company was spread too thin. The instruments that had been GR's bread and butter were competitively vulnerable, and that business had slowed to a crawl anyway. The Company's manufacturing department was struggling to adapt to the demands of the new systems business.

To add to Thurston's cares, Ivan Easton, whom he had bested in the contest for the presidency, was not planning to go quietly into the sunset. For one thing, he had invested more than three decades of hard work at GR, in Sales, in Engineering, as Chief Engineer, Vice President for Engineering, Senior Vice President, Treasurer, and a member of the Board of Directors. Still a young 57, Easton resented being put out to pasture. He and his supporters resented it even more when, in the 1972 Annual Report, Don Sinclair seemed to blame the Company's poor performance on failures chargeable to Easton. The following passage was particularly pointed:

> The time required to respond to an increase in demand was consistently underestimated, and expenses were permitted to increase too early, without adequate coordination......The need for this stronger coordination at the top-management level led to the adoption of the changes announced in my report of December 29, 1972 to General Radio stockholders and employees.

Since the only member of top management to be asked to leave was Easton, it must have seemed to him that he was being blamed for failures throughout the organization. But Easton, who was scheduled (per the year-end Sinclair memo) to leave the Board and GR at the April 20 stockholders' meeting, was not without recourse. A corps of retired employee stockholders was growing increasingly impatient over the Company's inability to buy back their shares, as had been the custom throughout GR's history. (In fact, the banks holding GR debt would not permit any such buybacks.) Thus people who had worked 20, 30, or more years for General Radio in the expectation of a comfortable retirement found their shares effectively frozen, with neither dividends nor a public market for the stock. Worse, book value, the traditional repurchase price, was actually dropping. Easton, who himself owned 7900 shares – more than 3 percent of the common shares outstanding – began lobbying the retirees to oppose the Sinclair slate. There was more: At a dinner during the annual IRE Conference in March, the engineering group leaders, most of whom had worked under Easton in the past, rallied to the support of their colleague.

Sensing the rising tide of pro-Easton sentiment, Thurston sought advice from Steve Stadler, a director and Easton's successor as chief financial officer, and from the Company's sole outside director, Jim Wright. Meeting at the Grason-Stadler plant in West Concord, they soon reached consensus: Ivan Easton would be invited to remain on the Board of Directors. But what about Sinclair's statement, in his December letter, that Bob Fulks and Peter Macalka would be added to the Board?

The reader will recall that Fulks, having been rebuffed in his efforts to convince Sinclair to support Data General and its new computer, was nevertheless authorized to launch the development of a GR computer, and now, five years later, this product, known formally as "System 2500" and informally as "the Fulks Computer," was nearing completion. System 2500 was a bus-structured, 16-bit general-purpose computer, equipped with a high-level language that promised to speed up test-program generation tenfold. Over its gestation period, the project had utilized the talents of some of GR's most able engineers. Dick Frank, a veteran GR group leader, managed the development, and Howie Painter, who had started his career in GR's Advertising Department and then moved to Digital Equipment, was rehired by Fulks to take over marketing.

Then, in January, with Thurston newly installed in the President's office, Don Sinclair, in a letter to stockholders, wrote the computer's obituary. "We have recently bitten off more than we can chew," wrote Sinclair, "and we have therefore determined that we must stop work on a GR computer." Although Sinclair signed the letter, there was little doubt the decision was Thurston's.

Fulks could not have been surprised when Thurston, in one of his first presidential acts, decided to shut down the computer project. With the Company bleeding badly, it was not an illogical move. The world, it could be argued, did not need another minicomputer, not even one as well crafted as the 2500. And GR, with hundreds of products in its bulging catalog, did not need another product line. But neither did the Company need to give its technology *wünderkind* one more grievance.

Bill Thurston

One does not scrap a heavy investment like the Fulks computer lightly, and the letter went on to suggest that the computer might be sold to another company "that can undertake responsibility for its commercial exploitation." That other company, in the scenario envisioned by Thurston, might be Mirco, whose President, John Walsh, had already displayed interest in GR. Accordingly, Thurston asked Fulks to forward an offer to Mirco: GR was willing to sell, as a package, the Fulks computer and the Time/Data subsidiary, now managed by Leo Chamberlain. Thus GR's two rising stars were both in a sense on the block.

In February, Fulks flew to Phoenix, where the offer was turned down cold. On his return, he was summoned to Thurston's office, where he was asked point-blank about his willingness to work as a member of the GR team. It was clearly "High Noon" in Concord.

Fulks resigned from GR in March, the story making the front page of Electronic News, and in April he was named President of Mirco Systems, a new organization formed to produce portable board testers. GR engineers

Bob Owen and Dave Nixon joined the new venture, and a few months later Bob Anderson, who had sold the 1790 so successfully in Europe, also joined the group in Phoenix.

The April 20th stockholders' meeting was preceded by a memo from Don Sinclair acknowledging complaints about stockholder meetings at which employees were forced to vote openly for or against their superiors. This meeting would be different: There would be, for the first time, a *secret* ballot, with provisions for write-ins. Shareholders also received a memo from Ivan Easton, explaining the events that caused him to stand for reelection to the Board, and another memo from Bill Thurston reporting that Peter Macalka had graciously agreed not to hold the Company to its earlier promise to add him to the Board, in order to give the Board a more "outside" cast. The new outside director would be Hardie Shepard, a Partner at Payson & Trask, a small New York venture capital firm. Shepard also had some industry experience at Hazeltine and Perkin-Elmer. Thurston, mindful of GR's need to raise equity capital, considered the addition of a Wall Streeter a plus. In addition to outsiders Shepard and Jim Wright, the slate included five insiders: Thurston, Easton, Sinclair, Stadler, and Quackenbos (Secretary). Quackenbos, it was explained, was essentially a place-holder in the expectation that a prospective lender (First National Bank of Boston) would ask for a seat.

The recommended slate won handily, though the presence of some write-ins (notably several thousand shares voted for Harold McAleer) must have turned a few heads. Given the turmoil of the previous few months and the cross-currents that must have lingered, it could not have been a very chummy Board.

GR had lost Fulks, but it still had a tiger by the tail in the 1790, along with a middle management team that was growing more comfortable by the day in the systems business. Succeeding Fulks as Vice President for Engineering was Harold McAleer, whose strengths included a solid technology base (MIT, of course), leadership ability, and, not least, a quick sense of humor. With Thurston's climb up the ladder and with Chamberlain removed to Time/Data, the sales stage was left to Peter Macalka and Dick Rogers. Macalka was Vice President in charge of worldwide sales, and Rogers was product manager for the Company's hot product, the 1790.

Harold McAleer

Sensing that the board testers required a specialized, dedicated sales group, Rogers, with Thurston's blessing, began implanting his own regional "system centers" within the Macalka-led sales organization. The first three systems centers were located in Santa Clara, Chicago, and Boston, and were run by salesmen John Zapf, Art Winterhalter, and Hal Barbour, respectively – the nucleus of a group that would become known as "Rogers' Raiders."

The systems centers were physically located in sales offices nominally under the supervision of Macalka, but Rogers' Raiders and their staffs (which included applications engineers) reported, of course, to Rogers, a situation that inevitably bred tension, as two sales groups worked side by side – one selling the fast-growing line of (relatively) high-priced board testers, the other selling lines that for the most part were in decline. The leaders of the two groups also saw their fortunes waxing and waning, with Dick Rogers' star generally waxing.

116

Although the loss of Fulks was regrettable, the Company still possessed abundant engineering strength. Talent was not the problem. A shaky financial condition was very much the problem. Debt now exceeded equity, and current liabilities exceeded current assets. Time/Data was improving but still not out of the woods. Micronetic Systems was an unmitigated disaster. The sales agreement with GR was terminated in mid-1973, and shortly thereafter the line of laser trimmers, battered by quality problems and fierce competition from Teradyne, was discontinued, leaving in its wake considerable wrangling over responsibility for service and ownership of parts stock. Micronetic Systems morphed through acquisition into a maker of wire-wrapping equipment and services, but it continued to go downhill throughout 1973 and 1974, until the bank seized the assets and effectively put the Company out of its misery. Thanks to careful footwork by Stadler and especially Lahanas all along the way, GR was able to escape without real financial damage. But the venture did consume a tremendous amount of management time, and the fiasco besmirched GR's reputation. Even in 1974, long after the laser-trim business had been folded, the Micronetic Systems letterhead featured the General Radio logo at the bottom of the sheet, with the words "An Associate of General Radio."

Grason-Stadler remained a bright spot. Its line of audiometers and related instruments rode a wave of new government (OSHA) regulations as well as the new Noise Control Act of 1972, administered by the Environmental Protection Agency. Grason-Stadler, alone of all GR operations, was profitable in both 1972 and 1973. Unfortunately, G-S was not large enough (its sales were less than $3 million) to offset the problems elsewhere.

Thurston, in trying to gain control over a Company undergoing a difficult transition, quickly spotted a serious systemic problem: a sclerotic management style. GR had long been wedded to the Committee format, and this model, Thurston realized, guaranteed that the best young talent would be driven from the Company, frustrated by the impossibility of achieving a consensus in support of any radical new idea. The problem, which had been so forcefully articulated by Fulks the year before, was compounded by matrix management, introduced by Sinclair. The combination of committees and matrices ensured that no single individual could ever be held accountable for anything.

So matrix management was abolished, and in July Thurston appointed a single manager to head each business area at the core company. From the 1973 Annual Report: "The appointment of individuals to lead our market/product areas reflects an important, fundamental change. GR has traditionally had a committee form of corporate management, but this has now been replaced by a more conventional, and more effective mode of operation, under which individuals, rather than committees, make the important decisions and are responsible for results." The individuals who were given this new burden of accountability included Dick Rogers (for test systems), Warren Kundert (the acoustic lines), and Ken Castle (industrial products), plus Leo Chamberlain and Rufus Grason, running the subsidiaries Time/Data and Grason-Stadler.

The dismantling of the matrix inevitably meant favoring one axis over another – in the case of acoustic products, engineer Warren Kundert over marketer Bob Boole. As a result, Boole left the Company, soon to begin a successful career at Analog Devices.

At a single stroke, then, Thurston was replacing a management style that had served General Radio well for decades, a style that was in the DNA of most of the Company's old-timers. How would people respond to the new emphasis on accountability? Before, if an individual slipped up, a committee was there to share the blame. Now, the errant individual would be in the spotlight. What would become of him or her?

To help GR management reshape its organization, Thurston hired the consulting firm Arthur D. Little, and "ADL" soon became a constant presence in Concord, devising a new "Corporate Quality Board" (boards were in, committees out) and generally putting its oar into every river and stream in the Company. Thus, while the new GR regime exalted the role of the individual, the consultants were usually hovering nearby.

The hoverers were in fact doing good work, educating GR's management, which had long been insulated from the real-world problems that beset most companies, including the realities of product life cycles. The vast GR product catalog ran the gamut, from ancient products in their harvest stage to test systems in their embryonic stage, and everything in between. With the help of Arthur D. Little, GR management began to examine each product line objectively, without reference to tradition. ADL also scored each operation (and thus its manager) on competence and efficiency, judgments that made it easier for Thurston to start upgrading his management team.

Despite the lingering effects of the competition for President and what most viewed as the forced departure of Fulks, Thurston gained support and respect with each passing month. For one thing, everyone saw him as a decent human being, soft-spoken, gentlemanly, never abrasive. For another, he had the right credentials: the MIT VI-A Master's degree, along with a stint in engineering, where he contributed to the design of the 1607 Transfer Function and Immittance Bridge, as well as the Company's "874" coaxial connector. Subsequent tours in Sales (the New York Office) and in Marketing added up to a nicely balanced background. His lack of financial skills had been addressed by the appointment of Stadler as Chief Financial Officer, but a lack of manufacturing experience could not be ignored, and, prodded by the consultants, he began looking around for an experienced manager to cover that base.

Thurston came into office lacking any zeal for the business of business. He saw himself, correctly, as a technologist who had learned a good deal about sales and marketing. Because his job required it, he would learn about debt and equity, return on investment, gross margin, mergers and acquisitions, working capital, public offerings, corporate litigation, and all the other baggage that went with the territory, but he approached it all with little passion.

In this regard he was following established GR precedent. Don Sinclair had even less appetite for business than had Thurston, and of all previous GR leaders only Henry Shaw (Chairman, but never President) could be said to have had a natural aptitude for business. In earlier times, this was not a serious handicap, but in the 1970s, many high-tech CEOs had MBAs to go with their engineering degrees, and Thurston would have to compete with them, on their ground. And he would have to accept a truth that flew in the face of all GR's settled theology: A good product, no matter how well designed, is not enough.

In October 1973, Leo Chamberlain came to Concord, bringing with him his new financial officer, Charles Petefish. Time/Data was on track to deliver a profitable year, and the financial reporting was vastly improved. There was still strong competition from Hewlett-Packard, whose worldwide sales network so often outgunned GR, but Chamberlain felt on solid ground as he met with Thurston and Stadler to ask that Time/Data's employee benefits package be tailored to the preferences of his California workforce. This was unacceptable to Thurston, who felt that benefits should be standardized throughout the Company, and equally unacceptable to Stadler, who rejected out of hand any request for special treatment from a subsidiary that had spilled so much red ink. Finally, with the two sides at an impasse, Chamberlain threw down the gauntlet, offering to resign if he was not to be supported. His offer was accepted on the spot.

It was an abrupt farewell for the 43-year-old Chamberlain, who had seemed marked for stardom from the day he joined the Company 18 years earlier. Brash, energetic, creative, dynamic – these were the adjectives usually applied to GR's one-time sales leader. But the road to the presidency of General Radio did not pass through Palo Alto, and in the course of three years in California he had lost his power base, the GR sales force. Now he was being forced out only six months after his engineering counterpart, Bob Fulks, had been ousted, also at the hands of Thurston. If there had been any doubt of Thurston's willingness to use the power of his office, they were gone by the end of 1973.

For Chamberlain, the dismissal from GR led to employment by computer-maker Rolm, where he rose rapidly to the position of Executive Vice President. Rolm was then bought by IBM, bringing Chamberlain considerable wealth and even greater satisfaction.

The turbulence at GR in 1973 made good copy for the trade press, but the real news was that General Radio under Thurston was on the cusp of a major turn-around. A born businessman he might not have been, but the numbers, especially compared against the dismal background of recent years, were breathtaking. Sales jumped 35 percent, to a record $44.7 million. The bottom line swung from a loss of $2.3 million in 1972 to a profit of $1.16 million in 1973. The balance sheet was still shaky, with debt exceeding equity, but the gap was narrowing.

Moreover, the 35-percent sales increase was accomplished with no gain in the Company's headcount. In fact it dropped, from 1640 to 1630, driving revenue per employee from $20,000 to $27,400.

Of the year's $44.7 million in sales, three-quarters came from two product areas: acoustics (broadly defined to include sound and vibration instruments, Grason-Stadler, and Time/Data) and component and circuit test, which included the fast-growing board-test systems. Although bridges, coaxial products, and stroboscopes continued to do reasonably well, other legacy instruments were feeling the effects of the semiconductor revolution, and it became clear that the Company now had two classes of products: (1) the growth products of the future and (2) cash cows to fund the investments in (1).

The changing face of the GR product line was manifest in *Catalog 73* (dates having replaced the traditional letter designators). Although the catalog was filled with the kinds of instruments, decade boxes, connectors, stroboscopes, Variacs, etc. for which GR was known, there were also pages of photographs of Volkswagen-sized systems – acoustic analysis systems, board test systems, wire-wrapping systems, cable test systems, the RATS anodize trim system, a new passive test system (the 2230), transformer test systems, leakage current test systems, etc. All in all, the 350-page catalog described a vast array of product offerings. A bound-in price list at the rear of the Catalog listed more than 1300 individual items, ranging in price from 10 cents (shorting link) to $10,610 (the Time/Data 1921). Those interested in larger systems like the 1790 were asked to submit their specifications and receive a quotation.

Of necessity, there was no longer a "General Radio look" to bind all the products into a cohesive whole. Mechanical designer Paul d'Entremont had repackaged most of the old black-crackle-faced instruments in new, gray wrappings, some of them featuring the clever "flip-tilt" cabinet, designed by GR's long-time chief mechanical engineer Henry Littlejohn, and the appearance of these products, particularly the bridges, would no doubt have pleased Melville Eastham. The talents of Littlejohn and d'Entremont were also applied to a few of the systems, but most of them looked like what they were: ad hoc, rack-mounted assemblies of instruments, computers, and peripheral equipment.

Thurston and other members of management knew that the Company could not afford to maintain a product line of more than 1000 items, most of which contributed little to the top line and less to the bottom line, but the issue of what to divest and when was saved for another day.

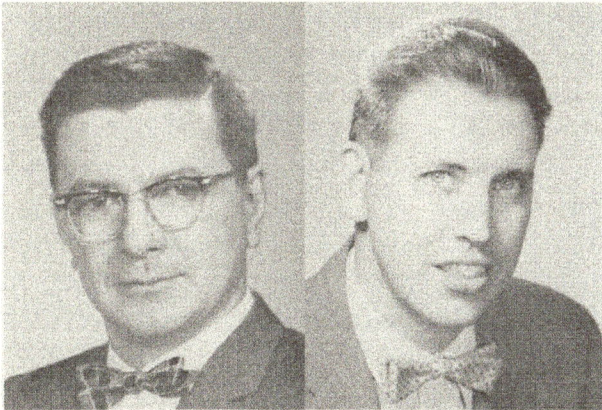

**Engineering titans. Above: Henry Hall and Mac Holtje .
Below: Arnold Peterson and Bob Soderman**

In the 1973 Annual Report's letter to stockholders, Chairman Sinclair understandably boasted about the Company's dramatic turnaround. Somewhat less understandably, the byline was his and his alone. Although he gave credit to the new management team, the meat of the report – the letter's sections on operations and finance - was presented unsigned. Of course, everyone close to GR knew that Thurston was at the helm, but he would have to wait another year before he would command the spotlight.

The 1973 Annual Report also hinted at the changing complexion of the officer corps. New Vice Presidents included one veteran - Mike Fitzmorris, the able engineering manager – and one new hire, Walter Hinds, recruited from General Signal to address the manufacturing deficiencies identified by Arthur D. Little. Hinds's arrival led to the departure of Clyde Horne, the erstwhile VP Manufacturing and a GR veteran. Another ADL suggestion, the strengthening of the personnel department and the broadening of its charter, led to the hiring of Richard Cambria, a human resources specialist from Exxon. At year-end, Charles Petefish was officially named President of Time/Data, succeeding Leo Chamberlain. More management changes were to come in 1974.

Chapter 19

The Turnaround

The years following the 1971 industry downturn were years of rapid growth for the electronics industry, and Thurston had taken office with the wind at his back. Still, he faced a mountain of difficulties.

Ironically, it would have been easier if the old General Radio, with all its glorious tradition, could have been erased from memory and a new enterprise formed around the board tester. Start-ups abounded in those days, and some of them became stock-market darlings in a few years. At GR, on the other hand, history, though ennobling, was baggage weighing the Company down. Long meetings were held and hundreds of pages of introspective prose were written to reflect on the kind of company GR was and to describe the kind of company it aspired to be. The new management team was determined to remake the Company, but it was spending an exorbitant amount of time agonizing over the transformation process itself. If it were an old house, it could have been torn down and a new structure built from scratch. But GR was not a house, but a collection of human beings with their own memories and habits and expectations.

Thurston's first year as President was good enough to turn most skeptics into believers, but much remained to be done. The debt burden was still a cloud over the balance sheet, and the Company would have to be dressed up before there could be a public stock offering. GR's success in the board test business was attracting more competitors. The Company still carried far too many product lines, some of which would have to be divested. The management team needed further strengthening in a number of areas. And, since Sinclair was about to complete his exit, the challenges would all fall to Thurston, as President and Chief Executive Officer. To emphasize the changing of the guard, Thurston asked for and received Ivan Easton's agreement not to stand for reelection to the Board in 1974. This, coupled with Sinclair's departure, meant that two seats would be open, and two outsiders were named as candidates: Wilbur Davenport, Chairman of MIT's Electrical Engineering Department, and Arthur D. Little consultant Bob Wright. Thus, at the 1974 Annual Meeting – held at a local theater rather than the cafeteria to accommodate an expanded list of employee-stockholders - the GR Board of Directors, which only three years before had been made up entirely of Company officers, was given a decidedly independent look, with four outsiders and three insiders. Thurston saw this as a key step in the march to public ownership.

By 1974 it was clear that the 1790, more than any other product, was remaking GR, from instrument maker to producer of ATE systems. This transformation touched every part of the Company. Salesmen used to selling technology now had to learn how to sell return on investment. Accountants used to collecting receivables in 30 or 60 days now had to negotiate with customers complaining that systems were not complete or were delivering unacceptable performance. Production planners used to controlling the complete, in-house assembly of every instrument now had to coordinate deliveries of computers and peripheral equipment from dozens of vendors. The concept of warranty service was redefined. Before, GR shipped instruments costing a few hundred dollars, and one or two percent of them might come back for warranty repair. Now, whenever a $100,000 system was shipped, GR and the customer were married for life. At least that's how it must have seemed, as the Company struggled with the transition.

But there was no going back. GR would wade deeper into the ATE waters year after year, until these waters seemed its natural habitat. Some of the instrument people slipped easily into their new roles. Rogers, Macalka, McAleer – all veterans of GR's instrument years, were now accomplished ATE managers, backed up by the likes of salesmen Eric Mudama, Hal Barbour, Bob Delzell, Tom Fricke, and others, all fighting for orders with an intensity the GR sales engineers of old never knew. Rogers, now General Manager of the board-test group, requested and received from Thurston the ability to price systems on the fly, depending on the competitive situation. It was a high-risk decision, which could have been disastrous, but it turned out to be a brilliant tactic.

Although the board test business was clearly the platform on which the Company hoped to ride to the next

126

level, the acoustics area was also seen as a growth business. Time/Data had turned around on the strength of successes in the structural dynamics and underwater acoustics fields, and new regulations pouring out of EPA, OSHA, and other government agencies meant new customers for sound-level meters. Grason-Stadler was a successful outpost in the medical arena, as it sold noise dosimeters and audiometer calibrators.

The 1974 results showed further revenue growth, to $49.5 million, a gain of 10 percent. Net income, on the other hand, soared, from $1.6 million in 1973 to more than $3.6 million, a dazzling 215 percent improvement. "Dazzling" was in fact the right word, as more than half of the profits had nothing to do with the Company's operations and everything to do with a change in accounting policy engineered by CFO Stadler. This change neatly shifted "certain indirect production costs" from the profit and loss statement, where they had been expensed, to the inventory account, where they no longer penalized earnings. Thus, while profits sparkled, the balance sheet showed inventories growing 51 percent on a 10-percent sales gain. The accounting change, which was entirely legal and duly blessed by Auditors Ernst & Ernst, could be seen as another step in GR's preparation for public ownership, as was the improving debt/equity ratio, now approaching unity. General Radio, for the first time in many years, was now beginning to assume the attributes of a company worth watching. It was profitable, the balance sheet was steadily improving, its Board had a majority of outside directors, and, most important of all, it had a stake in the ATE industry, by now widely recognized as one of the most exciting sectors of high technology.

Chapter 20

GenRad

In 1975, the name "General Radio" still had great value. To many thousands of people working in electronics, the words stood for innovation, quality, integrity, accuracy, reliability, and all the attributes most companies would have traded their souls for. To some, however, including Bill Thurston, the name was an echo of a past no longer relevant to the world of semiconductors and computers and automation. The Company did not make radios, and the term as Melville Eastham had used it had long since been replaced by "electronics." To hold on to such an anachronistic name would invite confusion – or even worse, derision. So Thurston in 1974 had invited the members of the GR community to submit their suggestions for a new Company name.

It is not clear who came up with the winning entry. More likely, a number of people converged on "GenRad." It was not, after all, a startlingly original idea. The Genradco Trust had been around for a long time, and there was obvious merit in a name that had both a futuristic ring and a remembrance of things past. The name "GenRad" offered other advantages. The familiar "GR" logo could be preserved, wrapped in a new package created by the design firm Chermayeff & Geismar. The new name also met one of Thurston's key criteria: The word "GenRad" meant absolutely nothing, leaving the Company the freedom to imprint in the public perception any persona it chose. So GenRad it was – with some urgency, moreover, since it was agreed that the new name should gain currency well before the Company's initial public stock offering, which now seemed fairly near.

Thurston, since he took over as President and scrapped matrix management, had been trying to streamline the organization and reduce the number of direct reports. In 1975, he created four product divisions, each with its own General Manager. Dick Rogers was named Vice President and GM of the Test Systems Division (formerly Component and Network Test). Acoustic products and Grason-Stadler were combined in the Enviromedics Division, under VP Rufus Grason. Time/Data contained to operate separately, under VP Charles Petefish, and GR's traditional products (instruments, Variacs, stroboscopes, coaxial products, synthesizers, precision standards, etc.) were placed in the Electronic Instrument Division, under VP Harold McAleer. Not much was expected of this catch-all division, but McAleer decided to make lemonade out of the lemons. He convinced Howie Painter, board test's man in Europe, to take over marketing for EID, then encouraged his engineering group to develop digital and linear integrated-circuit testers for the incoming-inspection market. McAleer had under his control some of the Company's most gifted engineers, including Dan Abenaim, Bill Kabele, and *bridgemeister* Henry Hall, who, assisted by engineering manager Dan Abenaim, circuit designer Bob Sullivan, and programmer Mike Gipe, designed a revolutionary new product, the 1657 Digibridge.

The Digibridge was born of Hall's realization that the algebra needed to cancel out the effects of phase differences in impedance measurements, while excruciatingly difficult to implement with conventional analog circuitry, was a relatively easy task for a computer. Hall and his team then settled on the new 6502 8-bit microprocessor, which enabled them to replace 27 adjustments on the instrument's predecessor (the 1685 Impedance Meter) with a single control (to set ac level). Dan Abenaim worked on the mechanical design, and Paul d'Entremont contributed a flashy package that stamped the Digibridge as a different kind of animal.

The first Digibridge, the 1657, was priced at $990, but as Hall, Bill Byers, and other engineers kept extending the product's accuracy and range, the price escalated, and the Digibridge began a long run, establishing itself on the roster of GR classics. Tens of thousands were eventually sold, cementing GR's position atop the impedance-measurement world.

The resurgence of the instrument line did little to ease tensions in the sales force, where Rogers' Raiders continued to bask in the glow of GR's continuing success in the board-test market and where instrument salesmen, sharing the same offices, simmered. These tensions were reflected in the growing competition between Peter Macalka and Dick Rogers. Macalka was the *de jure* leader of the Company's world-wide sales force, but Rogers' "Systems Centers" were installed like so many Trojan horses within the key sales offices. As board-test sales accounted for a growing share of the Company's revenues, it was clear that eventually Thurston would confront a difficult choice.

Another dilemma grew out of the functional overlap between Rogers's test systems and McAleer's instruments, some of which (like the IC testers) were in fact systems in miniature. In this case, a Solomonesque solution was found: If the component to be tested had two terminals, its testing rightfully belonged to McAleer. More than two terminals placed the device in Rogersville.

Meanwhile, the strengthening of the management team continued apace. Reflecting the broadening of the human resources charter, Personnel Manager Richard Cambria became Vice President, Personnel Development. CFO Stadler recruited a new Financial Vice President, James Gemmell, from Itek. Including Walter Hinds, now Vice President for Operations, six of the 10 vice presidents listed in the 1975 Annual Report had been employed at GR for less than five years. The rapidly changing face of the officer corps spoke volumes about the Company's break with its past.

Hinds's accomplishments in correcting the Company's manufacturing deficiencies were applauded by Thurston and others, and for a time it appeared that Thurston had found the ideal candidate to serve as a strong right hand and possible successor. But Hinds's fortunes would ebb and flow with time, and, although he held a number of senior management posts, his GR career probably peaked in his first few years with the Company. Later, there would be other candidates similarly anointed, but they, too, would flame out after a few years.

The electronics capital equipment business, which had rebounded smartly from a 1971 downturn, slumped again in 1975. GR, reacting quickly to order softness, released about 100 employees early in 1975, this layoff following a similar cutback the year before. Layoffs, unthinkable in the old General Radio, were now eminently thinkable, as financial pressures narrowed the margin for error. The layoff was unfortunate, but it was also an encouraging sign of a new fiscal discipline at the Company. Inventory, a chronic worry in years past, was being tamed by Hinds, and Stadler and Gemmell worked the receivables hard. A new, unsecured loan from Citicorp was used to pay off the Shawmut Bank. Salaries, in an era when high-tech paychecks were running in six figures, were quite modest. Thurston's salary was $57,000 in 1975, while the next two highest-paid officers, Stadler and Macalka, both earned less than $50,000. The restraint in setting executive salaries was reflected all the way down the ladder. There were, of course, no stock-option gains to sweeten the pot.

In July came another bout of self-analysis, this time in the weighty "GR Corporate Objectives and Strategies," intended as the first in a series of annual operations plans. In the introduction, Thurston acknowledged that the document was "essentially a statement of my views (developed in consultation with others) of where GR is today and where we should plan to go in the future." Since this was a time when the Mission Statement was a central element of every corporate catechism, the opus began with the following:

"GR's mission is to be a free-standing, healthy business enterprise with the central purpose of enabling its people to achieve substantial economic gains and other important accomplishments for the enterprise and its owners, and for themselves as individuals, within a broad essential market offering of electronic instrumentation and associated services. Efforts will be mainly focused on more narrowly defined areas of business, selected and handled in order to build strong market positions with substantial economic diversity, and the major functions performed will continue to be the surveillance of technology and customer needs, the definition of new products and services, their development, manufacture, sale and after-sale services, all managed so as to accomplish the objectives of the enterprise."

Some of this was pure boiler-plate (what company aims to be an unhealthy business enterprise?), but there was enough of substance to set the stage for the recitation of goals and strategies that followed, organized under the headings of Finance and Operations, Growth, Management, and People. The long and short of it was that the Company had to grow and to grow profitably in order to survive. Sinclair and Easton had said much the same thing in their 1967 treatise, but since then a fair amount of water (and not enough black ink) had flowed under the bridge. Said Thurston: "The present financial condition of the Company, though improved since two years ago, is still weak, without any substantial reserves or the ability either to increase debt financing or to raise equity either publicly or privately."

This time, however, the dire warnings were being heeded, and slowly, surely, the situation was improving. The 1975 Operations Plan was filled with management jargon *du jour*, but it also contained a fairly detailed blueprint for turning GR into a growing, financially strong, publicly owned company. Managers might or might not perform as Thurston expected, but no one would be able to say he or she didn't understand the marching orders.

Although the business environment in 1975 was sluggish, GenRad's numbers were respectable. Sales increased 8 percent, to $53.5 million, and net income was $2.3 million. Most impressive was the improved balance sheet, as equity grew to more than $18 million, versus total debt of less than $13 million. Minority interests in Time/Data and Grason-Stadler were bought out at year-end, and both subsidiaries were merged into the Company. The equity structure was simplified, with a single class of common stock replacing the previous hodgepodge of preferred and convertible voting and nonvoting shares. The Company was closing in on its goal of a public stock offering, viewed by all as the ultimate proof that the Company had arrived. The public offering was also high on the wish list of retired employees sitting on their frozen shares.

Other stockholders with their own agendas included the Genradco Trust, whose favored tax status required it to make charitable donations it could not afford, and MIT, which still owned the block of shares it received from Melville Eastham.

So Bill Thurston, in his short term as President, had racked up three straight years of profitability and three straight years of revenue growth. Market growth helped, but that was only part of the equation. The balance-sheet weakness, the manufacturing bottlenecks, the inventory problems had all yielded to the efforts of the new management team, and the Company, thanks to its hugely successful board-test hardware and software, had transformed itself from instrument dinosaur to systems powerhouse. If Thurston wasn't responsible for all that, who was?

1976 brought more management reshuffling. At Time/Data, Charles Petefish was replaced by Gus Lahanas in November. The operation, which had yet to live up to GR's expectations, was once again losing money as it struggled to compete against GR's old nemesis, Hewlett-Packard. Lahanas, who had become valuable to Thurston as a deal-maker, was dispatched to Santa Clara as a caretaker until a new general manager could be found. In another change, long-time Controller Walter Hill resigned and was replaced by Richard Millen, who, like VP Finance Gemmell, was recruited from Itek.

Gus Lahanas

The merger of Time/Data and Grason-Stadler into the parent Company, along with the sale of the Variac manufacturing plant in France (the rights were then licensed to a Swiss company), meant that, for the first time in a number of years, the corporate roster was purged of subsidiaries (except the European and Canadian sales units) and affiliates. There were now just four product divisions: the fast-growing Test Systems Division, under Dick Rogers, the Electronic Instrument Division, under Hal McAleer, Time/Data, looking for a permanent manager, and Environmedics, under Rufus Grason. The last-named unit was edging closer to medical electronics, adding middle-ear measuring instruments to its line of audiometers. While no one could question the value of the new instruments, which could help in the diagnosis of ear infections that plagued many children, this wasn't exactly what GR had in mind when it acquired Grason-Stadler six years earlier. Moreover, the board-test business consumed all the resources the Company could spare, and

134

there was neither the interest nor the appetite for excursions into the world of medicine.

The year unfolded roughly as planned, with one exception: Europe was a laggard. European Sales Manager Norbert Kuster, operating out of Zurich, ran into a dry spell, as the effects of the 1975 downturn lingered longer than in the United States. An additional factor was the same bipolar organization that existed in the U.S., with Peter Macalka, nominally Vice President Marketing and International, and Dick Rogers running worldwide board test sales – with both men reporting directly to Thurston.

Despite a sizeable revenue shortfall in Europe, total Company sales for the year set a new record at $54.6 million, versus $53.5 million in 1975. Net profit fell to just under a million dollars, less than half the previous year's net. Heavy R&D spending was partly offset by cuts in G&A and better productivity. The balance sheet continued to improve, the debt/equity ratio dropping another full point, to 39.3 percent. But the amount of debt ($12.5 million) was still uncomfortably large, with the average interest rate on the short-term portion sitting at 10.6 percent. The bank debt, moreover, came with a list of covenants, with which the Company was not in full compliance. But the banks, seeing that under Thurston the Company was climbing back from the edge of the abyss, were happy to waive the restrictions for the time being.

Chapter 21

All Systems Go

There could no longer be much doubt in Thurston's mind that the Company was on the right track, and with the confidence gained from his four-year winning streak, he moved decisively in 1977 to drive the Company to the next level. The simmering Rogers –

Macalka duel was resolved in favor of Rogers, who was named Vice President of a new Sales and Service Division, engineer Ralph Anderson succeeding him as Board Test Product Manager. The entire GR product line was consolidated in two divisions: Electronic Manufacturing Test (EMT), under Walter Hinds, and the Acoustics, Vibration and Analysis (AVA) Division, under Hal McAleer, who would manage this division from the Time/Data plant in Santa Clara. Time/Data, ever since its acquisition by GR, had been a problem child, overcoming the best efforts of Chamberlain and Petefish to reform it. Now, in desperation, GR sent two of senior staffers across the country to try their hand. McAleer had proved his administrative ability running the instrument division (EID), and as his Assistant General Manager the Company appointed Bob Soderman, a major talent most recently Engineering Manager at Bolton. If the combination of McAleer and Soderman couldn't save Time/Data, the thinking went, maybe it was hopeless.

With McAleer and Soderman installed at Santa Clara, Gus Lahanas returned to Concord as Thurston's deal-maker. And there were deals to be made, among them the sale of Grason-Stadler to Rufus Grason and a G-S colleague, Richard Vanderlippe, for just under $3 million.

Howie Painter, who had made the round trip from GR to Digital Equipment to GR, was named Vice President for Marketing for the EMT Division and the head of a new engineering group charged with investigating technology targets of opportunity ("a greenhouse for new ideas," according to Thurston).

The Digibridge, a quick success, was improved, and several bench-top IC testers (including derivatives of an instrument line acquired from Biomation) were introduced, along with several acoustic instruments and a new Time/Data system. But it was the functional board test line that was carrying the Company now. GR still sold coaxial connectors, Variac autotransformers, and stroboscopes, but the casual reader of GenRad's 1977 Annual Report would never have known it.

When the books closed on 1977, GenRad had unequivocally stamped itself as a growth company. Sales, for the fifth straight year under Thurston's leadership, set a new record, $70.1 million, an increase of 29 percent over 1976. Net income quadrupled, to $3.7 million, a 19.3 percent return on equity. (Total after-tax profits for the Company's five years under Thurston exceeded the total profits in the 20 pre-Thurston years.) Domestic bank debt was wiped out as two insurance companies bought $10 million worth of 15-year unsecured notes. Clearly, with respect to the long-awaited initial public offering, the ducks were now sitting in a row.

The Company bolstered its leadership position in the functional-test area by adding three new systems to the line: the 1795 for logic and two new systems for hybrid (analog plus digital) circuits. The board-test business, which GR had virtually invented, was now widely recognized as a growth sector, and GenRad, as the market leader, had attracted the attention of Wall Street. Investment bankers looking for a piece of the action began their pilgrimages to Concord to serenade Steve Stadler and Gus Lahanas, with CEO Thurston generally looking on from the sidelines.

But the spotlight also brought new competitors and reinvigorated old ones. Teradyne, whose L100 functional tester had been beaten back by the CAPS program-generating software, acquired a small Dallas software company called Digitest, whose LASAR simulation software was known to be very effective. LASAR, designed for military applications, originally ran on a large, time-shared computer, and it was thus no immediate threat to CAPS, but Teradyne obviously meant to distill the essence of LASAR and mount it on a stand-alone computer.

A more pressing danger to GenRad's board-test position came from a heightened interest in an approach that bypassed the simulation process altogether: in-circuit testing.

It was now widely recognized that the vast majority of board failures were caused by manufacturing defects: short and open circuits, misplaced or missing components, etc. It seemed obvious that the use of a high-priced functional tester to find a short circuit caused by a solder blob was outrageously inefficient, and this realization led to the creation of a new class of tester aimed squarely at garden-variety defects. In its simplest form, this was little more than a continuity tester, designed to find shorts and opens, and a full-bore functional tester was still needed to give the board its final blessing. Yet, even as a screening tool, the simple tester made sense, relieving the functional system of the dog work – and thus chipping away at the total market for the more expensive testers.

In-circuit testers looked at the board as an assembly whose components belonged in certain locations, connected to other components. They did not care about the board's functionality, and thus the test-programming burden associated with a functional tester disappeared. In its place, however, a new burden arose: the necessity of making physical contact with hundreds or even thousands of points on the circuit board. Thus, while the functional tester was happy enough to look at the board from its edge connector, the in-circuit tester required a custom fixture, usually a "bed of nails" to access the board's innards. In most cases, the test system makers were happy to leave the fixturing to mechanically adept companies like Everett-Charles.

The early entrants into in-circuit testing were Systomation, founded by an ex-GE employee named Gene Stanford, and Faultfinders, subsequently founded by the same individual. Both companies were located in the Albany, NY area. In 1974 a California company, Zehntel, shipped its first in-circuit tester, and by 1978 Faultfinders and Zehntel were the leaders in the small market. (Systomation had ceased to exist.) Other start-ups raced to establish positions, but they lacked the sales and service networks needed to succeed on a grand scale. Then Faultfinders was bought by Fairchild and given new credibility. Fairchild Test Systems, a division of the pioneering chip manufacturer, was already well known as a supplier of semiconductor test systems, battling with Teradyne for market leadership in that sector. The Faultfinders system was improved by Fairchild, and soon the improved in-circuit tester was installed on the floors of many manufacturers, including Digital Equipment. Fairchild later acquired the leading European board-test supplier, Membrain. Underscoring its intentions to become a major factor in the business, Fairchild combined its various board-test operations into a single unit called Factron.

The defection of DEC could not have been welcome news at Concord. Various factors have been cited to explain the loss of GenRad's largest and most prized account. One theory was that DEC had been removed from GR's normal sales force coverage and made a "house account" served from headquarters. But the real problem was that GenRad, in its campaign to achieve a stranglehold on functional board testing, had lost sight of the fact that its business was not functional testing, but finding bad boards. Thus, when a market discontinuity occurred, the Company was outflanked.

GenRad's initial response to the new challenge was the 2270, developed under Jim Skilling, with Bill Kabele as project manager. This system was quickly followed by the 2271, in which short-duration pulses were applied to the board's components through the bed of nails fixture, enabling the tester to isolate each integrated circuit and test it *in situ*. The approach, known as back-driving, had been pioneered by a small company called Testline (which, like Faultfinders, was bought by Fairchild) and first used with a bed-of-nails fixture by Zehntel. GenRad coupled the technique with enough memory behind each pin to permit the application of long patterns to digital ICs, plus automatic test generation software that created a stored directory of tests for each circuit.

The 2270 In-Circuit Test System

GenRad's new in-circuit tester and its experienced board-test sales force quickly gave the Company the same clout in that sector as it enjoyed in functional testing. Others came to the in-circuit party, as the approach was soon embraced by the industry as the wave of the future, but GenRad was to retain its leading position in the over-all board test market for many years, successfully warding off challenges by Teradyne, Fairchild, Marconi Instruments, Membrain, and others. Hewlett-Packard was also a factor, selling functional test systems that looked more like rack-mounted assemblies of instruments than integrated systems. But GenRad, burned so often by HP in the past, was not indifferent to the challenger from the west. Even if its test system was mediocre, its worldwide distribution and sales network was anything but.

Since their departure from GR in 1973, Bob Fulks and Bob Anderson had remained on the ATE stage, first as the leaders of Mirco Systems, then as founders of their own company, called Omnicomp. Omnicomp, based in Phoenix, made a portable board tester designed for field service applications. The development was funded by NCR, which was struggling to maintain the thousands of transaction terminals that had replaced its old cash registers. The Omnicomp tester performed well, and it was bought in quantity by its sponsor, as well as Sperry-Univac and ICL. Watching the success of Omnicomp's "suitcase tester" with interest was Dick Rogers. Something like that would nicely round out GR's board-test line, he reasoned, adding a market that the Company had previously ignored.

Consequently, GR signed an agreement giving it the right to sell the Omnicomp Portable Service Processor – and to manufacture the product after September 1979.

Chapter 22

GR Goes Public

In a watershed event for the old Company, GenRad completed an initial public offering of its stock on June 8, 1978, at $15 a share. The underwriter was Lehman Brothers. The number of shares sold was 800,000 (about 28 percent of the Company), of which 300,000 shares were sold by the Company, netting just under $4 million. The other 500,000 shares were sold by the Company's Profit-Sharing Trust and the GenRad Foundation (the old Genradco Trust), easing pressures on those institutions. GenRad stock was initially traded on the over-the-counter market, under the symbol GRAD.

Coincident with the public offering, the Company began paying a semiannual dividend of 5 cents a share. Very few technology companies paid dividends, on the assumption that the money was better spent invested in the business. In GenRad's case, however, about one fifth of the stock was still owned by retired employees, who did not participate in the public offering. (Holders of 300 shares or more were temporarily barred from selling.) The creation of a public market for their stock gave them hope, of course, but the dividend helped them put bread on the table.

Years later, an initial public offering (IPO) of a company's stock was a means of transferring great wealth to the senior management. Billionaires were sometimes created overnight by the process, which eventually reached absurd heights at the end of the twentieth century. The GenRad IPO created no billionaires. In fact, the total value of all the stock owned by all the officers and directors was less than $2 million. There were some outstanding options, to be sure, but the salary of each senior manager, including Thurston, was expressible in five figures. New England conservatism was still alive and well at GenRad.

The many new shareholders of GenRad had reason to be pleased with the Company's performance in 1978. Sales jumped to $84.1 million, a 20 percent gain (25 percent, if Grason-Stadler was eliminated from the calculation). Net income soared to $6.1 million, or $2.27 per share, versus $1.45. The stock price ranged from $15.25 to $24.50 a share, holding above the offering price throughout the year. The board test line, fortified by the new in-circuit systems, continued to roll, with Europe especially strong. In fact, a quarter of the Company's 1978 revenues came from Europe, where Rogers had made several personnel changes. European Sales Manager Norbert Kuster was replaced by Rob Held, who had joined GR in 1974 as a controller, and the center of European activity thus shifted from Zurich to Bourne End, England, where Held was based. John Zapf, who had been Western Regional Manager in the U.S., was moved to Munich to run Germany, reporting to Held. Rogers was aggressively moving pieces on his new chessboard, and the moves were paying off, adding to his growing reputation as GR's "go to" manager.

In giving Rogers total control of worldwide sales, Thurston had made a master stroke. There was little Rogers didn't know about the board-test business, and the board-test business was GenRad's future. To outside observers, including the small claque of securities analysts now following the Company, three people held the power at GenRad: Thurston, Senior VP and CFO Stadler, and Dick Rogers. Their positions gave them the most visibility, of course, but in this case the perception matched reality.

Since there is a finite amount of sales energy at any company, the concentration of effort in the board-test area left other products underserved. The other major product unit, the awkwardly named Acoustics and Vibration Analysis Division, actually ran in the red for the year, with Time/Data again the culprit. AVA Manager McAleer, assisted by Bob Soderman, was based in Santa Clara, where he could witness the shortcomings first-hand, but he was unable to correct them. The previous Time/Data management had been decimated in the wake of Petefish's departure, and most of those left were replaced by McAleer, often with talent imported from Concord. Bob Cvitkovich was brought west to head manufacturing, Larry Moulton for sales and marketing, Matt Pichon for finance. McAleer also snatched a bright engineer, Dick Benson, from Concord, as well as a drafting manager, Lee Smith. A new instrument-sized signal analyzer, the 2512, was added to the line, but the Division still depended almost entirely on sales of its large systems, and there simply was not enough revenue there to support the Division's infrastructure and its share of the Company's overhead. The problem proved so intractable that once, when Thurston stated a profit goal for Time/Data, McAleer responded, candidly, "It can't be done."

Time/Data excepted, the picture was brilliant at year-end 1978. Record sales and earnings and the public stock offering told only part of the story. The balance sheet was at last respectable. Inventory turns rose. Debt was down, both in absolute terms and as a percentage of capital. The Company was in compliance with all covenants. The product subsidiaries were gone and the divisional structure streamlined. No wonder that, for the first time since taking over in 1973, Bill Thurston was pictured in the Company's annual report wearing a big grin.

Chapter 23

The Money Keeps Rolling In

Thurston had decided that Stadler would be the Company's face on Wall Street. He enjoyed the routine, and of course he had a detailed knowledge of the Company's financial position. Thus, when GR held its first meeting for securities analysts since going public, at Boston's Museum of Contemporary Art on April 26, 1979, it was Stadler who introduced the Company and set the agenda. Thurston then held forth on the strength of GR's board test business, boasting that the Company's sales of functional testers in 1978 equaled the sales of the next five largest competitors combined. Walter Hinds then spoke, principally about the attractions of the 1731 Linear IC Test System, and Ralph Anderson gave a detailed analysis of the economic factors underpinning the market for automatic test hardware and software.

There was one more speaker on the program: Bruce Gladstone, representing GR's newest acquisition, Futuredata. GenRad's past experience with acquisitions was hardly encouraging. Of the two companies acquired in 1970, one, Grason-Stadler, had been divested, and the other, Time/Data, had fallen far short of expectations.

Yet acquisitions were a tried and true way for companies to expand their horizons, and GenRad, flushed with success, was in an expansive mood. Looking at it from the other end, a small company starved for cash could only regard GenRad, with a good name and an eminently marketable stock, as an attractive potential godfather.

Steve Stadler

Thus, when financially strapped, Los Angeles-based Futuredata came calling, it found Thurston and his colleagues ready to listen. Futuredata was an early (1975) entrant in the microprocessor development systems business. The sales projections were bullish. According to market researcher Dataquest, the 32,000 such systems in use at the end of 1978 would grow to 100,000 by 1982, with the average price of each system rising by 20 percent a year. Most microprocessor development systems, moreover, were designed for use with specific microprocessors, while Futuredata specialized in "universal" systems, where the growth would be even faster. Futuredata's only competitor in that sector was Tektronix, and a union with GenRad would, argued Futuredata's management, blunt Textronix's advantages in distribution and support. Thurston, a firm believer in management by consensus, ran the idea by senior management and the Board, and everyone signed on. Not only would the acquisition create a new revenue stream; a position in microprocessor development systems would give GenRad an advance look at the microprocessors of tomorrow. Thus, on February 28, 1979, GenRad

145

purchased Futuredata for 240,000 shares of stock, valued at about $5 million. The unit, renamed GenRad/Futuredata, was placed within the Electronic Manufacturing Test Division.

The growth projections for Futuredata were exciting, so exciting that GenRad overlooked a potential problem: The customers for microprocessor development systems were engineers. But GenRad's marketing and sales executives had turned away from the engineering laboratory, directing all their attention to the factory floor, where GR's test systems would serve as money-making tools. Slotting Futuredata within Walter Hinds's Electronic Manufacturing Test Division was hardly a recipe for success.

The addition of Futuredata was seen as one component of the remaking of GR. The other component was the shedding of old businesses whose growth had slowed or stopped. The catalog in 1978, 250 pages long, was stuffed with instruments, components, Variacs, stroboscopes, standards, and other relics of times past. A few instruments, including the Digibridge, paid their way. The stroboscopes, generating about $2 million a year in sales, were marginally profitable. The Variacs and the coaxial connectors, all quality products, could not hope to match the growth of the board testers and were thus destined to become a smaller and smaller piece of the pie. Thurston, in the 1978 Annual Report, called the tune: "Low-margin product lines not consistent with our longer-term market plans were phased out, divested, or managed through pruning and pricing to yield better results." The only divestitures to date were Grason-Stadler and the French Variac operation, but Thurston was preparing his little list of products that would "none of 'em be missed."

The catalog also included a line of bench-top IC testers designed for the incoming inspection market. The sales pitch promised buyers most of the performance of the big, production-line semiconductor test systems, at only a quarter of the price. Other companies had tried to mine this vein, with sad results. The customers were usually well aware just what performance was left out. Still, the 1731 Linear IC Tester, initially priced at $23,000, found enough takers to generate 6 or 7 million dollars in annual sales for several years. A line of digital IC testers, also aimed at the inspection market, yielded about half that.

With sales of $86.6 million in 1978, GR seemed poised to crack the $100 million threshold in 1979. In fact, it blasted through the mark with ease, racking up revenues of $115.3 million, a record for the seventh straight year. Net income soared to $9.1 million, or $2.91 per share, a 35-percent increase. Stockholders were happy, and to make them happier the Company increased the semiannual dividend to 6 cents. Analysts were writing glowing reports, and the stock climbed more or less steadily throughout the year, breaking $40 in the fourth quarter. (The gain for long-time stockholders was even greater than it appeared; the stock had split 3 for 2 since the public offering.) The trade press, which never saw a bandwagon it didn't like, hailed the Lazarus-like transformation of the old Company and lionized Thurston. *Electronics* posted a rave review under the headline "Born-Again GenRad Roars into the '80s."

The praise was deserved. In the woeful year of 1972, General Radio had stared bankruptcy in the face. It was losing money, and its balance sheet was a mess. A new, untested president was about to take over. Employee morale was low, and some of the key talent was rebellious. It had one card to play, a new circuit board test system.

Now, seven years later, GenRad was a highly profitable, fast-growing, publicly owned Company. It had shipped over 1000 board test systems and was the clear market leader in both the functional and in-circuit sectors of that business. The new-product engine was humming, turning out new versions of its famed CAPS software, new Digibridges, new benchtop IC testers for linear and digital devices, a new signal analyzer for structural engineers, a

147

new continuity tester for bare boards, and an improved portable board tester, the 2500, imported from Omnicomp.

   With a return on equity of 24.2 percent in 1979 and a stock-market valuation of well over $100 million, GR found its bankers friendly again, and a $25 million line of credit from New England Merchants Bank and Citibank replaced an earlier $9 million line.

The GRAPE Escape

In another of a long list of shameless acronyms beginning with GR, the Company dubbed one of its activities GRAPE, for GenRad Association for Personnel Entertainment. GRAPE's brief history reached its peak with a theatrical enterprise called "The GRAPE Escape," presented on October 26, 1979 at the auditorium of the Sentry Insurance Company, less than a mile from GR's Concord headquarters. The evening's highlight was a series of skits, culminating in a parody of corporate management, which included President Bill Thirsty, Treasurer Steve Stutterer, and Manufacturing VP Walter Behind, with Bill Thurston playing his alter ego and also contributing a piano solo. The show, whose impresario was engineer Dick Mortenson, also featured a chorus, a dance group, and a quartet, performing satirical songs written by Mortenson, Matt Fichtenbaum, John Lynch, and Tom MacKenzie. The GRAPE theatrical company reassembled the following year to present "Sentimental Journey," a humorous retrospective on the Company's 65-year history. Said the call for volunteers: "participation will be based on desire more than on talent."

   Long-suffering retiree stockholders were now able to cash out. Employees, now numbering over 2300, once again had a rich menu of benefits, including a profit-sharing plan, a bonus plan, a stock purchase plan, and, for some, stock options with real value.

Engulfed by an embarrassment of such riches, Thurston could have been forgiven had he held to a steady course, consolidating gains and further exploiting the potential of existing lines. But the world of electronics was exploding in 1979, and competitors, most of them sharing in the good times, could be expected to mount attacks. It was a time, Thurston believed, to stay on the offensive.

There was another factor. Despite the Company's rapid growth, GenRad's stock market value was barely equal to one year's sales. That was enough to satisfy the old-timers, but it did not create the kind of wealth that was expected by the younger generation, the kind of wealth that was sweeping Silicon Valley. GenRad was now respected by Wall Street, but something more was needed to make the Company a stock-market winner. It was time to look for new frontiers. It was a time to add sizzle to the steak.

And a time to exit businesses that no longer made sense for GenRad. The knife next fell on the Variac line of autotransformers, generating about $3 million a year in sales. The line, a GR staple for over 40 years, was sold in 1979 for $447,000 – a wash on the balance sheet.

Two new directors were named to the Board, replacing the departing Robert Wright and the retiring John Quackenbos. The new Board members were Wilson Wilde, President and CEO of the Hartford Steam Boiler Inspection and Insurance Company, and Earle Pitt, Chairman and CEO of the Foxboro Company. Replacing John Quackenbos as Secretary was Jack Steele, who also was named Corporate Counsel.

In choosing candidates for Board membership, Thurston relied heavily on instinct, often deciding, after hearing someone speak at an executive forum, that the person had the personal qualities Thurston deemed important. Of course, if there was a business rationale as well, so much the better.

The divisional line-up remained unchanged: Electronic Manufacturing Test under Hinds, Acoustics and Vibration Analysis under McAleer, and Sales and Service under Rogers. Tom MacKenzie, a quiet, talented engineer with 17 years of GR experience, was named Director of Operations for EMT.

GR and Teradyne

General Radio was founded in 1915 by a young self-taught engineer from Oregon, and over the next 40 years its mostly MIT-trained engineers created a formidable array of laboratory instruments.

Teradyne was founded in 1960 by a pair of MIT graduates, and over the next 40 years its engineers, many from MIT, created a formidable array of automatic test systems for the electronics production lines.

It was inevitable that the trajectories of the two companies would intersect, though at first it appeared that the two might go their separate ways, GR in board testing, Teradyne in semiconductor testing. Teradyne offered board test systems, and GR sold IC testers for incoming inspection, but in each case, these products were secondary to the core business. But that all changed in 1980. With the introduction of the million-dollar L200 combinational board test system, Teradyne mounted a major assault on GR's board test hegemony. In the same year, GR joined forces with a group of ex-Fairchild engineers to enter the market for large semiconductor test systems for the production lines – Teradyne's turf. Nick DeWolf, one of the founders of Teradyne, said at the time, "They have just bet the company."

.

Chapter 24

Going For Broke

Of the two acquisitions made by Thurston in this period, one, Futuredata, would come and go in short order, without making major ripples. The other acquisition, made at the end of 1979, would reverberate for many years thereafter.

It is easy to understand what attracted GenRad to the semiconductor test systems business. It represented a much larger market than board testing, and it was growing much faster. And if you believed that all circuit boards were destined to become integrated circuits (a fallacious argument, but superficially persuasive), then a maker of board test systems would have to move into semiconductor testing to survive. Finally, the makers of semiconductor production equipment basked in the glow that surrounded the semiconductor industry. At meetings sponsored by investment bankers, armies of securities analysts swarmed around semiconductor celebrities like Wilf Corrigan, Charlie Sporck, and Bob Noyce, and then, after they milked those sources, their next targets were the makers of semiconductor production gear – companies like Perkin-Elmer, GCA, Applied Materials, and Teradyne. There were few comparable forums for a maker of circuit-board testers, no sense of excitement, no matter how good a company's numbers were. Not that GenRad would enter a new business just for the glitter, but the Company, after less than two years in Wall Street's eye, had sampled just enough glamour to develop a taste for it.

The catalyst that would take GenRad into the world of semiconductor testing was a small group of engineers unhappy with their lot at Fairchild Test Systems and looking for someone to sponsor them in the formation of a new company. Fairchild was a pioneer in semiconductor testing. After being outdistanced by Boston-based Teradyne in the late 1960s, it had bounced back with a test system of unprecedented size and complexity, the Sentry. The Sentry series soon dominated the market for LSI (large-scale integration) testing, although Teradyne's strong positions in linear-IC and memory testing made that Company the over-all market leader. At the time the semiconductor test business was essentially a two-horse race, with a Japanese company called Takeda Riken (soon to rename itself Advantest) coming up on the outside track.

It is not known what caused the Fairchild group to defect. It may simply have been the entrepreneurial itch, common enough in Silicon Valley, where Fairchild was based. It may have been the fact that Fairchild's Test Systems Division, notwithstanding its success, was still a relatively small part of a large chip maker, and the talent may have felt underappreciated. Whatever the reason, the group approached GenRad with a proposition that seemed like the perfect platform on which to launch the Company into a new, vastly more exciting orbit.

The leader of the Fairchild band was an Englishman named Brian Sear. With a solid technical grounding, an engaging personality, and the ability to explain the complexities of logic testing with clarity (and a British accent), Sear was able to convince Thurston and his key officers to back the new venture. A few urged caution; Stadler and Gemmell, the Company's chief financial watchdogs, wanted to see a more convincing analysis of return on investment, and McAleer was skeptical. But Thurston would not be dissuaded. Then Sear made his pitch to the Board of Directors, covering three walls of a meeting room with flow charts. "It was the most impressive proposal of its type I'd ever seen anywhere," recalls one participant. The Board unanimously okayed the venture, to be named GenRad/STI.

The deal: On December 29, 1979, GenRad paid $40,000 for 80 percent of the new company and agreed to put up an additional $2 million for preferred stock in 1980. GR also agreed to provide $9,450,000 in loans over a four-year period. The agreement also specified performance standards under which GR would buy the remaining 20 percent of the start-up, starting in 1984. GenRad/STI would initially occupy space in Time/Data's Santa Clara plant.

It was a roll of the dice, but of course that's what high technology is all about, and Thurston and company had every reason to believe that the risk was worth taking. At first blush it appeared that the amount at risk was capped at $2.4 million, plus another $9 million-plus in loans. But, as GenRad would learn, that was just the ante to play in a game where the stakes could be astronomical.

The board test market, meanwhile, was heating up. The shift from functional to in-circuit testing was now in full force. In 1976, the functional test market was five times the size of the in-circuit market. By 1980, in-circuit sales had almost closed the gap, and in 1981 in-circuit took the lead, for good. There would always be a need for functional testers, particularly in the military arena, but most commercial customers found that the newer in-circuit testers gave them adequate fault coverage.

GenRad, within a few years of its initial foray into the in-circuit market, seized the lead, and it did so without skipping a beat in its functional test business. In 1981, the Company sold about $100 million worth of board testers, split evenly between functional and in-circuit systems. Its share of the functional market was about one-third. Of the in-circuit market, GenRad's share was 30 percent. It was the clear market leader in both sectors.

Not that the competition was soft. Teradyne, as the decade of the 80s began, made a bold move, combining in one system both functional and in-circuit capabilities. This enormously complex system, the L200, debuted at a trade show, carrying a price tag of one million dollars. It was the board-test equivalent of Fairchild's Sentry IC test system, and initially it met with similar derision. "The most expensive boat anchor in history," chortled one GR salesman at the trade show. "No one will ever pay a million dollars for a board tester," agreed others, including members of the press.

But the market proved the skeptics wrong, once again demonstrating, as in the case of the Sentry, that customers will pay up for performance. At a million (and more) a pop, Teradyne would sell over 100 of these systems in the next few years, leaving GenRad in the dust by 1983 – in the functional/combinational category. But the world was shifting to in-circuit test, and there GenRad would hold its lead for another decade.

1980 began with a bang. First-half sales were up over 40 percent versus the previous year's first half, and net income grew by more than 60 percent. Buoyed by the results, the Company went on an expansion spree. A 70,000-square-foot building conspicuously sited on Boston's famed Route 128 was leased to house the Sales and Service Division. Purchase agreements were signed for a 55-acre tract in Boxborough and for two properties in Littleton, near Route 495, billed as the State's next "electronics highway." One of these ("Littleton North") was an 87-acre site slated to accommodate the growth of the board-test division. The other ("Littleton South") was a 15-acre site meant for the Component Test Division. The Concord plant was expanded by 50,000 square feet. STI moved out of the Time/Data plant in Santa Clara and into new quarters in Milpitas. All in all, it was a head-spinning burst of energy at the once-conservative Company.

There was more. In March, there was an offering of 500,000 shares of stock at $42.50 a share, netting the Company $20.5 million. In May the Company bought Omnicomp, Inc., welcoming Bob Fulks and Bob Anderson back to the fold. In October the stock split 2 for 1. The semi-annual dividend was hiked to 3.5 cents, and, in January 1981, to 4 cents. (Readers recalling that the dividend at the time of the IPO was 5 cents must keep in mind 3-for-2 and 2-for-1 stock splits that intervened.)

In the same month, senior management gathered in Orlando for a strategy session. Not surprisingly, the mood was optimistic in the extreme. The considered opinion of the group was that sales would reach $428 million in 1983. Of this amount, $148 million, or more than a third, would represent sales at STI and Futuredata, two operations little understood by GenRad in 1980. Accepting the numbers at face value, this was obviously a huge jump from the $171 million projected for 1980, and some attendees wondered whether the management systems were in place to accommodate that level of growth. But it was hard to worry about it while orders were raining down on the Company. In fact, one agenda item for the Orlando meeting read: "Corporate jet? When?"

Thurston was an inveterate reader, and he was rarely without a book recommendation. At the Florida meeting, it was John Kotter's "Organizational Dynamics: Diagnosis and Intervention." GenRad's organizational style seemed always to be in flux, vacillating between centralized and decentralized formats (at the moment, decentralized was in), and Thurston was constantly expounding on new-found management theories, always emphasizing that his opinions were only opinions and inviting – nay, pleading for – arguments for or against them. Underlying his voluminous musings on the subject was the desire that all managers consider "the essential nature of the enterprise" in humanistic terms. This may be seen as an echo of Melville Eastham's philosophy, the difference being that, while Eastham had a spiritual partner in Henry Shaw, Thurston's essays on governance were deeply personal, the epistles of one man crying in the wilderness.

Thurston and three of his senior managers were understandably bullish at the Company's second annual meeting for securities analysts, at Boston's State Street Bank on May 6. The theme was GenRad's promise to empower "The Factory of the Future." Testing, in Thurston's vision, was the logical control point for the modern manufacturing operation, collecting and distributing test information that could be used to design better products, produce them more efficiently and to higher quality standards, track failures, control inventory, plan staffing levels, and in the process stamp GenRad as "the key information-gathering resource" in the electronics industry. The concept of testing as the strategic hub of the manufacturing universe would never be realized, but it would prove irresistible to Thurston and his successors, resurfacing again and again under a variety of mantras.

Howie Painter, Vice President for Advanced Development, followed Thurston, outlining the role GenRad-designed software would play in helping manufacturers optimize their test operations, and describing how the CAPS simulator might link engineering, manufacturing, and field service. The Omnicomp portable service tester was a key link in the chain, and Painter himself would soon be packing his bags for Phoenix, where he would run Omnicomp, renamed the Service Products Division.

Steve Stadler gave the obligatory financial presentation, and then Brian Sear painted a glowing word picture of GenRad's campaign to mount an assault on the semiconductor test market. The world of VLSI (very large scale integration) and custom chips was ready, explained Sear, for an entirely new architecture, based on tester-per-pin technology. The semiconductor test market, he said, would grow from $280 million in 1980 to $600 million in 1984, and the established players were handicapped by their legacy systems. The first of the new GenRad/STI systems would ship in early 1981, he predicted, at which time GenRad would "aggressively go after market share in the segment with the least competition" - a curious concept, when one thinks about it.

The organizational streamlining that Thurston had engineered since taking over was reversed in 1980, as the number of product groups doubled, to six. Dick Rogers continued to run the Board Test Division in Concord, the principal growth engine. Tom MacKenzie was named Manager of the Component Test Division, in Bolton. Howie Painter, as noted, was sent to Phoenix as head of the Service Products Division (nee Omnicomp). Futuredata, in Culver City, California, was rechristened the Development Systems Division, under Earl Jacobs. At the old Time/Data plant in Santa Clara, Eric Mudama ran the Vibration Analysis Division, and newcomer Brian Sear headed GenRad/STI in Milpitas. All were Vice Presidents except Sear, who was President of the STI subsidiary. The expansion of the organization chart could be seen as the inevitable result of the Company's growth, particularly by acquisition, but Thurston was also adding a layer of management, naming two senior vice presidents, Walter Hinds and Harold McAleer, to oversee the product groups. (Dick Rogers was a third senior VP, having been given that title in 1980.) More bureaucracy was added when each product group was given its own autonomous board of directors, chaired by a Senior VP – i.e., Hinds, Stadler, or McAleer. GenRad/STI was treated somewhat differently, with Bill Thurston chairing its Board and Brian Sear and Gus Lahanas as the other members.

The idea of divisional boards was borrowed from Kollmorgen, an old-line New England instrument company. At first blush, the new structure seemed unwieldy. Moreover, in diluting the authority of the division managers it came perilously close to the matrix management scheme that Thurston had wisely discarded long ago.

An Advanced Technology Division, under Bob Fulks in Phoenix (with Bob Anderson as Assistant Manager), was created as an R&D resource available to the product groups, and the Sales and Service Division, headquartered in the Company's new leased space on Route 128, was placed under Rob Held. A presence on Route 128, with GenRad signage, was proof positive, in case there were still any doubters, that this was not your grandfather's General Radio. In short order, the Company moved its headquarters staff out of Concord and into the three-story building on "the space highway."

By 1980, GenRad had shed its identity as an old-line instrument company and had become a rising star of the ATE industry, with a market-leading line of functional and in-circuit board test systems and a new group of semiconductor test system designers promising to capture a meaningful share of that market. The new Development Systems Division generated a certain amount of excitement as well, both for its revenue potential and for its strategic value. And much buzz surrounded the Omnicomp acquisition, which brought with it a portable field service board tester (the "suitcase tester") as well as the return of the prodigals Fulks and Anderson.

Then there were the legacy products: laboratory instruments, stroboscopes, sound and vibration meters, standards and decade boxes, coaxial connectors and accessories. Everyone knew these products were not part of GenRad's long-term future, but no one knew quite what to do with them. As we have mentioned, the Component Test Division had been expected to operate as little more than a nursing home for old instruments, but CTD engineers like Henry Hall had other ideas, and the Digibridge breathed new life into the impedance measurement area. Sound and vibration measuring instruments were placed under several umbrellas, including the Enviromedics Division and the Acoustic and Vibration Analysis (AVA) Division.

158

AVA was then split into AVA-West (the old Time/Data), rechristened the Vibration Analysis Division, under Eric Mudama, and AVA-East, covering the sound and vibration instruments and – simply because of expediency - all the odds and ends of the old General Radio. AVA-East was then given a fresh new name: the Precision Products Line (PPL) – which, considering its mission, was a bit like naming a nursing home Sunrise Village. In addition to the instrument, stroboscope, coaxial, and standards lines, PPL absorbed a telephone sales group called TelSel. TelSel had been formed by Ken Castle, a veteran instrument salesman and product-line manager, who saw telemarketing (as it would later be called) as an attractive alternative to personal sales calls, especially for lower-priced products.

The Precision Products Line, including TelSel, was based in the Bolton plant and was organizationally within the Sales and Service Division, run by Rob Held. TelSel was expanded somewhat to put more horsepower behind the effort to milk the old products and to sell the highly successful Digibridges, which, significantly, were not included in PPL's grab bag of oldies.

The products now clustered together in PPL had sales of about $24 million in 1980, or about 14 percent of the Company's total. The trend was downward, despite price increases. The marching orders were clear: Try to maintain volume while cutting expenses to the bone. There would be no new-product development. Weak sisters in the line would be weeded out. (The 1521 Graphic-Level Recorder was one of 10 products dropped in 1980.) PPL's products would be sold through TelSel and sales representatives wherever possible.

But the old warhorses – the Strobotacs, the 874 connectors, the sound-level meters, and the like – had decades of momentum behind them, and the flywheel would keep spinning almost independently of GenRad's effort (or non-effort).   The market for laboratory

159

instruments was shrinking, and competitors – smaller companies not distracted by the systems business - were underpricing GR, but to those looking for a good impedance bridge or sound-level meter, the General Radio name, even truncated, still had the ring of quality. So the sales of instruments, stroboscopes, and coaxial connectors rolled on, longer than most people expected. The instrument catalog would be pruned each year, but the discontinued products were of little consequence, and the survivors were profitable. And even $20 million a year in revenue was not to be sneezed at – especially when engineering and selling costs were practically nil.

Of the products assigned to PPL, the best-selling by far were the sound and vibration meters and analyzers. The world was growing increasingly aware of noise pollution from airplanes, factory machinery, traffic, and even rock concerts. Mine Safety Appliance was in the market with a competitive sound-level meter, but GenRad offered a full line of instruments: sound-level meters, vibration meters, octave-band analyzers, impact noise analyzers, and even a noise dosimeter left behind by Grason-Stadler. And then, of course, there was GenRad's *Handbook of Noise Measurement*, the field manual for thousands of soldiers fighting the war against excessive noise.

The stroboscope line, despite no direct sales effort whatsoever, reliably produced 2 to 3 million dollars a year in revenue, but the Company was busy looking for a buyer. Warren Kundert, meanwhile, was energetically exploring the chances of selling off the entire PPL business. All the divestiture efforts were orchestrated by Gus Lahanas, who was given a free hand by Thurston.

The off-site management meetings went on throughout 1980. In July, the site was Maine, the subject personnel development. A year earlier Thurston, perceiving a weakness in the Company's ability to develop management talent, hired John Ferrie as Director of

Training, reporting to Rick Cambria. Ferrie, a native of Ireland, had been director of international training at GTE Sylvania, and at GR he began enlisting the support of the Division managers and senior staffers in upgrading the training function. The next month, the subject was strategic planning and financing options, with Tom Piper, a Harvard professor (and future Board member) leading the discussions. Once again, the growth assumptions were heroic, but, with the stock now selling at more than $50 a share, there were few nonbelievers.

Another milestone was reached on November 19, 1980, when GenRad stock began trading on the New York Stock Exchange, under the symbol "GEN." It is curious to consider, looking back, that no other company – not General Motors, not General Electric, not General Telephone, not General Dynamics – had staked claim to the ticker symbol GEN. But they had not, and for the next 20 years "GEN" on the tape would stand for GenRad.

The Company, as it closed the books on 1980, looked unstoppable. The five-year bar charts on the first page of the Annual Report told a story of meteoric growth, and Thurston's letter to stockholders suggested that this was just the beginning. To those employees who lived through the crises of 1972, the transformation must have seemed incredible. What was more, the Company was just entering two exciting new areas – semiconductor testing and microprocessor development systems. Combine success in these two ventures with GenRad's market-leading board-test business, and a corporate jet or two would not be at all excessive.

To put the euphoria in perspective, it is worth noting that 1980 was a feast for virtually the entire U.S. electronics industry. The personal computer mania was about to erupt, spurring a huge investment in capital equipment. The United States semiconductor makers ruled the world, as did the U.S. suppliers of semiconductor capital equipment. Brian Sear's rosy projections for

161

GenRad/STI were entirely credible given the times, as was Bill Thurston's upbeat letter to stockholders. GenRad's customers were filled with optimism, and they were buying accordingly. How could GenRad not share their enthusiasm?

And yet.....a securities analyst poring over GR's 1980 numbers found that, despite a 40 percent increase in revenues, earnings per share inched up by only 5 percent, from $1.32 to $1.39. He or she could also see that inventories grew faster than sales, opening up an old wound that had its origins in the unwillingness of General Radio ("An Engineer's Company") to take asset utilization seriously. A study commissioned by Thurston showed that, while the inventory carried by comparable manufacturers averaged 170 days of sales, GenRad was carrying (and financing) 280 days' worth of inventories - a particularly heavy burden in the ATE business, where rapid obsolescence was a constant reality. The debt/equity ratio, though much improved under Thurston's reign, was starting to backslide. The summary table and bar charts at the beginning of the Annual Report boasted that stockholders' equity had soared from $42 million to $74 million in the course of the year, but those who dug deeper into the Report learned that over the same period total debt had grown from $24 million to $46 million.

Not that any of this was grounds for panic, or even much concern. GenRad, like almost every other company in the electronics industry, was investing in its future, which was presumably what its stockholders expected it to do. Thurston would have been the last person to admit to being a riverboat gambler. On the contrary, he took his stewardship of the old Company most seriously and without question judged his latest ventures to be prudent risks. But GenRad in 1980 was a Company eager to bury once and for all the image of a tradition-bound, stodgy New England institution, and in its eagerness it was joining the rush to the casino.

162

Chapter 25

Doug Hajjar Arrives

Although shipments grew throughout 1980, business tailed off in the second half, so that shipments fell from $52.2 million in 1980s' fourth quarter to $39.4 million in the first quarter of 1981. In earnings per share, the fall-off was even more pronounced: from 41 cents to 5 cents. When the first-quarter results were reported, the stock price dropped 3-3/8 points, to $27.50 a share.

Thurston, in remarks to stockholders, attributed the shortfall to a general softening of capital spending, heavy investment at the STI venture (now running almost $1 million per quarter), necessary additions to plant capacity, an increase in interest expense, and foreign currency exchange losses. To deal with the downturn in business, he imposed a 100-person layoff at year-end 1980, a one-week unpaid furlough, and freezes in hiring and capital spending. The layoff, which was borne entirely by the Board Test and Component Test Divisions, was explained as an attempt to reduce inventory levels.

The premier trade show for makers of semiconductor manufacturing equipment and materials was Semicon West. Held each spring at the San Mateo (CA) fairgrounds, it attracted some 30 or 40 thousand attendees, mostly from nearby Silicon Valley but with a heavy representation from other parts of the globe. GenRad had never participated, of course, but in 1981 the Company was there with all the hoopla it could muster. Billboards on the freeways and paid spots on the local radio stations proclaimed GenRad's debut at the Show, with its star attraction, STI's GR16 VLSI Test System. (Also in the GR booth were the 1731 and 1732 bench-top incoming inspection testers and a Digibridge, but little attention was paid to these.) Hawking the GR16 were Brian Sear, applications specialist Bob Huston, and sales manager Jim Healey, all three well known in the business from their Fairchild days. Meanwhile, everyone at GenRad anxiously awaited the shipment of the first STI system. It was behind schedule, but in this business that was to be expected.

Soon, two more GR16s were booked, and then two GR18s. The latter was a monster system that seemed almost unbuildable, but IBM was willing (with appropriate contractual safeguards) to take a flyer on it.

Japan was not yet the semiconductor powerhouse it was destined to become, but GenRad, especially with STI in the fold, could not ignore that market. Accordingly, in mid-1981, the Company formed a 50-50 joint venture to manufacture test systems in Japan. The partner was long-time GR sales representative Tokyo Electron Limited (TEL). The first products to be made at TEL-GenRad Ltd. would be in-circuit testers, but the obvious goal was to raise GR's profile in Japan, the better to sell semiconductor test systems.

Futuredata, now called the Futuredata Development Systems Division, was losing money, several of its key managers were jumping ship, and a key product was late and in need of additional funding. With one west coast operation already burning too much cash, Thurston decided that GenRad could not afford to stay in the development systems business. Thus, although Futuredata had been acquired only two years earlier amid much fanfare about its synergistic effects on GenRad's other businesses, now, Thurston explained, "the structure of the microprocessor development system market has changed, and we feel we can make better use of our opportunities by focusing our financial and management resources on our primary business areas." Translation: It just didn't work out. With Walter Hinds in charge as a caretaker General Manager, the division was put on the block in mid-1981. Its sales that year were about $11 million.

As Futuredata was headed out one door, Cirrus Computers, Ltd. was entering another. Cirrus, founded in the U.K. in 1978 by a group of engineers headed by Clive Crossley, out of ICL Computers, was a consulting organization active in design automation. Of particular interest to GR were a Cirrus simulator called HILO and a test-pattern generator called HITEST. Bob Fulks, impressed with Crossley's work (he had brought him to Phoenix to run manufacturing for Omnicomp and later advised him in the creation of Cirrus in England), suggested that GR buy an equity interest, Thurston enthusiastically agreed, and Gus Lahanas worked out the details. GR took an initial 25 percent stake, with an option on the other 75 percent.

Cirrus, for its size, managed a wide range of engineering projects at three UK sites, chosen to accommodate the preferences of Crossley's ICL associates who joined him. Crossley ran the operation from a headquarters in Fareham. In Uxbridge, an engineering team worked on the HILO simulator (purchased from Brunel University) and other software products, and in Manchester, another team under Roger Ball began writing custom test programs for Fulks's Portable Service Processor. Within a short time, Cirrus was collaborating with the board test and semiconductor test divisions in their efforts to expand their software bases.

But the big event of 1981 had nothing to do with corporate acquisitions or divestitures. In September GenRad greeted its new Senior Vice President, Treasurer, and Chief Financial Officer, W. Douglas Hajjar, and a year later said goodbye to Steve Stadler, who had been Thurston's financial right hand since1973 and a member of the Board for almost as long. Thus, for the first time in the long history of the Company, an outsider had been hired at the highest management level save one.

Doug Hajjar

The move had been telegraphed in a memo from Thurston dated November 24, 1980. In this memo Thurston appointed Stadler Vice President for Strategic Analysis and Planning, then closed with the following: "Because Larry Gemmell has decided to pursue his career outside of GenRad, Steve assumes direct supervision of Finance on an interim basis, while we conduct a search for an individual with outstanding qualifications, experience, and reputation to head GenRad's redefined financial function at the corporate level, reporting to me." This search led to the hiring of Doug Hajjar.

Although Stadler had managed the Company's financial affairs well during his tenure, doing most of the legwork for the initial public offering, Thurston saw finance as a corporate weakness. This was undoubtedly true, though the fault lay less with Stadler than with the historic inability of an engineering-oriented company to give issues like inventory control their proper attention. The solution, Thurston believed, was to hire a financial heavyweight, someone with a more conventional CFO background. The search led to Doug Hajjar, then on the financial staff of MA/COM (formerly Microwave Associates). MA/COM was planning to move its headquarters to Florida, and Hajjar, with Massachusetts roots, was ready to jump ship. An interview with Thurston led to a quick job offer, which Hajjar accepted, with a $210,000 hiring bonus presumably linked to money left on the table at MA/COM.

It was clear from the outset that Hajjar was an executive of boundless energy and ambition. He hit GenRad in full stride, dismantling the divisional boards of directors that Thurston had created only a year or two before, imposing a new monthly internal reporting regimen, and hiring a new Controller, Paul Coughlan. He was thus invading Stadler's turf, with Thurston's full sponsorship. So, after spending a short while as Senior Vice President for Strategic Planning, Stadler exited gracefully.

Hajjar's impact on GenRad was immediate and significant, and his timing was perfect, as the electronics industry, after a sluggish 1981, was recovering smartly. Thurston, regarding Hajjar as a breath of fresh air in the Company he was trying to rejuvenate, supported his latest protégé unstintingly, to the surprise of many who noted the obvious differences in style. Thurston was quiet, mild-mannered, self-effacing. Hajjar was flashy and a bit cocky. Nevertheless, the chemistry worked, at least for a while, and once again, as with Hinds, Thurston appeared to have found a strong right hand.

Stadler's departure left a vacancy on the Board, and the decision of Wilbur Davenport to move to Hawaii left another. Two academics were chosen to fill the slots: Professor Paul Penfield, head of MIT's VLSI semiconductor research program, and Professor Thomas Piper, Professor of Finance at the Harvard Business School. Thus the Board complement remained at seven, of whom six were outsiders.

Sales languished just below $40 million a quarter throughout 1981, until a fourth quarter spurt to $52 million. But the year-end pickup was not enough to save Thurston from the first loss year on his watch. Excluding a $4.7 million loss at the Futuredata Development Systems Division (now counted as discontinued), there was a slight profit, but this was scant consolation for Thurston, who glowered in his annual report photo, looking as if he had just eaten some month-old chicken salad. His letter to stockholders, after recounting the difficulties that had beset the Company in 1981 (primarily the impact of the economic recession), stoutly defended his decision to boost R&D spending from $14 million to $21 million in furtherance of "the projects we had embarked upon during 1979 and 1980." By which he meant, principally, the venture in semiconductor testing.

The stock market reacted badly to the 1981 results. Thurston's reputation as Company savior had been tarnished. And the balance sheet was not quite as lustrous as it had been. Still, it was only one bad year in the last nine, and most employees and the Company's watchers on Wall Street were betting on Thurston to restore momentum as soon as the business climate improved. And so he did.

1982 and 1983 were exhilarating years at GenRad. Sales and earnings soared, the excitement within the Company was palpable, and Wall Street took notice, concluding that the missteps of 1981 were an aberration, that Thurston, especially with Hajjar at his side, was indeed capable of carrying the Company to the billion-dollar level. The balance sheet was dressed up with the aid of two successful stock offerings ($19 million and $46 million), the ailing Development Systems Division (Futuredata) was dumped, bank credit lines were increased at favorable terms, the stock split (3-2) again, and the dividend was hiked. Happy days were back again.

The Company was pushed by a strong tailwind. The ATE industry was again in full gallop, with worldwide sales of in-circuit test systems growing more than 70 percent from 1982 to 1984. GenRad was the in-circuit market leader by a wide margin, and in functional board test it led Teradyne by a nose. Dick Rogers's Board Test Division, now renamed the Production Test Division, could do no wrong, it seemed, as it wheeled out one new successful board tester or option after another.

But there was more to GR's success than the tailwind. The primary source of GR's burst of energy in the 1982-1983 period was almost certainly Doug Hajjar. As a newcomer to GR and to the ATE industry, Hajjar inevitably ruffled some feathers among the Company's old guard, but most GR veterans could see that he had uncommon ability and enthusiasm, and it was clear that he was a doer, not a talker.

The GR-16 VLSI Test System

After only two years running GR's financial affairs, Hajjar could point to a balance sheet with $170 million of stockholders' equity, total debt of less than $18 million, and cash in hand of $27 million. He had improved the Company's relations with its bankers and with Wall Street. Small wonder that, in the1984 Annual Report, he cosigned the President's letter as Executive Vice President and Chief Operating Officer. To any outside observer, Thurston had clearly signaled that he had found his successor.

Offstage, while the Company's visible achievements were being roundly applauded, several problems were brewing. The most dangerous was the cash burn at STI. Despite the fact that ten GR16 systems were sold in 1982, the investments in that operation were sized, not to reality, but to the ambitious growth projections that Brian Sear rolled out. In his 1982 letter, Thurston acknowledged that at STI, "costs remained above planned levels," but in the same breath he boasted that "STI has emerged as the market leader" in its field. Despite the bleeding, work continued at a 120,000-square-foot addition to STI's Milpitas headquarters. Meanwhile, engineering work continued on the high-end GR18 system, as prospective customers encouraged the outlay. At one critical juncture, a senior IBM manager visited GR and said to Thurston and Hajjar, of the GR18, "We're going to make it happen."

There were mixed feelings in the officer corps about STI. While most, including Thurston and Hajjar, believed that a thrust into semiconductor testing was strategically necessary, the execution at the west-coast operation was clearly problematic. McAleer, who had seen the STI team close-up when he was based in Santa Clara, grew increasingly doubtful. Hajjar, despite having developed a close friendship with Brian Sear, agreed with Thurston that a change in leadership was required, and in 1983 Rogers was dispatched to California to manage the operation. It was too late, and with the move, moreover, Thurston was depriving the Company's crown jewel, its Production Test Division, of its long-time leader. In terms of talent as well as money, GenRad was willing to borrow from its board test division to try to save its semiconductor test venture.

From 1982 to 1984, GR's share of the total board test business slipped from 30 to 26 percent, while Teradyne's share grew from 18 to 20 percent and HP's climbed from 8 to 11 percent. Thus, while GR was still the hands-down market leader, the competition was not going away. And board test still paid the rent at GenRad.

Thurston's grand strategy for the Company, as articulated at every analysts' meeting and in every annual report, remained the positioning of ATE as the logical command center for the entire electronics manufacturing industry. His theme in the early 80s was a new version of the "Factory of the Future" that had been promoted in the 70s. This time it was IQMS, for Integrated Quality Management Systems. The rationale for IQMS was familiar: The key to an efficient, quality-driven manufacturing plant was a flow of information that interconnected the design process, the production line, and field service. Feedback loops would ensure that designs were testable and that failure data could be used to refine the manufacturing process and improve quality. In its broadest idealization, the information flow would control inventory, dictate purchasing levels, and even size the workforce. Here is how Thurston put it in the 1983 Annual Report:

"IQMS systems will monitor and manage the quality of every process in the product life cycle." And, elsewhere in the same report: "GenRad's specialty – test technology – ultimately would directly affect every aspect of a company's business."

Accordingly, GR unleashed a barrage of hardware and software to interface its testers to other elements of the electronics manufacturing plant. For board testers, there was TRACS (Test and Repair Analysis/Control System). For component testers there was SCAN (Semiconductor

171

Component Analysis Network). A new QMP (Quality Management Products) group, created in 1982, introduced CADMATE to couple board testers to computer-aided design systems. The Advanced Technology Development group in Phoenix, managed by Bob Fulks, joined forces with Cirrus Computers in the UK to create design-to-test links. An enormous amount of engineering was thus spent in the pursuit of Thurston's vision of IQMS. GenRad was certainly not the only ATE company to go down this road (Teradyne's BoardWatch product directly competed with TRACS), but the payoff, at least the payoff on the scale projected, never came. There were two roadblocks. First, the very large manufacturers who dominated every ATE company's customer base all had their own systems, designed in-house, for managing their production lines. Each of these systems was of course tailor-made for its owner, and the in-house engineers who designed it took understandable pride in their creation. For an outsider like GenRad (or Teradyne) to presume to know more about the real issues at hand was arrogant. Some customers nibbled at TRACS and SCAN, but most passed.

Second, the whole theology of IQMS put GR in competition with major computer manufacturers like IBM and Honeywell, who considered the manipulation of data to be their turf. To a computer maker, trolling its base for service revenue, a tester maker like GenRad was an upstart not to be tolerated.

The concept of helping designers arrange circuits so that they could be more easily tested was another matter. Here the test community could offer real help, and at the important ATE meetings there were always weighty papers by engineers from GenRad, Teradyne, and others on the subject of design-to-test and BIST (Built-In Self Test) innovations. The papers were sound, the audiences for the most part convinced, but all the scholarly work produced little revenue for the ATE makers.

The GenRad catalog in the early 80s was a litany of acronyms. In addition to TRACS, SCAN, CADMATE, IQMS, and QMP, there were PSP and LTS (Portable Service Processor and Logic Test System, respectively) from the Service Products Division (SPD). There was even a recycled acronym: GRAD, which at one time had stood for the General Radio Advertising Department, now meant the GenRad Advanced Development Group, not to be confused with the Advanced Technology Group (ATD) in Phoenix.

Although the keys to GenRad's future clearly were its prospects in board test and semiconductor test, there were other important contributors. In California, Eric Mudama had established such momentum for the GR line of vibration analysis products that Thurston dared to write, in his 1982 letter, "growth is expected to continue at an annual rate of 20 to 30 percent." The following year the Vibration Analysis Division was split in two. The old VAD continued to cover the structural analysis ground, while a new sub-group focused on circuit-design tools based partly on work done at Cirrus. McAleer's Component Test Division kept selling its bench-top testers at a healthy clip and introduced a precision version of its best-selling Digibridge and a new memory tester for the incoming inspection market. It also oversaw the refinement of SCAN, which provided datalogging and yield analysis for the bench-top 1731 and 1732 IC testers (but not for STI's GR16). In Phoenix, the Service Products Division, under Howie Painter, launched its 2620 Field Maintenance Processor and, later, the 2610 Universal Field Tester, called, hopefully, "the personal tester."

In 1982 Thurston named Bob Anderson to the post of Vice President for Corporate Marketing, with the mission of helping to make GR "the recognized international leader in supplying IQMS to manufacturers of electronic devices and equipment for use over the life cycle of their products." Anderson, who had been one of GR's

173

first board-test salesmen, was clearly back in the spotlight after returning to the Company from his Omnicomp detour.

Overseas sales accounted for 38 percent of the total in 1982, as the new GenRad-TEL partnership began to contribute meaningfully. TEL now manufactured in-circuit board testers in Japan, and STI was using its Tokyo office to promote the GR16.

Chapter 26

Thurston's Last Hurrah

The 1983 financial results were all that a stockholder could hope for. Sales were a record $227 million, net earnings were a record $19.6 million, stockholders' equity was a record $170 million. Debt was a mere $10.8 million, and the stock price hit a high of $46. The bar charts in the front of the Annual Report fairly exploded off the page.

Hajjar's hand could be seen everywhere. A stock offering added $46 million to GR's cash account and eased the strains on the GR Profit-Sharing Trust and the GenRad foundation by $8.3 million. Hajjar named Charlie Peters Treasurer in May and Controller in November. In the latter case, Peters succeeded anther Hajjar hire, Paul Coughlan, who became Vice President for Quality, a new position. Hajjar was now the face of the Company on Wall Street, with investor-relations specialist Ray McNulty at his side. Hajjar also became a conspicuous presence at sales meetings, where his cheerleading gave the crowd an enthusiasm and a spirit that hadn't been seen since the days of Leo Chamberlain. This was the era of Doug Flutie at Boston College, Hajjar's alma mater, and Hajjar burst on stage at one sales meeting sporting a jersey bearing Flutie's number 22. His specialty may have been finance, but

Hajjar, more than anyone else at the Company, knew how to turn a corporate meeting into a pep rally.

As sales and profits rained down during 1983, and as articles in the press began speculating that a billion-dollar GenRad was likely before the decade was out, management began laying ambitious expansion plans. In 1983, STI tripled its plant capacity, based on what Thurston forecast as "the major ramp-up of productivity scheduled for 1984." In Phoenix, the Service Products Division moved into a bigger facility. And a group in Concord began designing a new corporate headquarters and a new test systems manufacturing plant.

Why a new headquarters? First, the expansion possibilities in Waltham were nil. The leased building was too small, and no suitable land was available nearby. A return to Concord might have made sense but for an unfortunate land sale in the 1970s. A choice five-acre portion of the Company's 88-acre tract had been sold to a group seeking to build a medical office park. The five acres, on a rise overlooking the GenRad plant, would have made an ideal gateway to a new GR campus, but the land had been offloaded by Sinclair at a time when cash was scarce. The five acres aside, the Concord expansion possibilities were limited by traffic issues. Route 2, the east-west highway abutting the Company's land, was often congested, and access was problematic.

Second, the new, larger headquarters was intended to house a conference center and a training facility. A separate training facility in Framingham had opened a few years before, but it had not worked out, and there was much to be said for bringing customers to classrooms in a central corporate campus.

The Bird Watchers

Sometime in the early 1950s, a group of GR production workers banded together for a camping-out weekend in the country, which was such a success that it soon became an annual ritual. The organizers promoted the event as a gathering of a quasi-secret clan, dubbed "the Bird Watchers." In a way, this was the workers' answer to the stratification of "An Engineers' Company." Invitations were not extended to "the suits," and the Bird Watchers reveled in their status as a blue-collar band of weekend warriors. Eventually, however, the barriers fell, as engineers like Hal McAleer, Bob Fulks, and Leo Chamberlain proved that they were just the kind of closet rowdies that could contribute to the merriment.

The trips were generally by bus, the destinations often the vacation cabins of Bird Watchers in the White Mountains, Cape Cod, and Maine. The excursions were marked by serious beer drinking, poker games, singing, and general ribaldry, including initiation rites for new members, who, dressed in ceremonial feathers, were "hatched" from mock eggs.

The Bird Watchers were coy about their membership list, but it can be stated with some authority that the roster included Carl Uhlendorff, Paul Penney, Austin Corkum, Al Jones, Warren Newell, Charlie Kierstead, Emil Mohler, Bill Fish, Sid Beck, Larry Mounce, and Harold Meuse, as well as the engineers already mentioned. The roster of "El Presidentes" included Paul Penney, Hal McAleer, Dick Mortenson, Larry Pierce, and Billy Jones.

The Bird Watchers was one of the more durable of GR's institutions, lasting for more than 30 years. Then, like so many other things, the Bird Watchers fell victim to the hard times that engulfed the Company in its later years.

GenRad was only one of many companies looking for large, developable tracts in the area. To find suitable land and worry the new facilities into being, Thurston chose Jack Steele, GenRad's Secretary and General Counsel, and soon thereafter the Company closed on two choice parcels. For the new corporate headquarters, Steele's team closed on a 45-acre tract in Boxborough, near the intersection of Interstate 495 and State Route 111. For a planned new board-test campus, GenRad bought a 100-acre tract in Littleton, also near Interstate 495. Both sites were near enough to Concord so that personnel could be moved around without major disruptions, and both were on the circumferential Route 495, seen as a likely replica of the "space highway," Route 128.

Hajjar, realizing better than anyone that underneath the dazzling 1983 numbers lay a growing vulnerability to a business downturn, was nervous about the Company's planned new headquarters, a major project to be financed with a heavy mortgage. Thus he extracted from Steele a promise not to proceed farther down this avenue without Hajjar's approval – an approval that would never come. (Both the Boxborough and Littleton projects were aborted. The tracts were sold at a profit some years later.)

In mid-1983 GenRad completed the acquisition of Cirrus Sigma, the holding company for Cirrus Computers and Cirrus Designs, for about $4 million in cash and stock. These UK operations were proving useful to the parent Company, developing design software and simulation tools for the test-system divisions. The units worked closely with Bob Fulks's design team in Phoenix, and Fulks himself was a frequent traveler between Phoenix and London.

It was easy – too easy – to ignore the warning signs when the bookings were strong, the backlog growing, and the balance sheet brilliant. Well, perhaps not exactly brilliant. Inventories in 1983 grew by a whopping 38 percent "to meet expected demand in 1984," according to

Thurston. Another red flag was a 51-percent increase in accounts receivable. A surge in receivables may be a signal that buyers of test systems are withholding payment for incomplete or underperforming systems. Since 20 GR16 semiconductor test systems were sold in 1983, this system was a likely suspect.

In October 1983, at the International Test Conference in Philadelphia, GenRad officially took the wraps off its new "Complex VLSI Test System," the GR18. The specifications were impressive: a 40-MHz clock rate and 288 pins. IBM had already spoken for a system, and other customers were reportedly lined up. Meanwhile, the Semiconductor Test Division kept losing money at a fast clip, despite heroic efforts by Dick Rogers to control costs. Hajjar and a few directors were beginning to worry, but Thurston believed the take-off roll had passed the point of no return. In for a penny, in for a pound.

Chapter 27

The Wheels Come Off

There were no bar charts in the opening pages of the 1984 Annual Report, and the smile was gone from Bill Thurston's face. Sales were up by 10 percent, to $249.5 million, but net income dropped from $19.6 million to $11 million, or, on a per share basis, from $1.25 to 0.68. Amazingly, the annual dividend was increased from 8 to 10 cents during the year. But capital gains were elusive, as the stock price sank from a 1983 high of $46 to a low of $14 in the fourth quarter of 1984.

Once again, the balance sheet was flashing storm warnings, as inventories grew by 25 percent against the 10 percent sales gain. This, like the 32 percent increase in R&D spending, was explained as a necessary step to prepare the Company for an expected surge in orders, particularly at the Semiconductor Test Division. By the end of 1984, GenRad could report the installation of 52 VLSI Test Systems and the first shipment of the ambitious GR18. Paradoxically, the more systems STI shipped, the deeper the hole it dug for itself. The operation did not lack system design talent; the team that followed Brian Sear out the door at Fairchild was highly competent. At Fairchild, however, this team had handed its designs to a world-class manufacturing operation, which had cut its teeth on the Sentry systems. At GenRad's Semiconductor Test Division, the manufacturing group had its hands full assembling and testing the GR16, let alone the much larger GR18.

The letter to stockholders in the 1984 Annual Report alluded to "product introduction problems at our Production Test Division and manufacturing problems at our Semiconductor Test Division." These were of course the two divisions that would make or break GenRad, and one was stumbling, the other threatening to become a disaster. The letter said that these problems were "mostly" corrected, but people close to the Company knew otherwise.

At times of stress, it is not unusual for a CEO to shuffle the officer corps, and this is exactly what Thurston did in 1984, in an attempt to find the right lineup for the times.

First and most significant, Doug Hajjar was named Executive Vice President and Chief Operating Officer, while remaining Chief Financial Officer. Thurston's new responsibilities would include "long-term strategies, new product directions, human resource development, and quality issues." The message could not have been clearer if it had been posted on a billboard on the Company's Waltham headquarters: Thurston was phasing himself out, and Hajjar would soon become President. Conventional wisdom was united on this point, but conventional wisdom was wrong.

There was a flurry of other appointments, all orchestrated by Hajjar. Two outsiders were brought in to fill key positions. Glenn Pierce, an ex-IBMer, became Vice President and General Manager of the Sales and Service Division, succeeding Rob Held, who in turn succeeded Harold McAleer as head of the Component Test Division. And Joe Rivlin, an ATE veteran, signed on as Assistant General Manager of the Production Test Division (i.e., assistant to Ralph Anderson).

Clive Crossley, who had founded Cirrus Computers (now 100-percent-owned by GenRad), was named Vice President and General Manager of the Design Engineering Group, a mostly UK organization, with an outpost in California. Crossley's engineers were active on several fronts, feeding software to GR's board test, semiconductor test, and service product test divisions – while at the same time working on a number of "blue sky" projects – including, notably, a Manchester project, under GM Roger Ball, to test the electronics in Jaguar's new XJ6 automobile. In time this project would become a major success story.

The California outpost noted in the preceding paragraph was located in Santa Clara, under the direction of Eric Mudama, the erstwhile GM of the Vibration Analysis Division. Then, when Mudama was given the Service Products Division in Phoenix, displacing the departing Howie Painter, Paul Coughlan took over Mudama's old job. Completing the round robin, Harold McAleer succeeded Coughlan as the Company's top Quality officer.

The pieces were thus flying around the chessboard in 1984, as the problems worsened. And the chess master had cause for concern. Hajjar was smart and energetic, but he was deep in the mid-game now, and his position was deteriorating fast. Moreover, the unquestioning support he had always enjoyed from Thurston had begun to wane once

Thurston effectively proclaimed himself a lame duck CEO. The attention showered on Hajjar by the business and trade press could not have helped his cause.

A further problem for Hajjar, as he attempted to force change at GenRad, was, ironically, the fast-rising stock price he himself had helped to engineer. Some managers took the occasion to cash out, amassing considerable wealth and, along with it, the fortitude to oppose any of Hajjar's directives they disliked.

The Board of Directors was expanded from seven to eight in 1984 with the addition of Lawrence Mayhew, CEO of Data I/O Corporation and a former Group Vice President at Tektronix. The gears were thus set in motion for an attempted merger with Data I/O, an attempt that would consume much management energy a few years later, as GR looked for a life raft.

As it became increasingly apparent that GenRad's semiconductor test venture was dragging the Company down, Thurston and Hajjar huddled to examine possible avenues of salvation. One solution was the merger of GenRad with an established semiconductor-test-system maker, a company that could lend credibility as well as manufacturing resources to GR's struggling operation. One obvious candidate was LTX, a company founded in 1976 by a Teradyne executive named Graham Miller and a team of Teradyne engineers. Miller, an Englishman, was technically strong and an excellent salesman, and his Company's sales had skyrocketed from less than $10 million in 1979 to more than $100 million in 1984. Its fortunes were thus soaring while GR's were wobbling. More important, LTX's sales were entirely in the linear, or analog, test area, and were thus complementary to STD's digital offerings. LTX was based, moreover, in the Boston area, a short drive down Route 128 from GR's Waltham headquarters.

Hajjar, in the course of his travels on the financial relations circuit, had come to know Graham Miller well, and the two had hit it off, talking casually every now and then about the benefits of uniting their two companies. Then, in mid-1985, the talks grew serious, and Hajjar and Miller mapped out a planned merger. Thurston would be Chairman of the combined company, Miller President and CEO, and Hajjar COO and CFO.

Hajjar thought it a match made in heaven. Thurston was not likely to object, he thought, inasmuch as he was spending less time on GenRad matters and more on political affairs. (He was a Director of the Massachusetts High Technology Council.) The role of Chairman, on a glide path toward retirement, seemed perfect for Thurston. Or so it seemed to Doug Hajjar.

But when the plan was put on Thurston's desk, he balked. In Hajjar and Miller, who had drawn up the merger plan without his input, he saw a twosome who, he feared, would force his early exit from the new company. Nevertheless, he agreed to let Hajjar present his plan to GenRad's Board of Directors. Hajjar did so, and he obtained what he took as the Board's green light to proceed.

Hajjar then quickly put the final pieces in place, drafting a press release to be issued the day after Labor Day. Just days before, however, he was asked to meet with Thurston at the latter's home in Harvard, MA. At that meeting, Thurston informed Hajjar that the merger was off, that the Board had reconsidered and had now joined Thurston in opposition. Hajjar's reaction was curt and decisive: On the day after Labor Day, he said, a news release would report either a planned merger or Doug Hajjar's resignation. Thurston did not back down, and Hajjar was gone.

He quickly became CEO of Telesis, a Boston-area computer-aided-design (CAD) company, taking with him Bob Fulks and Glenn Pierce. Thus GR had lost, at one fell swoop, its Executive Vice President, its Chief Operating Officer, its Chief Financial Officer, its Vice President in charge of Advanced Technology, and its Vice President for Sales and Service. Also joining the group of defectors were financial trouble-shooter Bob McAuliffe and board-test product manager Joe Prang.

Like Leo Chamberlain before him, Doug Hajjar's ouster from GenRad was a springboard to better things, as Telesis was purchased by Valid Logic, which in turn was bought by Cadence Design, with Hajjar's star rising at every step. The scenario was not unlike the tale of Leo Chamberlain, forced out by Thurston years earlier and similarly enriched by his ensuing career.

The Hajjar-led exodus came at the worst possible time for GenRad – in a year that Bill Thurston characterized, in his letter to stockholders in the 1985 Annual Report, as "the most difficult and challenging year in GenRad's history."

No one could argue with that. On a 12 percent sales dip, the Company posted a net loss of a sickening $52.3 million. On the balance sheet, retained earnings plummeted from $78 million to $24 million. Most of the accumulated earnings of 70 years of GR history were thus wiped out in a single year.

Inventory write-offs, severance costs, and plant-closing charges contributed to the massive loss, as the excesses of the past few years came home to roost. In his letter, Thurston pointed to a worldwide slump in test-system sales, and 1985 did indeed see a pullback by the industry deep enough to explain GR's 12 percent sales downturn. Harder to explain was how a 12-percent sales dip could translate into a $52 million loss.

One answer was that the sales decline was greater than the full-year statements revealed. Fourth-quarter shipments of $49.6 million in 1985 compared with fourth-quarter shipments of $85.6 million in 1984. At year-end, then, the sales collapse was not 12 percent but 42 percent.

Another answer was GR's spending spree in the early eighties, which left the Company highly vulnerable. Still another was Thurston's failure to appreciate the magnitude of the bet he was making on Brian Sear and his semiconductor test team.

In what Thurston called the most difficult year in GenRad's history, stockholder dividends were maintained, to the tune of $1.6 million.

In the wake of Hajjar's departure, Thurston took control of day-to-day operations and set out to craft yet another complete reorganization of the Company. This time there would be but two business groups: Electronic Manufacturing Test and Semiconductor Test, the former under Dick Rogers, the latter under Bob Anderson. Two other Group Vice Presidents were named: Joe Rivlin, running sales and service, and Harold McAleer, heading a Design Engineering Group now based in the U.K. and California. Hajjar's CFO role fell to Treasurer Charlie Peters, who was named a Vice President.

The organizational reshuffling included the merger of the Component Test Division, under Rob Held, and the Production Test Division, under Ralph Anderson. Rogers's initial decision was to place the expanded Production Test Division under Anderson. But then, persuaded that the challenges in board test could best be met by a marketer (Held) rather than an engineer (Anderson), Rogers reversed his decision. Anderson was to be VP for Advanced Technologies, but in fact his career at GenRad was effectively over. A year later he left, becoming Engineering Vice President at BTU Corporation.

GR had for years supported design engineering staffs in Phoenix (under Fulks), in Santa Clara (under Eric Mudama and then Dave Wharton of Cirrus), and at three separate UK locations. That many non-revenue-producing operations could no longer be carried, and Harold McAleer's formidable challenge was to stop the bleeding. McAleer moved to England and soon saw that the Fareham operation, in a new, lavishly appointed plant, was the chief bleeder, and he moved Crossley out and named himself manager. Three Cirrus engineers reported to him: John Bowthorpe in Fareham, Dave Wharton in Santa Clara, and Richard Bosworth in Manchester, where engineers continued discussions with Jaguar regarding a tester for automotive electronics.

Thurston, closing in on the traditional retirement age of 65, was now forced to consider the issue of succession once again. Realistically, there was a short list of inside candidates: the four Group Vice Presidents. Of these, Anderson and Rogers, heading the two dominant business groups, appeared to be the front-runners. Of course, an outsider was always a possibility. Thurston, after all, had plucked Hajjar from outside only a few years earlier and had quickly brought him to within an inch of the presidency.

The rest of the 1985 officer corps at the end of 1985 included Gus Lahanas, CFO Charlie Peters, Planning VP Russ Craig, Eric Mudama, still running Service Products in Phoenix, Rob Held, heading board-test ("Massachusetts Operations") under Dick Rogers, and Paul Coughlan, heading Structural Test. Controller Vin Carolan and Counsel John Hurley rounded out the list.

The following officers listed in the 1984 report were gone in 1985: Ralph Anderson, Clive Crossley, Bob Fulks, Doug Hajjar, Glenn Pierce, Brian Sear, and Jack Steele.

As GenRad's condition worsened, Thurston put the Company into a crash dive. A seven-day unpaid furlough and a pay freeze were starters. Then, in December 1985, the Company laid off 525 employees, or 19 percent of its workforce. Since another layoff earlier in the year had trimmed 10 percent, the Company was shrinking fast.

In 1985, GR's board-test sales accounted for 63 percent of its total revenues, and GR could still claim market-share leadership. But in the LSI/VLSI portion of the semiconductor test market – the market served by the

185

Semiconductor Test Division, GenRad was still an also-ran, with a share of less than 7 percent. This was of course far removed from the projections rolled out by Thurston and Brian Sear a few years earlier. Despite massive injections of cash and the best efforts of Rogers to rescue the operation, STD was still gushing red ink. Thurston had indeed "bet the Company" in entering the semiconductor test market, and in 1985 it looked like a bad bet.

In naming Hajjar Executive Vice President and Chief Operating Officer, Thurston had announced that his own proper role lay in the area of strategic planning and that day-to-day management of the Company's affairs was best left to someone else. The same rationale was invoked in 1986, when Dick Rogers was given the same titles that Hajjar had won two years earlier. Thurston and Rogers were pictured together in the 1986 Annual Report, and they co-signed the letter to stockholders, just as Thurston and Hajjar had in 1984.

In the 1986 report, Thurston again tried to finesse the situation at the Semiconductor Test Division, claiming that "in 1986, as in 1985, GenRad was the leading U.S. vendor of VLSI test systems in the over-$600,000 market segment." The key to this extravagant claim was the modifier "U.S.", which allowed Thurston to exclude not only the Japanese suppliers Advantest and Ando, but Fairchild Test Systems, now owned by offshore-based Schlumberger. Such artful logic was also the basis for the claim that "Semiconductor Test (ST) had a successful year" – a claim recognized by insiders as well as many outsiders as wishful thinking.

Responsibility for the Semiconductor Test Division now rested with Group Vice President Bob Anderson, who, despite the developing crisis at Milpitas, chose to continue living in Phoenix. Day-to-day operations in California were supervised by Rick Tippett, who was named General Manager. Tippett's strengths lay in operations, and it was hoped that his skills, combined with Anderson's experience in sales and marketing, would stabilize the struggling division. By this time, however, the GR16 and GR18 systems were widely known to be problem-ridden, and attempts to extend the line by adding new systems (GR125, GR160, GR180) were handicapped by the Company's deteriorating market position. Through the end of 1986, GenRad had shipped more than 100 VLSI test systems, but the losses were staggering. After 1986, GenRad's semiconductor test sales started a sickening nosedive toward an ignoble end.

Board test was another matter. There, the Company successfully warded off a competitive thrust from Boston rival Teradyne. In 1986 it even launched a counterattack against Teradyne's best-selling L200 line of combinational test systems. GR may not have been the first into the combinational market – as it was not the first into the in-circuit market - but its reputation and, more important, its array of software tools were enough to give its new 2750 board test system a quick burst of orders.

Board-test product direction, with the departure of product manager Joe Prang, fell to Richie Faubert, who had managed the 2750 project and who in 1986 was named Vice President for New Product Development. And with the promotion of Rogers to the executive suite, Rob Held gained complete control of the all-important board-test business. Held and Faubert were thus recognized as stars of the shrunken officer corps. Three Senior Vice Presidents were named in 1986: CFO Charlie Peters, Thurston's long-time aide Gus Lahanas, and Bob Anderson, still presiding over the failing semiconductor test division. The only other line officers were Tippett at STD and Eric Mudama, running the Service Products Division in Phoenix.

At this time, Senior Vice President and long-time officer Harold McAleer decided to call it a career at GenRad and took an early retirement offer.

A major 1986 development was the sale of a $57.5 million, 25-year convertible subordinated debenture in May. The proceeds from this offering enabled the Company to dress up its balance sheet, so that by year-end the Company's cash on hand exceeded its short-term borrowings. The bond bore a 7.25-percent coupon, and the conversion price was $14.375 per share.

The financial results for 1986 were grim, though Thurston could and did point to some improvement. Sales were down again, to $204 million, and the Company suffered a net loss of just under $30 million. Through layoffs, early retirements, and attrition, the Company managed to shed more than 1000 employees in the space of 15 months. The dividends were finally eliminated, and the large tracts of land in Boxborough and Littleton were sold, at a profit of $4 million. The rented space on Route 128 in Waltham was vacated, and the Company's headquarters moved back to Concord. The dreams of grandeur had changed to plans for retrenchment.

Despite the relief provided by the convertible bond issue, the Company's financial position remained precarious. The outlook for the Semiconductor Test Division was bleak, not only because of its own missteps, but also because of changes in the competitive landscape. LTX, a leader in the linear/analog IC test business, was making inroads in the digital area through its Trillium subsidiary, most notably by the capture of the Intel microprocessor-testing business. Trillium's chief marketer was a semiconductor-test veteran named Jim Healey, who was recruited from GenRad by Graham Miller. Teradyne, with strong positions in digital, analog, and memory test, was snapping back fast after a 1985 slump. Advantest and Ando were blocking GenRad's attempts to crack the Japanese market. Megatest, a relative newcomer, had begun to penetrate Texas Instruments and IBM with its new VLSI tester. And Fairchild Test Systems, now renamed Schlumberger Test Systems, was as strong as ever.

(Schlumberger had bought the entire Fairchild organization, then sold the semiconductor operation to National Semiconductor, retaining the test-equipment operation.) Most of these players had deep pockets, and GenRad clearly did not.

In 1987, Thurston was thinking about the previously unthinkable – GenRad's exit from the semiconductor test business. A number of exit strategies were on the table. One was merger with a partner able to share the burden. Another was sale of the division. The third was simply closure of the operation.

Bob Anderson, at Thurston's direction, spent several months trying to sell the ailing operation. He also made a last, vain attempt to persuade IBM, the godfather of the problematic GR18, to fund the development of a next-generation test system, the GR300. But IBM was not buying, and the last hope vanished. Of course, Anderson's efforts inevitably spread the word that GenRad was ready to throw in the towel, and VLSI test sales plummeted from $27.3 million in 1986 to less than $4 million in 1987. (The operation's peak sales were $31.8 million, in 1985.) In August, GenRad finally bit the bullet, closing its Semiconductor Test Division and ending a painful chapter in its history.

As the year wound down, Thurston informed the directors that, at the January Board meeting, he would recommend either merger with a larger company or the selection of an insider to replace him as CEO. A third possibility, he noted, was the initiation of a search for an outside successor.

At least two merger propositions were floated during 1987. One involved Data I/O, whose CEO, Larry Mayhew, sat on GenRad's board. Data I/O, based in Washington State, was a leader in the PROM programming business. Its sales were about $65 million a year. Only with the most optimistic assumptions of its sales growth and GenRad's could a merger have made any sense. So, after the merger details were thoroughly examined in the spring of 1987, they were dropped.

The other merger candidate was LTX, now a major factor in the semiconductor test business. A few years before, Doug Hajjar and LTX founder and CEO Graham Miller had almost walked down the aisle together, but Bill Thurston scotched their wedding plans. Now, with Thurston on the brink of retirement and GenRad's position weakening, Shearson Lehman drew up detailed plans for the merger of the two companies, called, in typical M&A-speak, Adam (GR) and Eve (LTX).

Meetings were held, attended by Gus Lahanas, Charlie Peters, several LTX executives, and the Lehman intermediaries – but not by Thurston or Miller. Graham Miller, it appeared, was blowing hot and cold on the idea of merging with GenRad – mostly cold. His apathy was understandable; LTX was flying high, the board test business was not especially appealing to him, and GR's semiconductor test business was worthless to him. So Adam and Eve were quietly banished from Eden.

There were other suitors in the wings, among them GR's historical *bête noire* Hewlett-Packard, Teradyne, and the British board-test competitor British Marconi. HP conducted a thorough due-diligence review of GR's operations, and for years thereafter there were those at GenRad who were sure that it was solely an espionage mission.

Thurston feared, probably with cause, that a merger with a larger company like HP, Teradyne, or British Marconi would be followed by massive layoffs at GR, and he thus approached the prospective merger partners without enthusiasm. But the deal-breaker was usually price.

Sales recovered somewhat in 1987, to $194 million, but a small operating profit was swamped by a loss of $39 million at the Semiconductor Test Division, counted as a discontinued operation. (Under pressure from the SEC,

STD was subsequently reclassified as a continuing operation, so the bottom line was in fact red in 1987.)

In all, the Company lost more than $119 million in the three years from 1985 through 1987, wiping out retained earnings and then some. Only the $57.5 million convertible sold in 1986 stood between the Company and ruin. Surveying the sorry situation, some officers opted for early retirement packages, others began to demand a change at the top. Of course, Thurston was now 65 and on the eve of retirement – but far from ready to give up the reins completely. He intended to have a vote, preferably the deciding vote, on the Board's selection of a new CEO.

To an outsider, looking at the photo accompanying the President's letter in the 1986 Annual Report, the choice was obvious. Standing behind a seated Bill Thurston was Dick Rogers, the new Executive Vice President and Chief Operating Officer. Of course, Thurston and Hajjar had shared the same pose in 1984, and then, quickly, Doug Hajjar was gone.

On the day after Thanksgiving, as the GR-LTX merger plan was falling apart, Thurston, with Board approval, offered Bob Anderson the job as his successor. Anderson's salary would be higher than Thurston's, and there would be an employment contract. The news hit Rogers hard, and he and board-test GM Rob Held made their displeasure well known, composing a "white paper" outlining their grievances. It was a throw of the dice, and Rogers and Held lost. On January 4, 1988, both resigned, and on the same day Bob Anderson was named the new President and CEO of GenRad. Like their predecessors Hajjar and Chamberlain, Rogers and Held went on to successful careers elsewhere.

Thus ended the Thurston presidency. He had much to be proud of. He took over in 1972, with the Company *in extremis*, restored sales growth and profitability, took the Company public, and made GR the world leader in its core business, circuit-board testing. But he was leaving with the Company again in great difficulty, owing chiefly to the hemorrhaging of cash at the semiconductor test operation. It would be unfair to hold Thurston solely accountable for the decision to enter chip testing. The Board of Directors was equally enthusiastic about the initial investment and equally supportive of Brian Sear and his team, at least at the outset. And Doug Hajjar, Thurston's right hand in the early 80s,was a strong advocate, seconding Thurston's resolve to stay the course, as did most of the Board and senior management. As the losses deepened, some of the early enthusiasts jumped off the wagon, but Thurston remained hopeful, for far too long, that GenRad would become a power in semiconductor testing.

The news in 1987 was not all bad. The new high-end board test system, the 2750, was introduced, and 20 were booked during the year. The Company's total board test sales increased by about 9 percent, and contributed to a record year-end backlog of $35 million. A strong line of software products, including the highly successful HILO logic simulator out of Cirrus, underscored the Company's long-running tag line "The Difference in Software is the Difference in Testers," although there were complaints from within that new software products were being rushed to market before they were ready.

Meanwhile, Hewlett-Packard was preparing to attack GenRad's bread-and-butter business. As mentioned, GR's board test sales grew by 9 percent in 1987, but HP's board test sales were up 27 percent. In board test, GR was twice HP's size, but it would take HP just six years to close the gap.

Chapter 28

The Anderson Years

I n endorsing Bob Anderson as his successor, Thurston was choosing the GR insider who most closely resembled him in background and style. An MIT VI-A engineering graduate whose career path had led through sales and marketing positions, a soft-spoken, mild-mannered executive, Anderson slid easily into Thurston's position, with little discernible break in continuity.

Bob Anderson

Anderson was also added to the Board of Directors, of course. In the wake of the failed attempt to merge GR into Data I/O, the CEO of that Company left the GR Board and was replaced by Bill Scheerer, a senior executive at Bell Laboratories. Scheerer and Thurston had met the year before while on vacation in Maine, found that they got along, an invitation (by Anderson) followed, and Scheerer joined the Board in 1988, remaining a Director until the Company was acquired in 2001.

As Anderson took the helm, his agenda was clear: Costs had to be trimmed. Investor confidence had to be rebuilt. Most important, the Company would have to reinvigorate its technology base, particularly in board test. The board test market was not as fast growing as the semiconductor test market, but it was still a growth business. More important, it was GenRad's business – and GenRad's business to lose. In 1988 GenRad held 24 percent of the total worldwide board test market, compared with Teradyne's 19 percent and Hewlett-Packard's 13 percent. Trailing HP was Schlumberger-Factron, the latest incarnation of the Fairchild board-test business. (Schlumberger had rechristened its semiconductor-test and board-test units Sentry and Factron, respectively.) The competitors were all well heeled, but in board test GR was clearly the Company to beat. Its installed base was huge, including thousands of 1790 and 2210 testers, along with the new 2750. Compaq Computer, one of the fastest-growing electronics manufacturers in the world, owned more than 60 GenRad in-circuit testers, and competitors who tried to penetrate the account quickly found that Compaq was solidly in the GR camp. So tight was the bond, in fact, that Compaq collaborated in the development of a higher-performance, higher-pin-count board tester, the 2282, subsequently deploying this system on its surface-mount lines in Texas and Scotland.

Under Anderson's leadership, the Company added to its board test lineup in 1988. In addition to the 2282, the Company introduced the 2752, designed to upgrade the huge (1500-plus) base of 1790 testers. Similarly, a GR-EXCEL package was intended to add combinational capability to the 2276. The software engineers were busy, too: Version 2.0 of TRACS was unveiled, to speed board-repair operations. And, for the high-end 2750, there was a new software package christened GENESIS, a tortured acronym standing for GenRad Environment for Strategic Independent Software. GENESIS also incorporated its own logic simulator, and it greatly added to GR's luster as a technology leader. (The technology was moving fast, however, and the 2750, GENESIS, and TRACS would all require constant upgrades to keep pace.)

Anderson also made sure that other revenue streams were fortified. Three new Digibridges were introduced, along with a new Random Vibration Controller (2530) and, most significantly, new capabilities for its automotive diagnostic tester, based in England and now shipping in volume to Jaguar Motors. The tester was in fact a custom product specifically designed to test the electronics in a Jaguar XJ6, but GR saw this as a business with enormous potential.

To address the cost side of the ledger, Anderson closed the Phoenix operation and moved the unit, called the Small Test Systems Group, to Concord, incurring a charge of $10 million. Bolton manufacturing operations were consolidated in Concord.

Anderson's vision, as articulated in the Annual Report, was less ambitious than that of his predecessor. The Company had been chastened since the days when it proclaimed itself the natural nerve center of the manufacturing universe. Offering a refreshingly candid retrospective, Anderson was able to write, "CIM, Computer Integrated Manufacturing, became the buzzword. It was going to solve everybody's problem. It hasn't yet."

At year-end 1988, GenRad employed 2000 people. It was the leader in its core business. Its stock sold for about $7 a share, against a book value of about $4. Debt, consisting mostly of convertible bonds, was manageable. Income taxes on future profits would be shielded by a $113 million tax-loss carry forward. Without question, the Company had suffered greatly from its adventure in semiconductor testing, but all in all, the situation was far from hopeless.

In 1989, Hewlett-Packard's board test sales shot up 20 percent, while GR's sagged slightly, as did the over-all market. HP's market share was now 16 percent, still well below GR's 23 percent, but HP, with the advantage of its vast worldwide sales and service network, was coming on strong. Teradyne, at 19 percent, was also a strong competitor. The Boston-based company, with sales of $483 million, was now much larger than GenRad ($205 million), and it was also financially strong. To counter its more muscular competitors, GenRad could point to one major advantage: To HP and Teradyne, board test was a sideline. HP's core businesses were instruments and computers, while Teradyne was primarily a maker of semiconductor test systems. At GR, board test was the ball game.

In mid-1989, a mild slump in the U.S. computer industry, a key part of GR's sales base, inflicted great damage on the Company's board test bookings. The order flow from Compaq and other customers was cut to a trickle, and Anderson was forced to lay off more than 100 employees and mandate 12 days of unpaid leave for the entire workforce. Particularly hard hit was an old standby, the 2276, now handicapped by an inadequate pin count and an uncompetitive price. The 2276 was also being squeezed between lower-priced MDAs (Manufacturing Defect Analyzers) and higher-performance systems reaching down-market. The gross margins on the system were good enough to allow GR to cut the price of the 2276, but it was too little, too late.

Anderson looked for other opportunities to husband the Company's resources. For instance, recognizing that the TEL-GenRad operation in Tokyo would never pay off, he sold GR's interest to its partner, netting $600,000.

New-product development was not on the cutting block. The 1989 crop included a new high-throughput board tester, the 2286, new versions of HILO and TRACS, a higher-pin-count 2750, and an ISDN software package for use with the 2276XP telecommunications device tester.

Periodically, it seemed, GR would develop a heightened appetite for "business relationships" – quasi-partnerships that promised the benefits of synergy to both participants. Anderson caught the bug in 1989, heralding a list of "partners in innovation," which included Computer Integrated Modular Manufacturing (CIMM), Logic Modeling Systems (LMS), and Cimflex Teknowledge. Then, for good measure, the Company made an outright acquisition, buying, for 408,000 shares of GR stock, Structural Measurement Systems and promptly housing it within the Structural Test Products Division. Little of consequence came from any of these deals.

The final scorecard for 1989 was not pretty: Sales dropped 8 percent, to $189 million, and the bottom line was printed in red ink for the fifth straight year. A total of $131 million in losses had been recorded in the years from 1985 through 1989, leaving the Company with retained earnings, over its 74-year history, of minus $55 million.

As the Company entered the 90s, it faced two monumental challenges. First, the board test business was slowing to a crawl. Second, Hewlett-Packard was threatening to dislodge GR from its leadership position, as it had so often in the case of other GR product lines.

The competitive threat was ominous, but GenRad had fought off good competition ever since it entered the ATE business almost 20 years earlier. HP and Teradyne were competent and then some, but GR held the high ground, and its board test technology was solid. It would be difficult, but GR could compete.

The deceleration of market growth was something else again. There was no escaping the fact that board test was no longer a high-growth business. There was irony here: Twenty years before, GR had cast aside the instrument foundation on which the Company was built, on the grounds that an annual growth rate of four or five percent was insufficient as a wealth creator or a career platform. Now the instruments were mostly gone, and the board test business, the new girl in town back in 1970, was showing her age, growing four or five percent in a good year, and often less than that.

The figures, as reported by the foremost market researcher, Prime Data, tell the sad story. From 1976 through 1981, the board test market's average annual growth rate was 76 percent. From 1981 through 1986, the annual growth averaged 13 percent. From 1986 through 1991, the period through which Bob Anderson found himself struggling, the board test market grew, on the average, about 3 percent a year. Even that meager growth was largely driven by low-cost testers made by Zehntel and others – a market in which GenRad did not participate. Meanwhile, the Company was spending 14 percent of every sales dollar on engineering – money to develop more new products for a sluggish market of which it held a declining share. Yet there was no alternative. Board test systems represented more than 75 percent of the Company's total revenues – more, if one added the software products that tagged along. The board-test market was no longer a dynamic business, but the technology was still damnably complex, with new curve balls and new customer demands pushing the envelope. Teradyne had seized the high ground in the functional area with its L290 series, and that threat had to be countered. Many customers wanted to revert to "rack-and-stack" testers (the new term of art was "open architecture"), using instruments linked by a VXI bus, and that had to be addressed. New SCAN technology – design techniques to enhance testability – required further investment, for here again Teradyne had moved ahead of GenRad. TRACS, GenRad's successful board-test tracking software, had been updated as version 2.0, but it lacked an interface to new 32-bit testers. HP and

Teradyne both competed in that space, and they were pricing aggressively. The new 2750 high-end test system, in which so many hopes were invested, needed a higher pin count to accommodate the larger ASICs coming along. The new GENESIS software platform, also a major element of GR's future board-test strategy, was proving user-unfriendly, and the interface would have to be redesigned to make the platform more intuitive and easier to use. Fixturing, an ever-more critical part of the test installation, was clearly outside GR's competence, and a relationship would have to be forged with at least one outside supplier. All that was just to take care of present business; at some point, a next generation system, referred to within the Company as "HHH", would have to be developed.

The list of vital engineering projects seemed endless. And it all had to be funded out of a $30 million R&D budget – money spent, not to push the frontiers of technology, but simply to stay alive.

The reader may well wonder how the board test market could turn so sour so fast. First, industry-wide efforts to improve manufacturing quality – efforts that GR helped to spearhead – were bearing fruit. When first-pass board yields were 20 or 30 percent, manufacturers had no alternative but to buy more test systems to diagnose the mounting volume of bad boards. Bad boards meant tied-up inventory, shipping delays, unhappy customers, and, probably, horrendous field repair costs. The lower the quality, the higher the board test sales.

Now, however, industry, taking a page from the Japanese model, had embarked on a crusade to raise quality, and first-pass board yields had jumped to the 90 percent range. Result: Fewer bad boards and fewer testers required to process them.

The situation was markedly different from that prevailing in semiconductor ATE. There, Moore's Law dictated that device complexity and speed raced ahead, doubling every year or two, and new generations of test systems were needed to keep pace. This was not so in the board-test universe, where test systems often did useful work for 10 years or more.

Another factor contributing to the slowdown was the increasing outsourcing of board manufacture to contract manufacturers, whose operations were models of efficiency and who drove their capital-equipment suppliers hard on price.

But is the growth rate of a given technology market something over which a company has no control, or should companies stimulate growth by innovative engineering? Take the computer market, for instance. Over its history, each time the growth rate slowed, some company – Digital Equipment, IBM, Apple, Dell – did something exciting and different to revive it. The market changed, the players changed, but the growth was always there, because companies made it happen. In board test, there were fewer and fewer innovations. Zehntel introduced a low-cost tester called the Z1800, which was programmed by a personal computer, assembled out of a Heathkit-like parts kit, and sold over the telephone. Several thousand of these testers were sold by a sales team with pep-rally fervor, but then the Company was bought by Teradyne, and the pep rally ended. GenRad kept improving its board test hardware and software, but the advances were all incremental; there was no real breakthrough. It must be remembered that, during the critical years from 1980 through 1987, when board test market growth was slowing but still respectable, GenRad was diverting treasure and talent into its semiconductor test venture. It is worth speculating what might have been if the investment at STI had instead been channeled into board test and if Dick Rogers had not been reassigned in an effort to save the sinking California operation. It is possible, though of course not certain, that GenRad might have engineered a major advance and changed the whole course of board test history.

But Anderson in 1989 had to deal with reality, not might-have-been, and the reality was that the Company was foundering, and a board test recovery was unlikely to come to the rescue. Looking across the Company's product landscape, there was little else that offered meaningful help. The design automation program (chiefly the HILO simulator) was successful but lacked critical mass. The catalog still included stroboscopes and acoustic instruments, both fading fast and candidates for divestiture. Impedance-measuring instruments were still a GR strong suit, with thousands of Digibridges in use throughout the electronics industry. These products paid their way, and the technology could be used in modules designed for a VXI-bus cage, but the market was small, and competitors were nipping at GR's heels. Other offerings in the instrument product line ranged from feeble to moribund. GR had found out, as had other ATE suppliers over the years, that the incoming inspection market was always smaller than logic said it should be, and the1730-series of testers and the GR125 IC tester were candidates for the axe.

The Company's line of so-called quality management products (QMP), based on TRACS, was considered promising, especially with the arrival of OPUS, a new architecture to port TRACS to a 32-bit host, but here again, the hope vastly exceeded any realistic revenue forecasts. In a 1989 strategic plan, QMP's vision of the future was described in an especially fanciful projection: The world would invest $100,000 to $150,000 to manage each of its 15,000 PC-board production lines, reasoned the author, creating a potential of between $1.5 and $1.8 billion for QMP's products.

In 1988, the Company's QMP revenue was $1.5 million.

As Anderson saw it, GenRad desperately needed an exciting new market opportunity, removed from the core business, but still within range of GenRad's technical

201

competence. The outreaches to other companies ("partners in innovation") were part of the search.

Two attractive growth opportunities engaged Anderson's attention and enthusiasm. One was automotive testing, which had already been successfully launched by one of the Cirrus teams in England. The other was the automatic testing of liquid crystal display (LCD) panels.

In Manchester, England, GR's Automotive Test Products (ATP) Division, under a succession of general managers – Roger Ball, Richard Bosworth, and Peter Palmer – had studied the automotive electronics area closely, in consultation with engineers at Jaguar Motor Cars. Jaguar's popular XJ6, introduced 20 years earlier, was having problems coping with the proliferation of electronic devices "under the bonnet." The Cirrus engineers got on well with their Jaguar counterparts, and soon the Manchester crew was at work on systems, not only to diagnose problems in the service bay, but also to configure cars on the Jaguar production line (e.g, by programming PROMs on the engine control module).

Then, in the fall of 1989, an event occurred that created a step-function improvement in GR's chances to make something out of this business. The event was the purchase of the British auto manufacturer by the Ford Motor Company. Suddenly there was a reasonable chance of using the Jaguar business to open doors throughout the Ford-Europe organization, and a remote chance of leveraging that into business with the parent Company in Detroit.

By this time, it was no secret that the automobile industry was "going electronic," and other test companies were fishing in the same waters. In Detroit, a small army of Hewlett-Packard engineers was encamped at Ford, developing computer-controlled test systems for Ford's U.S. product line. Across the Atlantic, the engineers at Ford-Europe sized up the investment their Detroit colleagues were making and opted for the less expensive, but still more than adequate, test technology available from GenRad. Thus Anderson had just the kind of new business opening he had sought. He was understandably excited and before long was shuttling between Concord and the two UK operations involved, Fareham and Manchester, with frequent stops at various Ford-Europe sites. Could automotive test be the spark that reignited GenRad's growth? The positives: The Company already had a foot in the door, and the engineers at ATP included some of the Company's best. Also, GR's reputation in Europe, dating far back to its General Radio years, was excellent. And beyond Ford, there were several other car makers in Europe, all having problems dealing with electronics. The negatives: ATP was based 3000 miles east of Concord, and day-to-day oversight was impossible (the comparison with STI, 3000 miles west, was inevitable). And GenRad was in no position financially to fund a major development program, as HP most certainly was. Assuming GR achieved a measure of success in Europe, at some point HP could be expected to play hardball. It had not escaped GR's notice that HP and Ford had representatives on each other's boards of directors.

Anderson decided that the positives outweighed the negatives, and he wholeheartedly supported the efforts of the UK group.

The eighties had not been kind to GenRad. The Company began the decade on the heels of 10 straight years of record sales, record earnings, and a stock price in the forties. Exactly 10 years later, as the Company closed its books at the end of 1989, sales were stagnant, there had been five straight years of losses, retained earnings had shrunk from plus $35.5 million to minus $55 million, and the stock price was hovering around $5 a share. Most people attributed the reversal of fortunes to the misadventure in semiconductor testing, and there is obviously some merit in that argument, but it is also true, as we have noted, that the board test market had slowed to a crawl. In fact, the bet on Brian Sear and his team could be seen as springing from the same impulse to diversify that was now leading the Company to fund ventures into automotive electronics and LCD testing. The difference was that these new probes were controlled investments, not money pits.

Board test sales peaked in 1988, then began a slow, steady decline, despite a flurry of new product announcements. Most of the engineering budget was invested in two system families. The 2280 series of high-performance testers included systems with a variety of in-circuit and functional capabilities and pin counts, all addressed to production-line applications. The top-of-the-line 2750 series, with which GR staked its claim to technological supremacy, won quick market acceptance, and gave the Company a flicker of hope. At the low-priced end, the 2270 series competed with manufacturing defect analyzers, typically priced well under $100,000 – and dropping fast.

The GR board-test lineup was, as usual, backed by a broad arsenal of software weapons, including TRACS, HILO, GENESIS, and an array of allied products developed in partnership with other companies. The allure of software products was obvious: the margins were good, the competition highly fragmented, and the tie-in possibilities attractive. Still, the engineering dollars flowing into GR's design automation products was substantial. GenRad, in its reports to shareholders, made much of the fact that it was spending at least 15 percent of sales on R&D. A cynical interpretation of that boast was that the R&D percentage was high, not because the Company was investing so much in technology, but because the sales harvested from that investment were so low. It's a conundrum well known by every high-tech CEO.

In 1989 GR sold $154 million worth of board testers, still comfortably ahead of Teradyne ($129 million) and Hewlett-Packard ($106 million), but Anderson could see trouble ahead. The computer industry was putting the brakes on spending, the competitors were discounting aggressively, and GR's P&L and balance sheet made heavy personnel cuts inevitable.

Chapter 29

Hard Times

W hen Bill Thurston announced the appointment of Bob Anderson as his successor, he simultaneously reported the departure of two senior officers, Dick Rogers and Rob Held. This left significant holes in the organization; Rogers had been COO and Executive Vice President, while Held ran the worldwide sales and service organization. Thus Anderson faced not only the difficulties that the market and the competition were handing him, but the necessity of building a new senior management team. He inherited two senior vice presidents, Gus Lahanas and CFO Charlie Peters, along with Richie Faubert as VP for Product Development, Jim Lynch as VP Human Resources, and Art Winterhalter, VP for Marketing and Sales. Anderson brought Rick Tippett, who had run STD in its final days, to Concord as VP Operations. With the retirement of Gus Lahanas in 1990, the VP corps was slimmed down to four: Faubert, Peters, Tippett, and Winterhalter.

Sales dropped again in 1990, to $179 million, and the loss deepened, to $21 million, or $1.22 share, including the effects of write-offs and restructuring charges. The stock price chart reflected the deterioration of the Company's fortunes, and in the second half of the year

GenRad stock, still listed on the New York Stock Exchange, often traded below $2 a share. A Company with $180 million in sales had a market value of about $35 million. This attracted the attention of at least one investment house, which began accumulating the stock, hoping for a turnaround.

Topic A during this period was the Search for a Winning Strategy, and a number of Management Group meetings were convened to explore alternatives. Actual and potential partnerships were examined, the automotive and LCD test businesses were analyzed, and some saw growth possibilities in the Structural Test Products area. Some people still clung to the idea that the Company's software products – HILO, TRACS, etc. – could be the platform for building a future in design automation business. But it was universally agreed that the board test business, though necessary to defend, could not create the new, fast-growing, profitable enterprise everyone wanted. There was a growing feeling that HP was unstoppable, and GR's self-confidence took a further beating when a Walker Customer Satisfaction Survey ranked GR systems behind those of HP, Marconi, and Schlumberger-Factron in two key components of reliability - MTBF (mean time between failures) and MTTR (mean time to repair).

The reliability feedback did not indicate that GR was slipshod, but rather that the world was changing, with competitors driving hard on quality and customers raising expectations. In fact, the GR culture historically emphasized quality, and under Thurston and Anderson quality was always a top priority. When Anderson became CEO, he immediately brought Jim Lynch east from Milpitas as Vice President for Human Resources and Quality Deployment, and Lynch masterminded GR's TQM (Total Quality Management) program, with positive results. He also orchestrated the Walker Customer Satisfaction Survey, which, notwithstanding the reliability ratings, indicated that 62 percent of respondents would buy from GR again, while only 11 percent would not.

The campaign to shape a new corporate strategy was waged under the direction of Carole Prest, who was given the title of Director of Strategic Marketing and Corporate Development. Prest had become a key member of Anderson's management team, since the Company's future depended on the successful reordering of its priorities. The "Corporate Development" part of her portfolio was inherited when long-time GR stalwart Gus Lahanas retired. Anderson had sized up Prest as one of the brightest people in the Company, and he had full confidence in her ability to handle a broad range of responsibilities. Prest, with a Physics degree from Mt. Holyoke and an MBA from Harvard, joined GR in 1985 and had been Marketing Manager and Program Director for Quality Management Products (TRACS) before moving into the corporate strategy area in 1992. She quickly seized control of the territory, and within a year she became the first woman in the Company's long history to be named a Vice President.

The balance sheet at year-end 1990 showed about $13 million in cash and almost $60 million in debt, with the $57 million convertible bond (now standing at $48.7 million, owing to repurchases) proving to have been a providential transaction in 1986.

In 1991, Anderson was jolted by the departure of Senior VP and CFO Charlie Peters. Peters was widely known and respected, and it was only a matter of time before he moved along to a better opportunity elsewhere. The elsewhere turned out to be the area's leading electric utility, Boston Edison, which offered Peters the post of Chief Financial Officer. Peters understandably accepted the offer, and Anderson turned to headhunter Hedrick and Struggles to help him find a new CFO.

This search led to the hiring of Bob Aldworth, who quickly replaced GR's long-time auditor, Ernst & Young, in favor of Arthur Anderson. Ernst had been GR's auditor for as long as anyone could remember, from the days when it was Ernst & Ernst, but Aldworth felt that a new set of auditing eyes would be helpful, and it is probable that some cost savings were also in prospect. There was no loss of credibility, as AA's reputation was just as solid as Ernst's.

At about the same time Jim Lynch decided to return to California, where he accepted an offer from Sun Microsystems to head that Company's quality program. His place as head of Human Resources at GR was taken by Steve McCarthy, formerly head of training.

Anderson, watching with growing unease as key officers like Charlie Peters and Jim Lynch left GR for what they perceived as greener pastures, decided to take steps to bolster morale. Several senior engineers were cause for special concern. The engineering force had certainly not escaped the downsizings of recent years, and more engineers would soon be laid off. Yet a core of senior engineers was essential to any hopes to reestablish technical preeminence. Thus, partly as a preemptive move, Anderson in 1991 initiated the GenRad Fellows Program ("to honor senior technologists for their exceptional achievements in the field of design and test technology"). Two of GenRad's top engineers, Henry Hall and Malcolm Holtje, were named the first two Fellows. Hall was the Company's resident expert on impedance measurement, while Holtje had developed a wide range of products in the industrial electronics field and headed GR's microelectronics laboratory, the source of monolithic circuits that lay at the heart of many GR systems and instruments. The Fellows program was hardly unique, of course. The IBM Fellows program was well known, and other companies had traveled the same path. Yet Anderson should be credited with understanding, more than any of his predecessors and more than his ATE competitors, the importance of publicly recognizing the contributions of outstanding engineers. It was fitting that GR ("an engineer's company") took the lead in this area – despite the sea of troubles that beset the struggling Company.

In March 1991 the GenRad instrument era officially came to an end with the sale of the Precision Products Line to a start-up called QuadTech for $6.32 million. (The potential buyers also included Keithley Instruments, represented by the retired Harold McAleer.) The book value of the line was $3.4 million at the time of closing. The products involved included impedance bridges and standards – the lineal descendants of Melville Eastham's General Radio Company – as well as stroboscopes and acoustic instruments. For three quarters of a century the electronics world had looked to GR for the best in laboratory instruments, and now the end had come. Rights to use the GenRad and General Radio names were included in the sale, and QuadTech sold the "General Radio" Digibridge^{TM}, megohmmeters, and other instruments for a number of years before selling the lines to IET Labs in 2000 and 2006.

Things went from bad to worse in 1991. Sales slipped further, to $156 million, and the loss, including restructuring charges and inventory write-downs, was $39 million. The restructuring included the termination of 400 employees. Shareholders' equity at year-end was about $3.5 million, or $2 a share, and over most of the year the stock traded at about that price – a shocking reminder of how far the Company had fallen.

Board-test products represented almost 90 percent of GenRad's revenues in 1991. The Company kept upgrading its board test systems and adding new ones, spending 15 percent of sales on engineering. The products were excellent but the market was weak, with industry sales of in-circuit testers, GR's lead products, sagging 6 percent. The competition was as aggressive as ever. GR was still the market leader, with a 21-percent share, but Teradyne at 19 percent and Hewlett-Packard at 16 percent were closing in. The former's strength lay in functional and combinational testing, much of it in the military/aerospace area, while HP was attacking GR head-on with its 3070 in-circuit test system, featuring a scalable architecture.

The GR9000 GENEVA Test System

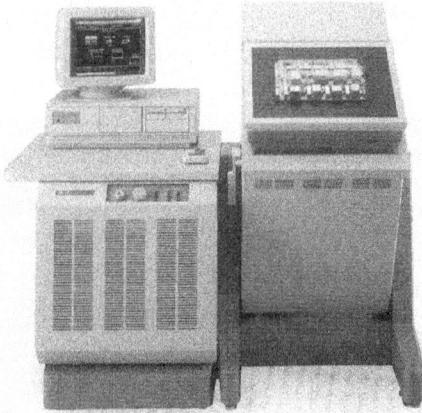

The board–test line was augmented in 1991 with the introduction of the GR9000, a system featuring the increasingly popular VXI bus "open architecture," called, in its GR iteration, GENEVA. The system was aimed at telecommunications equipment makers, at the time spending substantial sums on line-card production. But this business was being hotly pursued not only by Teradyne and HP, but by LTX and other ATE suppliers, and GR would find that the low-hanging fruit had already been picked.

Meanwhile, the Design Automation Products group, based in the U.K., kept upgrading the GR line of simulators. HILO 4, introduced in 1990, was chosen by a number of customers as their simulation standard, and an logic synthesizer acquired from Aptor, a Swiss company, further strengthened GR's hand. But design automation products, while winning bragging rights, would never achieve enough sales volume to make a difference in the

Company's fortunes. For that kind of impact, the two great hopes were automotive test products and LCD panel testing

LCD testing was a long shot. The idea was born of a request from GR's long-time Japanese representative, Tokyo Electron (TEL). Liquid crystal displays were on the brink of a market explosion as computer components, but one issue threatened to derail the train: No one could make the things. At least they couldn't make them economically. The yields were abysmally low, a few percent, and worse, the bad units weren't found until they had been loaded with added value. TEL wondered if GenRad could design and build a tester that could find defects in the LCD panels early in the manufacturing process. After a couple of brainstorming meetings, they sent GR a corner of a broken substrate to experiment on.

LCD technology is based on control of the light transmittance of a thin layer of liquid crystal material polarized by an applied voltage. An LCD substrate controls the voltages on a matrix of thousands of pixels, or electrodes, by means of tiny field-effect transistors, each located at the intersection of a horizontal (gate) and a vertical (drain) line, in an architecture not unlike that of a semiconductor memory. Henry Hall, GR's veteran bridge

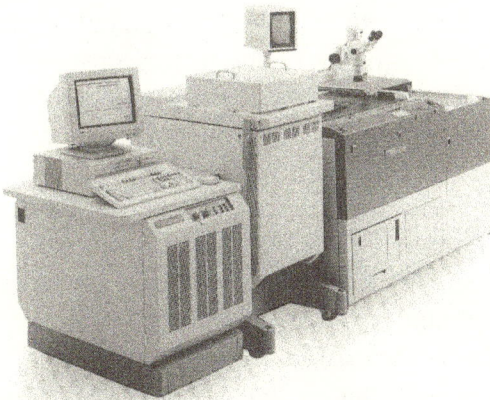

The GR-TEL GTS-1 Test System

211

designer, found that he could detect a small change in the capacitance between a drain line and a gate line as the transistor was turned on or off. This finding led to the launch of a new development project called "Looking Glass." At that time, the panels to be tested were small, only four by five inches, having 480 gate lines and 640X3 (three for each color) drain lines, for a total of 921,600 pixels. The panel was accessed through a prober supplied by Tokyo Electron.

The system, which measured both capacitance and conductance, was useful in spotting "hard" faults (opens and shorts), but not sensitive enough to detect "soft" faults such as transistor leakage. At the time, however, the LCD makers were desperate for anything that promised to increase yields, and the GenRad project plowed ahead. A test system, the GR-TEL GTS-1, soon took shape, with Hall and Paul Pillote designing the hardware and Sharon Albertini leading the software team. The GTS-1 was able to test the 921,600 pixels in about two minutes, an eternity in the broader field of semiconductor testing, but quite acceptable in the LCD world.

Only a few of these systems were sold. GR's window of opportunity closed when LCD manufacturers improved their manufacturing processes and yields, and as the emergence of laptop computers and the promise of an LCD television market pushed panel sizes steadily upward, forcing a wholesale rethinking of the testing problem. The electronics of the GR system was easily scalable, but the mechanics (i.e., the prober) was not, and GR's foray into the LCD market was abandoned.

"Looking Glass" thus never amounted to much, but the project was certainly a justifiable attempt to find a new growth market to spur GenRad's sales. If the Company had the resources to mount an all-out development effort, the outcome might have been different. As it was, there was only one bullet in the gun – Henry Hall's expertise in impedance measurement – and it was not enough.

212

Automotive test prospects, on the other hand, were improving steadily. Ford's acquisition of Jaguar had the desired effect, and in October 1991, Ford signed a production agreement with GenRad to equip Ford's entire European dealer network with its diagnostic system, called the FDS 2000. The system was born of a $9 million development contract awarded to GR by Ford. With the electronics content in automobiles poised to soar from $600 to $2000 per car in the coming decade, here at last was the kind of growth market the Company needed to offset the losses in board test.

In three years under Anderson's reign, GenRad had losses totaling more than $66 million. Some of the red ink could be attributed to write-downs resulting from the excesses of the past, and the top-line slide was largely a reflection of a stagnant board-test market, but the results were what they were, and pressure on the CEO was growing to turn the ship around. The stock price ranged, in 1991, from a high of $4.50 to a low of $1.50, and the stockholders were growing restless. These included west coast investor Husic Capital Management, owning 8.1 percent of the Company, and a New York investor, Basil Regan of Regan Partners, who kept adding to his position throughout the year.

The angst of institutional shareholders like Basil Regan was channeled to the Company through its investment banker, Lehman Brothers, to Board member Ned Martin. Martin, who had been closely associated with GR as a corporate counsel with Hale and Dorr, had joined the Board at Anderson's invitation in 1989, after leaving Hale and Dorr for a Washington law firm. When Lehman Brothers and its Wall Street clients wanted to vent about GR's poor performance, they found Martin a sympathetic listener.

It is often said that a CEO's responsibility is to run the company, not to inflate the stock price. This is nonsense. The stock price can't be ignored. It is the ultimate scorecard. It directly affects the value of the options held by key employees. It affects the vulnerability of a company to a takeover. It even serves as a yardstick of staying power in the minds of customers. Most important, GR's $2 stock price effectively closed the door on equity financing as the balance sheet deteriorated.

It was a difficult market environment for GR's competitors, too, but the best of them were insulated from disaster. Teradyne's equity, at the end of 1991, stood at over $300 million, almost 100 times GenRad's, and HP was a financial powerhouse. Barring a windfall from its automotive or LCD venture, or a sudden, violent upturn in board-test spending, the outlook for GR could hardly have been bleaker.

GenRad's long-term sales decline continued in 1992, although the cost-slashing imposed by Anderson in 1991 reduced the net loss to $7.4 million, or 42 cents a share. In the fourth quarter the Company finally posted a profit for the first time in several years, scratching out a penny a share.

There was some good news. The U.S. Marine Corps gave GR the largest single contract in its history, a $14.2 million order for digital test subsystems, based on the GENEVA platform. The GR9000, the telecommunication test system introduced in 1991, was purchased by several equipment makers, including GTE and Nokia. Most significant of all, Jaguar agreed to equip its worldwide dealer network with the FDS 2000, developed jointly by GR and Ford.

The board test line was bolstered by the addition of two combinational testers, the 2283 and 2284, priced under $100,000, or less than one-tenth the price of the first combinational tester, Teradyne's L200, introduced 12 years earlier. This highlighted another market depressant: Prices of all electronic products were inexorably falling, year after year, so that more systems had to be sold just to hold sales level.

GenRad once again held the number one position in the board test market, but 1992 was the last year the Company could make the claim.

Then, at the end of 1992, the Board decided, at a meeting in England, that the plight of the Company was desperate, that shareholders' complaints could no longer be ignored, and that the time had come to find a new CEO.

Thus Anderson, in his letter to shareholders in the 1992 Annual Report, reported that the search was on for his successor. Someone with a new perspective was needed, and the candidate could not be found in the existing officer corps. This group had been significantly thinned in the past few years, and by 1992, Anderson was left with only three vice presidents: Aldworth, McCarthy, and Prest, none of whom was considered CEO material.

The Board that pondered these matters was a congenial group that cared deeply about the Company and about corporate governance (before the term became fashionable). Jim Wright, Wilson Wilde, and Paul Penfield had served for years. Bill Scheerer and Ned Martin were relative newcomers. They were to a man agreed that Anderson was a man of talent and unquestioned integrity. But the Company was sinking, and the buck stopped at the President's desk.

Chapter 30

Jim Lyons Takes Over

The search for a new CEO, led by Directors Ned Martin, Paul Penfield, and Jim Wright, eventually led to a 59-year-old executive named James Lyons, at the time the President of Harry Gray Associates, an investment firm formed by the retired Chairman of United

215

Technologies Corporation. Lyons had at one time been the chief strategic officer of UTC, and his career also included stops at Xerox, Carrier, and, more recently, a stint as CEO of American Medical International, a $2-billion company. He was used to playing on big stages, and GenRad was a relatively small company with big troubles. As he performed his due diligence, he found that, for all its problems, GR retained an excellent reputation in the electronics industry. In fact, he found that there were many people – customers and suppliers, notably – who were pulling for the Company to turn itself around. Needless to say, the cheerleaders also included stockholders like Basil Regan of Regan Partners, who was enthusiastic about the prospect of securing the services of Jim Lyons.

Lyons knew he would not be walking into a comfortable situation. He had been around the track enough times to realize that, for every officer who would welcome a change at the top, there would be another who would expect him to fall on his face. He was, after all, a complete outsider, not just to GR, but to the test and measurement business and in fact to the world of electronics. The last three GR presidents held engineering degrees from MIT, and there were still a few who regarded GR as "an engineer's company." On the other hand, the downside wasn't that bad. If he failed, the blame arguably belonged to his predecessors who left the Company in shambles. If he succeeded, he could earn a small fortune via stock options, as well as great satisfaction. The risk-reward ratio wasn't bad.

And so, in June of 1993, Jim Lyons became the seventh president in GR's 78-year history. He immediately began remaking the Company, starting with the officer corps. After engaging consultant McKinsey & Company to help plot a new course, Lyons hired a member of that firm, Sarah Lucas, as Vice President for Strategic Planning and Analysis, a post previously held by Carole Prest. Prest, after a short tour running the board test group, left the

216

Company. John Bulman, a Director of Sales, was promoted to Vice President, Sales and Service. Lucas and Bulman, along with CFO Aldworth and Treasurer Shephard, constituted the entire top management team in 1993.

Jim Lyons

Any new CEO taking over a distressed company will seek to write off everything the auditors and the SEC will allow, and Lyons was no exception. He announced, in the 1993 Annual Report, a worldwide restructuring program "and other unusual charges" that would cost $41.8 million, in order to eliminate "the accumulated debris of prior business decisions that did not come to fruition." Here and in meetings with securities analysts, Lyons took an unsparing view of his predecessors' legacy.

He also declared unequivocally that GR had two, and only two, core businesses: board test and automotive test. The instrument lines had been sold, the semiconductor test business was a distant though painful memory, and the LCD test venture proved to be a dry hole. There were other bits and pieces of the old GenRad – Design Automation and Structural Test Products - but Lyons made it clear that he intended to prune the Company of businesses that did not fit his strategic vision.

The initial reaction of Wall Street was mildly positive. The stock reached a four-year high of $6.25 in the fourth quarter of 1993. To the securities analysts, Lyons was a new breed of GenRad CEO. In Thurston and Anderson, the analysts had seen two very decent people without any visible passion for the business of business. Not since the days of Doug Hajjar, a decade before, had a GR spokesman been someone who knew how to "talk the talk" of Wall Street. Lyons was a master of the art, painting word pictures of a Company that was performing to "established metrics" and dealing with "shifting paradigms." The portfolio managers were clearly not yet sure that GenRad would become a much better Company, but one thing was sure: It would be a much different GenRad.

In addition to sizzle, Lyons had some red meat to serve, including new orders for its FDU 2000 automotive diagnostic tester, now sweeping Ford's large (9300 dealers) European network. The new lower-cost 2280 "e" series of board testers was launched late in 1993 and garnered multiple-system orders from Northern Telecom, General Instrument, and GR's most faithful customer, Compaq. But the real news of the year was an order from IBM for eight board testers for its Greenock, Scotland, plant. This order followed a head-to-head shoot-out versus arch-rival Hewlett-Packard, which subsequently grumbled that the deck was stacked, because IBM was comparing an existing HP tester against a new GR system gussied up by GR's best programmer.

GenRad's commitment to open-architecture board testers was underscored by the October release of the GR1000, the latest member of the GENEVA family. And the latest iteration of TRACS, also unveiled in October, offered customers the capability of networking board testers made by other suppliers as well as by GenRad. Obviously, this spate of new products announced in late 1993, less than six months after Lyons arrived at Concord, was in the mill while Anderson was CEO, so, notwithstanding the "accumulated debris," Lyons started his tenure with the advantage of a reasonably healthy engineering program.

The financial results for 1993, the huge write-off aside, showed improvement, with sales up about 11 percent, mostly on the back of the Ford-Europe business and shipments of test units to the U.S. Marine Corps for its MCATES program. Orders of $144 million trailed shipments of $159 million, however, leaving year-end backlog at a razor-thin $19 million, about eight weeks' worth of shipments. The balance sheet was horrendous, with stockholders' equity now standing at minus $45 million.

Most ominously, Hewlett-Packard's sales of board testers jumped more than 30 percent to $141 million, while GR's board test shipments edged up 2 percent to $131 million. Thus, despite the win over HP at IBM, GR was no longer king of the board-test hill. Moreover, Hewlett-Packard, apparently stung by the resurgence of a competitor they had counted out, launched a legal attack on the Concord Company, alleging that GenRad's Open Xpress technology, used to detect open circuits on surface-mount boards, infringed patents held by HP and incorporated in its competing TestJet technology.

For Lyons, 1993 was dress rehearsal. In 1994, he began a top-to-bottom Company overhaul. By year-end, 80 percent of all his direct reports were people he had hired within the previous 12 months. The Design Automation Products business was sold in March, and a year later Structural Test Products was jettisoned as well. Total receipts for both operations: less than $2 million.

Sales fell by about 9 percent, to $144 million, but the bottom line was positive for the first time in 10 years, and orders rose to $157 million, suggesting better days to come. The stock market applauded by lifting the share price to the $5 to $7 region over most of the year. Net income for 1994 was $5.4 million, or 27 cents per diluted share. At the new GenRad, said Lyons in his 1994 stockholders' letter, there was a commitment to "sustained quarterly profitability," and, based on his first full year in office, many people inside and outside the Company were beginning to believe that Jim Lyons was exactly the tonic GenRad needed.

Profitability was also a sign that repeated layoffs in recent years – including a 12 percent cut in the workforce at the end of 1993 - had finally brought the workforce, now about 1000 strong, to equilibrium. And the Company finally began shedding some of its excess plant space. The Company had been real-estate-heavy for a number of years, with idle plant space in Massachusetts, California, and the U.K. The Fareham, England plant was sold in 1994 for $1.7 million, and in January 1995, the Bolton, Massachusetts plant was sold for $2.1 million – a pittance, by today's standards, for an attractive, 254,000-square-foot plant on 85 acres near Route 495. Part of this facility had been leased for a time to QuadTech, the purchaser of GR's instrument lines. Some costly real estate remained on the books, including the Milpitas, California former home of the Semiconductor Test Division, with a lease running through 1998, and a plant in Maidenhead, England operation leased through 2013 but subleased through 1999.

Margins improved in 1994 because of a more favorable mix of product shipments. Board-test profits were hardly obscene, but they were higher than those yielded by the Ford-Europe diagnostic systems or the Marine Corps test units. The automotive business was a mixed bag: On the one hand, the potential sales volume was enormous, especially if the Ford-Europe business could be leveraged into a worldwide deal. On the other hand, automobile manufacturers were notorious for squeezing their suppliers. The Marine Corps (MCATES) business was not quite as bad, but strong competition was on hand to keep GR honest. Teradyne had major long-run contracts with the Navy and the Air Force, and the ever-present Hewlett-Packard was a player, too. The Marine Corps program was GR's only military contract of size, bringing in revenues of $12 to $15 million a year – too small to ignore, but not large enough to justify heavy forward investment. The MCATES program was also winding down, and it was hard to see similar targets of opportunity in the military area.

International sales in the 1992 through 1994 period ranged from 55 to 58 percent of the Company total, with Europe the major contributor. In 1994, in fact, Europe alone accounted for just under half of total worldwide sales. The growing Ford-Europe business was a major factor here, but hardly the only one. GenRad had long been a powerful presence in the European board-test market, and the Company's position in Europe, fortified by offices in Munich, Milan, Paris, and Zurich, held up impressively even as sales slipped elsewhere. Worldwide, GenRad was under siege from Hewlett-Packard, and the numbers were not encouraging. In 1994, HP took about one-third of the market for board-test systems, while GR's share slipped to less than a quarter. The comparison would be worse in 1995, as GenRad, despite a valiant effort to stem the tide, could not deal with the much greater sales horsepower of its old rival.

As Lyons entered his second year as President, he began forming his own team of senior officers and recasting the Board of Directors. Aldworth was out as

Chief Financial Officer, and George O'Brien, a Lyons hire, was in. Director Wilson Wilde was out, and two new Directors were in: Adriana Stadecker, a Boston management consultant, and Russell Gullotti, CEO of National Computer Systems.

In 1995, Paul Penfield, the Head of MIT's Electrical Engineering faculty, and Jim Wright, an attorney and a director for more than 20 years, both left the Board, having been advised that investors wanted "new blood" and would vote against their reelection. The new blood consisted of four new members: William Antle, CEO of Oak Industries; Lowell Hawkinson, CEO of Gensym; Ed Zschau, a lecturer at Harvard and a veteran of the electronics industry; and, most surprisingly, Dick Rogers – the very same Dick Rogers who had piloted GR's board test business for years in the 70s and 80s, at one time becoming Executive VP and Chief Operating Officer. Bill Thurston, in turning over control to Bob Anderson in 1988, had ousted Rogers, and now the wheel had come full circle. The talented executive was now President of Tokyo Electron America, the U.S. wing of the large Japanese equipment supplier and GR sales representative. Thus Jim Lyons was acquiring the advisory services of one of the world's most knowledgeable ATE executives.

In 1995 the personnel whirlwind intensified. Daniel Harrington, a financial executive, was recruited from Waters Corporation as VP for Financial Planning in April and less than a year later became CFO, replacing George O'Brien. And a horde of new Vice Presidents joined the officer roster: Philip Charlton, Paul Geere, Philip Service, and Kenneth Harris in Europe; Michael Schraeder, VP Sales and Service; William Schymik, VP Technology; and Louis Zollo, VP and Chief Information Officer. The contingent of new vice presidents in Europe underscored the growing importance of the automotive test business, now called Advanced Diagnostic Solutions (ADS), and in presentations to Wall Street Lyons often made this business the centerpiece of his sales pitch – for good reason. Jim Lyons instinctively knew what buttons to push to excite an audience. Board test, while still the heart of GenRad, was, to most of the analyst corps, a tired story, while the automotive electronics business was fresh. Moreover, it inspired the kind of projections (think of the volume!) the analysts revel in. The fact that GenRad stock touched $10 (briefly) in 1995 - for the first time in many years - was not due solely to strong operating results; Lyons was creating the image of GenRad as a major turn-around story.

The 1995 Annual Report, for instance, featured quotes from three Wall Street professionals. Basil Regan of Regan Partners, who had supported the hiring of Lyons from the start, waxed rhapsodic, with this:

"Jim Lyons and his management team have accomplished one of the fastest and best executions of a turnaround that I have seen in my 20+ years in the investment business. I am convinced that the Company is now poised for double-digit revenue growth."

Similar sentiments were voiced by executives from Morgan Stanley and Munn Bernard – both, like Regan, large shareholders.

But, hyperbole aside, the numbers were improving steadily, and bar charts were revived at the opening of the 1995 Annual Report, showing dramatic growth in market capitalization and margins. The turnaround, however, lagged in one key respect: Sales had been on a $150 million plateau for five years, and in fact 1995's top line trailed those of 1991 and 1993. The margin improvement was not illusory, but it was engineered by cost cutting, not sales growth. The layoffs and restructuring were major factors, but Lyons, working with three different chief financial officers in his first three years, missed few opportunities to strengthen the balance sheet. In January 1995, for instance, the Company announced a revision to its defined-benefit pension program. Thereafter, while employees would retain their vested benefits to that point, there would be no further accrual. This single change generated a "curtailment gain" of just under $2 million.

Now that the Company was profitable, it could start taking advantage of its huge tax-loss carryforwards. At year-end 1995, these amounted to more than $155 million, which translated into a net deferred tax asset of over $75 million. (Tax laws limited the size of the benefit, depending on estimated future profitability.) Thus, except for minimal foreign tax liabilities, essentially all the pre-tax profits flowed straight to the bottom line.

With a new Chief Financial Officer came another change in auditors, as Arthur Andersen was replaced by Price Waterhouse.

Although no one could have known at the time, the country, the electronics industry, and GenRad in 1995 were on the brink of a period of frenzied growth. The country was actually moving toward a budget surplus, with politicians and economists wondering what to do with the excess tax revenues. The electronics industry was being catapulted forward by the Internet and by the digitization of cameras, music players, and virtually every physical phenomenon. The emergence of China as a manufacturing titan added fuel to the fire. And in Concord, Jim Lyons set the stage for the fireworks to come, openly predicting "double-digit growth." Once again, he was able to deliver on his promise.

Chapter 31

The Last Climb

I n 1996 GenRad delivered the double-digit sales growth Lyons had promised, along with record profits. Revenues were by no means at a record level (in fact, at $184 million, they were some $60 million below the 1984 record), and the sales gain of 15.6 percent, while impressive by GR standards, still left the Company far behind HP in board-test market share. Still, fairness demands that Lyons's achievements be measured against GenRad as it was when he arrived on the scene. Sales and margins were up, and the stock, which had traded in a range of 2 to 6 dollars in 1993, hit a high of $23 in the fourth quarter of 1996. The most dramatic change was visible on the balance sheet, where a debt of more than $60 million in 1993 stood at zero at the end of 1996. As the stock price flew by the $14.38 strike price of the convertible bonds, the Company forced conversion of these into common stock, and as a result, the GenRad balance sheet was cleaner than it had been in decades. It was no wonder that the image of GenRad as a solid turn-around situation took root on Wall Street.

In his short tenure as CEO, Lyons had announced, almost annually, a "new senior management team." Heading the 1996 arrivals was Paul Pronsky, an old associate of Lyons and now GR's fourth Chief Financial Officer in four years. Bob Aldworth, George O'Brien, and Daniel Harrington had all served as CFO under Lyons, and all had left for one reason or another.

Lyons identified six executives as members of his latest senior management team: In addition to Pronsky, there were Sarah Lucas, VP and Chief Strategic Officer; Kevin Cloutier, VP and General Manager of Electronic Manufacturing Systems (i.e., board-test); Paul Geere, running Advanced Diagnostic Solutions (automotive test); Lori Hannay, VP Human Resources; and Michael Schraeder, VP Sales and Service. Of these, only Geere and Cloutier pre-dated Lyons at GenRad; the others were hired by him.

Board-test sales recovered somewhat in 1996, driven by a flurry of new products: the high-pin-count 2287L test system, the GENEVA-based GR4000/GR3000 platforms for modem testing, a new optical board-inspection system called VISION, and, for the automotive market, a PC-based diagnostic system and a portable trouble-shooting tool. As was typical of GenRad, the new hardware was accompanied by a barrage of new software offerings, including a suite of "vectorless" software tools, which notably included OpensXpress, the open-circuit software that had been at the center of a contentious patent fight against Hewlett-Packard. The litigation was settled in 1995 under terms better than GenRad had reserved for, adding $1.3 million to its bottom line for that year. More important, it removed an obstacle to future sales of OpensXpress.

The reader will recall that at various times in GenRad's later history, the Company had undertaken to characterize the test function as the hub of the entire electronics manufacturing process, using shibboleths like "Factory of the Future" and "Integrated Quality Management Systems" and acquiring small specialist companies that could contribute to the vision. For reasons that have been covered here, the reality never lived up to the expectations, but the allure was always there, and it seemed to resurface whenever a business upturn provided the wherewithal to indulge the appetite. In 1996, Lyons bit, just as Thurston had done twenty years earlier. GenRad henceforth would supply not just board test systems, but solutions spanning the entire manufacturing process, from design through product introduction through process management. To make it all happen, Lyons announced four acquisitions during 1996. All were small, and taken together they did not overburden the balance sheet. The real cost, as is often the case, lay in management talent diverted from other opportunities.

Test Technology Associates (TTA) and Testware, based in Texas, supplied customer test programming, test-fixture integration, and other services sold to users of board testers made by GenRad and its competitors. GenRad agreed to pay at least $2 million for TTA, with additional incentive payments over the next three years. For Testware, GenRad paid 80,000 shares of stock plus some cash.

Mitron, based in Portland, Oregon, was also in the software development business, notably through a product called CIMBridge, the framework through which design, test, assembly, quality control etc. would be integrated. It was through CIMBridge that GenRad hoped to make its next run at the "factory of the future." For this Company, GenRad paid just over a million shares of stock, valued at about $15 million.

Field Oriented Engineering, AG had been the contract developer of GenRad's TRACS III software, the latest version of a program that had been a GR offering for a number of years. TRACS enabled its users to collect, analyze, and otherwise process test data to improve the quality of its products and the efficiency of its manufacturing. FOE consisted of a small team of software developers located in Zurich. In acquiring "certain assets" belonging to this team, GenRad was essentially locking up the software rights to a key product, in return for a relatively small amount of cash and stock.

The elimination of debt from the balance sheet, together with a higher stock price, meant that a variety of financing options were now open to Lyons. With the stock at $20 a share, the market valued GenRad at well over a half billion dollars, or almost three years' sales. The banks were suddenly more hospitable, and a stock offering was not out of the question. (In one year, stockholders' equity had skyrocketed from minus $23.2 million to plus $63.7 million, an astonishing swing of almost $90 million.) Most important to the employees, real wealth was being created again. More than 1.5 million shares were optioned at strike prices between $4.38 and $7.75.

In Europe, meanwhile, the Advanced Diagnostic Solutions (ADS) operation was moving ahead on several fronts. The seeds planted several years before at Jaguar had turned into a worldwide business, thanks mostly to Ford. Saab chose GR to develop a package of digitized parts catalogs, technical manuals, and other documentation. The FDS2000 portable diagnostic system developed for Ford was now deployed in 80 countries, with some 8000 units talking to service technicians in 20 languages. And at Jaguar, where it all began, ADS was moving from the service bay to the assembly line, supplying a system for Vehicle Configuration and Test (VCATS). Other customers for ADS products included BMW, Aston-Martin, and British Airways. Total ADS revenues were still only in the $30 million range, but in terms of potential – and talking points for the securities analysts – ADS was a goldmine.

The Marine Corps project (MCATES), on the other hand, was fading fast, with sales in 1996 of only $1.1 million, versus $9.3 million in 1995. This collapse was turned into a plus by Lyons. Although the Company's total sales gain in 1996 was less than $25 million, Lyons could correctly refer in the opening of his Annual Report letter to "$32 million in new commercial revenues."

In 1997, the electronics industry began its rocket-like climb to the stratosphere, and GenRad along with it, as buying of board test systems – and especially the more expensive, high-pin-count versions – accelerated. As computer makers and others outsourced manufacturing to contract manufacturers, GenRad was quick to cultivate this new market, unleashing a number of hardware and software offerings geared to high volume and high complexity. As a result, GenRad's share of the board test market actually jumped in 1997, by about five percentage points, while Teradyne gave up a point and Hewlett-Packard was flat. In absolute terms, HP was still number one by a comfortable margin, but no one could doubt that GenRad was back in the hunt.

The other core business, the testing of automotive electronics, was also doing well, with a new software contract inked with Ford and with new European customers signing on to the expanding line of products out of the ADS group in Manchester, England. Thanks partly to ADS, the international portion of GR's revenues held at more than 50 percent.

In mid-1997, GenRad ended its long, mutually rewarding association with the Town of Concord, selling the plant and grounds that had been its home for 40 years and moving into leased space in Westford, Massachusetts, near Route 495 (and near a site acquired and then sold some years earlier). The new GenRad headquarters and board-test plant occupied a modern, 230,000-square-foot, two-building complex in a campus setting a few miles north of Concord. The term of the lease was 15 years.

The move, along with a late-1996 move of the ADS site in Manchester, was costly. A new, unsecured, five-year, $12 million loan was negotiated, with most of the money earmarked to furnish the new Westford headquarters, and total spending on property, plant, and equipment in 1997 was just under $25 million. The shift from owned to leased space in Massachusetts did improve the balance sheet, but the Company recorded a gain of only $4 million on the sale of the Concord property. The location was choice, and the acreage was large, but the Concord complex was starting to show its age, and a number of potential buyers (including Teradyne) looked it over and passed.

The engineering budget was focused on three major programs: the redesign of the line of in-circuit board testers, GR's bread-and-butter product line; enhancements to the CIMbridge software suite acquired with Mitron; and the design of a new optical board-inspection system (GR VISION). As circuit boards became ever denser and the components less accessible, the market demanded alternatives to electrical testing, with optical and X-ray systems the leading candidates.

The 1997 results were nothing short of remarkable, especially to those observers who had suffered through the Company's past woes. Sales jumped almost 30 percent, to $236.8 million, and bookings increased even more. Net profit was a staggering $41.3 million, as the tax loss carryforwards continued to take effect. Had normal (statutory) income tax rates applied, the Company's tax liability would have been $13.2 million. But after the adjustments and reversals were netted out, the Company found itself with a tax *credit* of $3.5 million, so that almost $17 million of the $41 million was courtesy of the tax laws – which GenRad applied to their maximum benefit, as indeed it should have. Even without this gain, moreover, Lyons could rightfully point to an outstanding year.

As the decade of the nineties began, GenRad stock traded at about $2 a share, so that stock option gains for employees were nonexistent. Now, in the fourth quarter of 1997, with the stock trading in a range between $34 and $23 a share, serious money was on the table. At year-end, some five million option shares were outstanding, at an average exercise price of $12.88. (A few fortunate employees had options with a strike price of $3.25.) For those not holding options, there was an employee stock purchase plan, offering the usual 15 percent discount from the lower of the year's starting or ending price. Thus, for GR's 1388 employees and thousands of stockholders, Jim Lyons was the man of the year in 1997.

After the solid turnaround executed by Lyons and his management team, a slight sales decline in 1998, from

$236.8 to 224.8 million, did not seem particularly worrisome. But the $12 million decline in shipments brought a huge negative swing on the bottom line, from 1997's $41.3 profit to a loss of $13.7 million. This despite heavy layoffs (230 people) in the second and third quarter and cessation of manufacturing activities at Manchester. The layoffs, of course, brought one-time severance charges, as did the Company's decisions to drop its VISION line of optical board testers and to recognize difficulties at Testware and TTA.

In 1998 GenRad acquired Industrial Computer Corporation (ICC), a software company based in Atlanta. The rationale was a reprise of an old siren call: the notion that GR's test systems could, with the proper software tools, serve as the center of the manufacturing universe. This time the "Factory of the Future" was reborn under the label of Manufacturing Execution Systems (MES), with ICC's Shop Floor Data Manager (SFDM) the product that would take GR "beyond electronic assembly into box build, distribution, and inventory control.......providing integration with ERP (Enterprise Resource Planning) systems." GenRad purchased ICC on April 7, on the heels of a profitable first quarter (its only profitable quarter in the year), for 1,237,917 shares of stock, valued at the time at about $36.6 million. (Later in the year, as losses accumulated and the stock price sank, Lyons and his Board authorized the repurchase of one million shares for about $15 million.) At the same time, GR purchased a small Scottish company, a unit of Valstar, which provided integration services for ICC's SFDM software. The price was $3.2 million in cash.

The ICC acquisition, which was apparently orchestrated directly by GenRad, triggered a lawsuit by unhappy ICC investors. The suit was filed on May 27, 1998 and was settled about a year later, at a cost to GenRad of $7 million (net of $4 million covered by insurance).

231

With the acquisition of ICC, Lyons created a third business unit, called GR Software (GRS), based in Atlanta under Stephen Holford. This unit, whose products included TRACS and CIMBridge as well as ICC and its SFDM software, accounted for $16.6 million in sales in 1998. The other two business units, board test (EMS) and automotive test (ADS) contributed $176 million and $32 million, respectively.

The decline in board test sales, about 3 percent, was in line with the over-all market. Hewlett-Packard was still the 800-pound gorilla, but GR's market share seemed to have stabilized at a respectable 25 percent. The GENEVA platform, aimed at the VXI-bus market, continued to do well, as did the 2280 flagship line of board testers and a new, low-end system called Viper. Another new system, called Pilot, took GR into the "flying prober" business, in which an automatic test probe" flew" around a circuit board to contact the various test nodes

A 30-percent decline in ADS shipments reflected the lumpiness of the business, in which large orders, especially from Ford, created volatility. But this business was essentially healthy and promising. During the year ADS opened a 50-person office in Detroit and formed a partnership with Daimler-Chrysler to develop diagnostic software. And even in the soft year of 1998, Ford bought more than $20 million worth of GR's products and services, making it GR's only customer to account for 10 percent of sales.

The realignment into three business units meant that GR now had a "big three" of operating officers. Michael Schraeder was given the title of President, EMS, Paul Geere was President of ADS, and Stephen Holford became Chief Operating Officer of GRS. The year brought yet another Chief Financial Officer, as Paul Pronsky was replaced by Walter Shephard. Thus, in his six years at the helm at GenRad, Lyons had a total of five different chief financial officers.

Lyons's appetite for acquisitions, combined with a down year in sales, left the Company with a year-end balance sheet that, while still healthy, was starting to show a few warning signs. Intangible assets, partly goodwill resulting from the ICC acquisition, jumped from $7.1 million to $35.7 million. The share count, despite the buyback, grew by almost 2 million. Debt was still a modest $6 million, and the $25 million credit line was expanded to $50 million. But the main concern had to be the fate of the ICC acquisition, hinging on a new product expected to be completed in late 1999. The product, a Unix-based version of SFDM, was said to be 69 percent complete at the time of acquisition, but this and other technical matters were taken largely on the word of ICC management. Technical issues, said GenRad, in the 1998 10-K, "were addressed primarily by engineering representatives from ICC along with the Company's independent valuation advisors." These advisors were not identified.

Acquisitions, as GenRad well knew, are fraught with risks. The most recent examples were Testware and TTA, acquired by GR in 1996 accompanied by great expectations. In1998, conceding that these expectations had not been met, GenRad bit the bullet, taking a $4.9 million asset impairment charge to cover its bad bet.

As initially reported, the Company's net income for the second, third, and fourth quarters were all losses. A subsequent resolution of a dispute with the SEC (relating to charges incurred with the ICC acquisition) led to a restatement that deepened the second-quarter loss and pushed the fourth quarter into the black. The restated numbers for the year showed a loss of $13.7 million, versus an as-reported loss of $9.1 million.

Despite the 1998 results, Lyons was upbeat in the Annual Report, assuring readers that "1999 will be a year when we demonstrate that we are not only back on track, but at a decidedly more positive growth trajectory."

Chapter 32

Boom

A more positive growth trajectory indeed. In 1999, all the records tumbled. Sales topped $300 million, and net income was a mind-boggling $47.5 million. Orders topped shipments, debt was reduced, stockholders' equity climbed by more than $40 million - all this while the headcount barely budged.

Although sales grew at all three of the Company's business units, 1999 belonged to ADS, where sales exploded to more than $100 million, compared with $32.3 million in 1998. In fact, of the Company's over-all revenue gain of $77 million, $70 million (91 percent) was contributed by ADS, which shipped 10,000 copies of its new WDS 3500 tester to Ford, a $65.9 million bonanza. The downside was the effect of this business on margins. Ford, pressed by Japanese competition, was relentless in squeezing its suppliers, and GenRad was forced to accept thin margins on the WDS 3500. With ADS representing a growing share of the Company's sales (34 percent, up from 14 percent) over-all gross margins slipped, from 52.8 to 46.6 percent. Ford was also largely responsible for a 24-percent jump in accounts receivable, explained by the Company as due to "customer demands for favorable terms." Still, with $47.5 million falling to the bottom line, no one was complaining about niggardly Ford.

Curiously, as sales and earnings soared, the stock price did not, and during the year the Company repurchased another million shares, for $18.7 million, bringing the total bought under the 1998 authorization to slightly over 2 million shares, at a cost of $33.7 million. With 1999 earnings per diluted share of $1.60, the repurchase looked like a bargain.

GR's Last Home, in Westford, MA

Of course, securities analysts were aware that the Company's effective tax rate was one percent, as the tax loss carry-forward still sheltered profits. The Ford business was exciting, and Lyons expressed confidence that more of the same would come in 2000, though he warned that annual shipments of 10,000 testers should not be expected. The fall in gross margins was a negative. GR's board-test business, still representing more than 60 percent of the Company's revenues, grew by 7 percent in 1999, but Hewlett-Packard grew more, and sales of GR's high-ticket functional testers were falling rapidly.

Then there was the new, Atlanta-based GR Software. The new product expected from the ICC group was still not complete as 1999 ended, and the target date was moved back, to the summer of 2000. Nevertheless, revenues from GRS grew from $17 million to $23.6 million in 1999, and management hoped, reasonably, that the higher-margined software business might offset the low-margin automotive business, at least to some degree.

Jim Lyons was now 65 years old. In his six years as CEO he had overseen a remarkable Company turnaround. In his first six full years at the helm, GenRad earned a net profit of $120 million on sales of $1.24 billion. In the preceding six years, the Company lost $123 million on sales of $1.03 billion. The tax-loss carry-forwards tilt the comparison, and the economy in the late 90s provided a tailwind, but Lyons's performance was still extraordinary.

The turnaround was delivered by a management team largely of Lyons's creation; of the officers listed in the 1992 Annual Report, only Shephard, then Treasurer, was still on board in 1999. In the years since, Lyons had shuffled his management team often, appointing, as has been mentioned, five chief financial officers, including Paul Pronsky, who left the Company in 1999. Also departing in 1999 was Sarah Lucas, whom Lyons had hired as GR's chief strategic officer shortly after taking over.

The Board was also recast by Lyons. Five of the six directors on the 1992 Board were gone. Only Bill Scheerer overlapped the pre-Lyons and Lyons periods.

With the ICC and Testware additions still question marks, one might have expected Lyons to take a more jaded view of acquisitions. Instead, he began meeting with the Company's bankers, negotiating a new line of credit to $125 million, with $75 million   earmarked for further acquisitions. This deal was signed in March 2000.

The round of acquisitions that followed, with the concomitant increase in debt, should be seen in the context of a period of unprecedented growth in the electronics industry. The Internet was now established, and new technologies were remaking the worlds of commerce, communications, and entertainment. Companies like Cisco Systems were growing exponentially, and stock prices were soaring. It would all end badly, as it usually does, but at the time Lyons, in the afterglow of GenRad's hugely successful 1999, could be forgiven for raising the stakes. His own money was on the table, too, since he owned more than a million shares of GenRad stock, making him the third largest holder, after Morgan Stanley and Basil Regan. Regan and the man he had praised as CEO now owned more than 10 percent of the Company.

Lyons might have ridden off to retirement triumphantly if the electronics boom could be sustained for a few more years. But it could not, and GenRad was soon hurtling toward an inglorious end.

Chapter 33

Bust

The ink was barely dry on GenRad's new $125 million line of bank credit before a new round of the acquisitions began. In March, GR paid $49 million in cash to acquire Nicolet Imaging Systems and its affiliate, Sierra Research Technology, collectively called NIS. The Company's attraction was x-ray technology used in the inspection of circuit boards. A month later GR bought a Swedish company, Autodiagnos, involved in automotive electronics testing, for $26.7 million in cash.

In between the signings of those two acquisitions, on April 9, GenRad announced the appointment of a new Chairman, President and Chief Executive, Robert Dutkowsky – an earlier choice who had begged off some months before. Dutkowsky came to GR from IBM, via EMC, where he had run its Data General division. At 45, he had won a reputation as a no-nonsense executive, more interested in results than in style. To persuade him to jump, the Board approved an option grant of a half million shares, a base annual salary of $500,000, plus a hiring bonus of

$125,000. Lyons, meanwhile, was given an earned bonus of $350,000 and a lump-sum payment of $2,625,000, plus benefit continuation for three years and immediate vesting of all options

As luck would have it, the most explosive boom in the history of the electronics industry was topping out just as Dutkowsky landed at GenRad. Just after signing on, he met on a Sunday afternoon with CFO Walter Shephard and heard the bad news: The Company would miss its first-quarter numbers by a mile, and the year looked extremely doubtful.

In the event, GenRad made money in 2000 (*everybody* made money in 2000), and sales would climb from the first quarter's disappointing $66.4 million to a fourth quarter $109.4 million, but behind these numbers the Company was actually in free fall. From the first to the second quarter, for instance, sales jumped from $66.4 million to $87.3 million, but net income plummeted from $18.1 million (mostly extraordinary items) to a loss of $1 million. The third quarter was roughly at break-even, and a fourth-quarter shipments spurt of more than $30 million (to $109.4 million) generated a profit of only $4.4 million. For the full year, operating income dropped from $49.1 million to $19 million, despite a 13-percent sales increase.

Sales and income volatility was to be expected in the ATE business. More serious was the debt picture. Thanks to the acquisition spree and to further ballooning of inventories and receivables, total debt, which had stood at only $6 million at the end of 1999, was a horrendous $93.5 million as 2000 ended. Of this amount, $63.8 million had been spent on acquisitions; the rest went into working capital. This debt, owed to a consortium of eight banks, carried interest charges that ranged from 8.66 to 10.5 percent, and it was collateralized by all the Company's assets.

In early 2001 Dutkowsky scrambled to put out fires, closing a west-coast office, cutting headcount, and outsourcing printed-circuit-board assembly. But by mid-year the stock market was in a full-scale rout and customers were starting to panic, pulling back on capital expenditures. Watching this with growing unease were GenRad's bankers.

On May 1, the GenRad Board held a special meeting by teleconference to discuss financing options, which were few. One avenue favored by many high-tech firms at the time was the issuance of convertible bonds, and the Board authorized Dutkowsky and his management team to investigate this option. It took only a week or so to decide that the convertible route was iffy at best, and on May 10 GenRad informed the lead bank, Fleet, that the convertible deal was out. At that point, the banks, as of May 15, agreed to waive GR's covenant defaults through June 15 – at which time the banks wanted to hear how they were to be repaid.

On May 30, the Board authorized the engagement of an investment firm, William Blair and Company, to help the Company explore merger alternatives. There were soon several prospective acquirers, and by the end of May confidentiality agreements had been signed with three of these suitors, but none of the discussions reached the due-diligence stage.

Then, in early June, Dutkowsky and his CFO Shephard were en route to New York (by automobile; cash was too tight to fly) when, at a McDonald's in Westborough, Dutkowsky's secretary phoned to tell him that George Chamillard, Teradyne's CEO, was trying to reach him. Dutkowsky promptly returned the call, and a dialogue began, culminating in the meeting in Waltham described at the start of this book.

As the downturn in the electronics industry turned into an all-out collapse, Dutkowsky engaged a New York crisis management specialist and pressed the banks to extend the default waiver beyond June 15. The second waiver was granted, through September 28, and the Fleet

Bank installed a representative of its "workout group" in an office adjacent to Dutkowsky's, presumably to monitor cash outflow. The banks also collected a fee of $483,000 for their willingness to grant the loan waiver, with another $483,000 due in September.

In the second quarter, the operating losses in the four reporting segments totaled $50.6 million, and corporate expenses and restructuring charges ran this figure to $62.2 million. To make matters worse, the tax-loss carry-forwards that had smiled on the Company for several years now turned against them. In valuing these tax benefits, the Company, under FASB accounting rules, had to assess the probability of future profits against which the tax benefits could be taken. When profits were pouring in, the probability was high, as was the value of the tax benefits. Now, with the Company hemorrhaging red ink, the value of the tax benefits disappeared. It was a non-cash event, but it did hit the balance sheet hard, to the tune of $35.9 million in the second quarter. The total first-half loss, including the reversal of the tax benefit and some minor currency losses, was an almost unimaginable $113.9 million. For the second quarter, the Company reported a loss of $98.1 million on sales of $54.5 million. The balance sheet, at June 30, showed cash of $5.9 million, and debt of $85.5 million, which was termed current because it was now subject to demand.

The discussions with Teradyne progressed quickly, and, on July 10, with Goldman Sachs as advisor, Teradyne made an initial offer to acquire GenRad for $6.00 to $7.00 a share. A GenRad Board meeting was held on July 20 to assess the Company's bleak prospects, including the possibility that the banks would force GR into bankruptcy at the end of September. On that day, GenRad agreed to discuss merger exclusively with Teradyne through the end of July. Over the next 10 days, there were the usual negotiations over the price and other conditions of the merger. Then, on August 1, the two companies signed a definitive merger agreement. A press release was issued the next day.

The terms would give GenRad stockholders 0.1733 share of Teradyne stock for every share of GenRad stock. The closing price of Teradyne stock on August 1 was $35.10, of GenRad's stock, $4.00. Based on these prices, Teradyne was paying $6.08 for each share of GenRad. A month or so later, after the September 11 disaster, Teradyne's stock price would be $24.12, reducing the value of 0.1733 Teradyne share to $4.18. Based on Teradyne's closing price on August 1, when the agreement was signed, Teradyne paid about $260 million for GenRad, including the assumption of about $85 million in GenRad debt.

The deal was wrapped up in late October, and on October 27, Teradyne CEO George Chamillard addressed GenRad employees at Westford to share with them his thoughts on the difficulties they all faced and what had to be done to succeed.

GenRad was merged into Teradyne's Assembly Test Division, giving the combined operation the mass it needed to compete with Agilent. The Division was placed under Bob Dutkowsky, but in less than a year he was off to his next opportunity, as CEO of a software company, and the Division was placed under Teradyne veteran John Casey, who was succeeded by Jeff Hotchkiss, another long-time Teradyne employee, and it is has since taken over the leadership position in the board-test market. Old black-and-white photographs of General Radio scenes grace the walls of the Teradyne site in North Reading, and a General Radio museum, including classic instruments and treasured archives, has been preserved. A number of GenRad employees now work for Teradyne, and the many GR retirees, who in 2001 came within an inch of losing all their benefits, remain covered, courtesy of Teradyne.

General Radio's life spanned 86 years, 4 months, and 12 days. During that time it helped lay the foundation for today's electronics industry. The technical achievements of its engineers were central to the development of radio and television, from the day when Armstrong built his first superheterodyne receiver using a General Radio variable condenser. To hundreds of thousands of engineers in the twentieth century, "GR" was the supreme authority on electronics technology, and the *General Radio Experimenter* their bible. The Company was and remains a legend.

Afterthoughts

W hat lessons can be learned from the life story of this great company? The first is a lesson taught by Melville Eastham and Henry Shaw, and it is this: If you hire the best people you can find and treat them as well as you possibly can, good things happen. If you have read this book through, you know that GR's people were exceptional and that they were generally very well treated.

A second lesson is that acquisitions in high tech rarely justify the risks. If a company has a bulletproof balance sheet it may make sense to bet a few chips to add a new technology or a new product line. But the bet must recognize the odds that the acquisition will be a failure. Risk-taking is mandatory in high tech, but trying to enter a new area with a team of new people is a recipe for disaster. It's even chancier when the new team is physically remote from the core company.

GenRad was not the only company to run aground on these shoals. Acquisitions are seductive, offering the promise of growth beyond what can be achieved organically. The rationale is usually a presumed synergy, an argument that makes sense in mergers of banks or retail stores, but only rarely in high tech. GenRad's most successful new-business ventures, Variacs, stroboscopes, coaxial connectors, and of course board-testing, were all the results of in-house projects staffed by engineers already on the payroll.

The acquisition-related debt burden that brought GenRad down in 2001 was taken on at the worst possible time, just as "irrational exuberance" was propelling the stock market to insane heights and setting up an implosion of historic dimensions. Within a few months, euphoria turned into panic selling and the steepest business downturn most high-tech observers ever experienced. In hindsight, one can question whether it was prudent of GenRad to place itself in so vulnerable a financial situation, but we are all geniuses after the fact. Had the high-tech boom continued for a few more years, would GenRad have recovered and gone on to new heights? We will never know.

Another lesson is the importance of planning for management succession. At GR, the transition from one CEO to the next often seemed to be ad-libbed, with the retiring CEO and Board scrambling to find the right person to take the reins. This is somewhat surprising for a Company that had always given so much attention to policies, objectives, and management processes.

But, to repeat what has been said, of the thousands of high-tech companies born during the twentieth century, only a very few survived as independent entities as long as General Radio. So, whatever the mistakes of its leaders, spending too much time examining them is a bit like performing an autopsy on a man who dies at age 110. You can find out why he died, but it might be more profitable to find out why he lived so long.

Appendix 1: Sales, Earnings, 1915-2001, as reported

	Sales (K$)	Net (K$)
1915	0.38	-3.6
1916	12	-3.3
1917	54	-10.8
1918	407	12.5
1919	155	-3.5
1920	101	0.5
1921	146	1.8
1922	658	169
1923	728	186
1924	1130	243
1925	1012	123
1926	975	129
1927	756	52
1928	645	56
1929	934	259
1930	843	145
1931	593	-17
1932	515	-84
1933	554	32
1934	676	25
1935	908	75
1936	1189	170
1937	1350	120
1938	997	56
1939	1263	98
1941	2579	197
1942	3834	67
1943	4559	206
1944	4508	136
1945	4411	153
1946	2977	146
1947	4707	324
1948	4610	380
1949	4489	324
1950	4915	333
1951	7098	343
1952	8412	391
1953	9784	403
1954	8216	474
1955	8508	449
1956	11234	658
1957	12581	659
1958	11951	596

1959	13333	523
1960	15828	803
1961	16298	731
1962	17465	838
1963	17682	785
1964	17425	755
1965	19259	844
1966	22228	945
1967	22972	973
1968	24919	600
1969	25527	304
1970	26096	46
1971	29112	244
1972	33105	-2303
1973	44656	1157
1974	48961	3649
1975	53208	2347
1976	54288	925
1977	70100	3740
1978	86647	6308
1979	115393	9104
1980	157669	11053
1981	169324	-1772
1982	188020	8786
1983	226611	19630
1984	249451	10990
1985	218304	-52254
1986	177059	-29895
1987	193771	-37045
1988	205859	-6238
1989	188906	-6090
1990	179349	-21114
1991	156391	-39081
1992	142609	-7406
1993	158704	-43797
1994	143915	5419
1995	153567	12410
1996	183545	27335
1997	236761	41295
1998	224789	-9068
1999	301948	47494
2000	341655	21647
2001 (6 mos)	116930	-110087

Index

Abbe, Ernst, 30
Abenaim, Dan, 86
Advantest, 152
Agilent, 2
Albertini, Sharon, 212
Aldworth, Bob, 207
Allen, Dave, 86
Anderson, Ralph, 136
Anderson, Robert, 70
Ando, 188
Antle, William, 222
Aptor, 210
Arguimbeau, Larry, 25
Armstrong, Howard, 4
Autodiagnos, 237
Ball, Roger, 165
Banana plug, 10
Barbour, Hal, 116
Beck, Sid, 176
Benson, Dick, 143
Beranek, Leo, 44
Biomation, 136
Bird Watchers, the, 176
BIST, 172
Blair, William, 3
Bolton plant, 63
Boole, Bob, 76
Boonton Radio, 64
Bosworth, Richard, 185
Bowthorpe, John, 185
Broadcasting, birth of, 15
Brown Bridge, 36
Brown, Cyrus, 6

Brown, Ken, 108
BTU Corporation, 184
Bulman, John, 217
Burke, Charles, 17
Cabot, George, 8
Cambria, Richard, 124
Canobie Lake, 60
CAPS, 108
Carey, Charles, 41
Carolan, Vin, 185
Casey, John, 241
Castle, Ken, 79
Chamberlain, Leo, 67
Chamillard, George, 1
Charlton, Philip, 222
CIMBridge, 227
Cimflex Teknowledge, 197
Cirrus Computers, 165
Cirrus Designs, 177
Cirrus Sigma, 177
Clapp, James, 21
Clapp, J. Emory, 7
Clapp-Eastham Co., 6
Clayton, John, 59
Cloutier, Kevin, 225
Coaxial connectors, 46
Compaq Computer, 196
Computer Automation, 107
Computerwrap, 102
Concord plant, 50
Corkum, Austin, 176
Corrigan, Wilf, 151
Coughlan, Paul, 167

Crawford, John, 17
Crossley, Clive, 165
Crowell, Steve, 66
Cvitkovitch, Bob, 85
d'Arbeloff, Alex, 105
Data General, 88
Data I/O Corp., 181
Davenport, Wilbur, 125
Dawes, Howard, 59
DeBlois, Steve, 81
Delzell, Bob, 94
d'Entremont, Paul, 85
Depression, the Great, 22
DeWolf, Nick, 86
Digibridge, 129
Digital Equipment Corp, 87
Digital General, 107
Digitest, 137
Dramatic Society, GR, 43
Duratrak, 50
Dutkowsky, Robert, 1
Eastham, Jesse, 47
Eastham, Melville, 4
Easton, Dr. Mahlon, 31
Easton, Ivan, 42
Eddy, W. O., 7
Edgerton stroboscope, 26
Electro Scientific Ind., 36
Emery, Ralph, 6
Epsco, 55
Everett-Charles, 138
Experimenter, The, 17
Factron, 139
Fairchild Semiconductor, 65
Fairchild Test Systems, 139
Faubert, Richie, 187

Faultfinders, 138
Ferrie, John, 160
Fichtenbaum, Matt, 85
Field Oriented Eng'g, 227
Field, Robert, 21
Fish, Bill, 176
Fitzmorris, Michael, 70
Fleet Bank, 239
Fluke, John, 64
Ford Motor, 202
Frank, Dick, 64
Frequency standards, 21
Fricke, Tom, 126
Fulks, Bob, 68
Futuredata, 144
Geere, Paul, 222
Gemmell, James, 130
General Electric, 65
General Radio museum, 241
General Radio News, 31
GENESIS, 185
GENEVA, 210
GenRad, name, 128
GenRad Fellows, 208
Genradco Trust, 63
Gensym, 222
Gilman, Martin, 42
Gipe, Mike, 129
Gladstone, Bruce, 144
Goebel, Peter, 85
Goldman Sachs, 240
GRAD, 83
GRAIL, 77
GRAPE Escape, 148
Grason, Rufus, 89
Grason-Stadler, 89

GREIFS, the, 37
Gross, Ervin, 45
Gullotti, Russell, 222
Haas, Rene, 108
Hajjar, Doug, 163
Hall, Henry, 61
Hannay, Lori, 226
Harrington, Daniel, 222
Harris, Kenneth, 222
Harry Gray Assoc., 215
Hawkinson, Lowell, 222
Healey, Jim, 164
Held, Rob, 142
Henkels, Lutz, 108
Hewlett-Packard, 51
Hinds, Walter, 124
Holford, Stephen, 232
Holtje, Mac, 66
Holtzer-Cabot, 8
Horne, Clyde, 124
Horton, J. Warren, 18
Hotchkiss, Jeff, 241
Hull, Lewis, 18
Hurlbut, Ed, 110
Hurley, John, 185
Husic Capital Mgmt, 213
Huston, Bob, 164
ICL Computers, 165
IET Labs, 209
Industrial Comp. Corp, 231
Initials, 56
Institute of Radio Engrs, 45
Ireland, Fred, 34
Jacobs, Earl, 157
Jaguar Motors, 180
Johnson, Knut, 9
Jones, Al, 176

Jones, Billy, 176
Jorrens, Peter, 85
K Plan, the, 23
K. Dixon, 102
Kabele, Bill, 129
Karplus, Eduard, 26
Keithley Instruments, 209
Kierstead, Charlie, 176
Kollmorgen, 157
Kundert, Warren, 76
Kuster, Norbert, 135
Lahanas, C. J., 89
Lamson, Horatio, 14
LASAR, 137
LCD testing, 211
Lehman Brothers, 141
Lewis, Frank, 40
Little, Arthur D., 65
Littlejohn, Henry, 122
Locke, Errol, 13
Looking Glass, 212
LTX, 181
Lucas, Sarah, 216
Luscomb, O. Kerro, 7
Lynch, John, 148
Lyons, Claude, 71
Lyons, James, 215
MA/COM, 167
Mabrey, Dr. Roy, 31
Macalka, Peter, 63
MacKenzie, Tom, 148
Marconi Instruments, 140
Marconi, Guglielmo, 4
Martin, Ned, 213
Mayhew, Lawrence, 181
Mayo, Lawrence, 13
McAleer, Harold, 64

McAuliffe, Bob, 183
McCarthy, Steve, 208
McCouch, Gordon, 64
McElroy, Paul 14
McKinsey & Co., 216
McNulty, Ray, 174
Megatest, 188
Membrain, 107
Meuse, Harold, 176
Mico Instrument Co., 48
Micronetic Systems, 96
Midoriya Associates, 90
Millen, Richard, 134
Miller, Graham, 181
Mine Safety Appliance, 160
Mirco, 105
Mirco Systems, 141
MIT Radiation Lab, 40
Mitron, 227
Mohler, Eric, 176
Monitor Instruments, 102
Morgan Stanley, 223
Mortensen, Dick, 148
Motion pictures, 19
Moulton, Larry, 143
Mounce, Larry, 176
Mudama, Eric, 86
Munn Bernard, 223
Nat'l Comp. Systems, 222
Necco girls, the, 37
Newell, Warren, 176
Nicolet Imaging, 237
Nixon, Dave, 77
Noyce, Bob, 151
O'Brien, George, 222
Olsen, Ken, 87

Omnicomp, 141
OPUS, 201
Orthonull, 61
Osborne, Dave, 86
Ovington X-Ray Co., 7
Owen, Bob, 77
Packard, David, 18
Packard, Luke, 42
Painter, Howard, 113
Palmer, Peter, 202
PDP-8 minicomputer, 87
Penfield, Paul, 167
Penney, Paul, 176
Petefish, Charles, 120
Peters, Charles, 174
Peterson, Arnold, 44
Pexton, Larry, 53
Pfaffman, Fritz, 90
Pichon, Matt, 143
Pierce, G.W., 14
Pierce, Glenn, 180
Pierce, Larry, 176
Pillote, Paul, 212
Pilot, 232
Piper, Thomas, 167
Pitt, Earle, 149
Powers, Nelson, 66
Powers, Phil, 68
Prang, Joe, 183
Prest, Carole, 207
Pronsky, Paul, 225
Quackenbos, John, 115
QuadTech, 209
Radiophon, 74
RATS, 96
Raytheon, 65

Regan Partners, 213
Richmond, Harold, 14
Rivlin, Joe, 180
Rogers, Dick, 81
ROLM, 121
Sarnoff, David, 45
Schlumberger, 188
Schraeder, Michael, 222
Schymik, William, 222
Scott, H. H., 27
Sear, Brian, 152
Semicon West, 163
Sentry test system, 154
Sette, Dick, 85
Shaw, Henry, 11
Shephard, Hardie, 115
Shephard, Walter, 232
Shockley, William, 52
Sierra Research Tech., 237
Sinclair, Donald, 34
Skilling, Jim, 77
Smith, Lee, 143
Smith, Myron, 34
Snook, John, 94
Soderman, Bob, 60
Spectral Dynamics, 102
Sporck, Charlie, 151
Stadecker, Adriana, 222
Stadler, Steve, 89
Stanford University, 52
Stanford, Gene, 138
Steele, Jack, 149
Storer, Tracy, 103
Stroboscope, the, 26
Struct. Meas. Systems, 197
Sullivan, Bob, 129

Sun Microsystems, 208
Sylvania, 65
Systomation, 138
Takeda Riken, 152
Techware, 95
Tektronix, 92
Telesis, 182
Television, 20
Telpar, 106
TelSel, 159
Teradyne, 65
Test Technology, 227
Testline, 139
Testware, 227
Texas Instruments, 65
Thiessen, Arthur, 41
Thoma, Frank, 94
Thurston, Bill, 46
Time/Data, 89
Tippett, Rick, 186
Tokyo Electron, 91
Tour-Lab, the, 77
TRACS, 171
Transitron, 65
Trillium, 188
Tucker, Frank, 41
Tuttle, Norris, 25
Uhlendorff, Carl, 176
Unit instruments, 48
Vanderlippe, Richard, 136
Variac, 27
Viper, 232
VISION, 226
Walker survey, 206
Walsh, John, 114
Waters Corp., 222

Watrous, Ralph, 6
Western Electric, 65
Westford, move to, 229
Wharton, Dave, 184
Wilde, Wilson, 149
Wilson, Harold, 62
Winterhalter, Art, 116
Worthen, Charles, 18
Wright, James, 97
Wright, Robert, 125
Zapf, John, 116
Zehntel, 138
Zeiss Works, 30
Zollo, Louis, 222
Zshau, Ed, 222
Zwicker, Ashley, 9